Keeping It Finer

WHAT IT MEANS TO BE A FINER WOMAN IN THE 21ST CENTURY

ANTHOLOGY

Zeta Phi Beta Sorority, Incorporated Centennial Commission
1734 New Hampshire Ave. NW, Washington, DC 20009
CentennialCommission@zphib2020.com • www.zphib2020.com

Keeping It Finer: What it means to be a Finer Woman in the 21st Century; Anthology

Rhonda Lawson, Centennial Project Visionary and Acquisitions Editor
Doris McAdams Stokes, Copy Editor
Jylla Moore Tearte, PhD, Project Director
Malica Fleming, Cover Design

ISBN 978-0-9963832-1-9 (Paperback)
ISBN 978-0-9963832-2-6 (Kindle)
ISBN 978-0-9963832-3-3 (iPad/Nook/Kobo)

Crystal Stairs, Inc., Publisher
Printed in the United States of America

Zeta Phi Beta Sorority, Incorporated

ESTABLISHED JANUARY 16, 1920

This Anthology is Dedicated to the Founders

| Arizona Cleaver Stemons | Fannie Pettie Watts | Myrtle Tyler Faithful | Viola Tyler Goings | Pearl Neal |

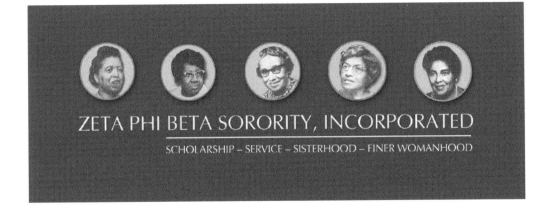

ZETA PHI BETA SORORITY, INCORPORATED

SCHOLARSHIP – SERVICE – SISTERHOOD – FINER WOMANHOOD

CONTENTS

THE VOICES OF ZETAS

Archonettes on Finer Womanhood

AFFIRMATIONS OF FINER WOMANHOOD

PERSONAL REFLECTIONS ON FINER WOMANHOOD

CONTRIBUTORS

ZETA DOVES

YOUTH VOICES: YOUTH AUXILIARY MEMBERS— ZETA PHI BETA SORORITY, INC.

Pearlettes (4–8 years old) on Finer Womanhood. 118

Amicettes (9–13 years old) on Finer Womanhood. 180

Archonettes (14–18 years old) on Finer Womanhood. .260

Foreword

Rhonda M. Lawson

In my 21 years as a member of Zeta Phi Beta Sorority, Inc., I have met many different Sorors from many different walks of life. Many have had varying opinions on the direction of the Sorority. Just as many have had different opinions on community service, scholarship, and even sisterly love. Yet, nearly all of them agree that our defining principle is Finer Womanhood. In fact, I remember going through Course of Study back in 1993 when my Big Sister stressed that Finer Womanhood was to be listed first when reciting our principles, and with so much sass that anyone within earshot would recognize and understand its importance. Well, she didn't say it with quite those words, but that was how I took it!

If you ever want to start a philosophical debate within Zeta, ask the question, "What does Finer Womanhood mean?" In listening to these discussions, I've found that although nearly all Sorors find Finer Womanhood important, opinions differ as to what it truly is and when it should be used. Some may liken a Finer Woman to Proverbs 31, while others credit the lessons learned from their mothers. But what of the young lady who might have been taught that Finer Womanhood begins and ends with her looks? What about the young lady who doesn't regularly read the Bible? Still yet, how does a Soror display Finer Womanhood when dealing with difficult, often life-threatening situations?

This anthology helps to answer many of those questions. The Sorors in this book vary in age, experience, and backgrounds, but their views on Finer Womanhood are equally profound. From the highest leaders of Zeta to our undergraduates, from a World War II veteran, to teachers, to business women, to students, every woman represented between this book's covers shares a story that each of us can relate to.

I invite you to explore the wisdom of our International President Mary Breaux Wright, as well as five of our Past International President. Sit at the knee of our Zeta Doves, some of whom have dedicated more than 60 years to our beloved Sisterhood. Reflect with Sorors who found Finer Womanhood to be a process that they continue to undergo well into their adult years.

You will find yourself laughing, crying, and sometimes even celebrating as you read these stories, but most of all, I pray that you will walk away from this book with a nugget of knowledge that you can apply to your own Finer journey. As we move into our Centennial year, I pray that this book will be a blessing to our Sisterhood, as well as a blessing to each of you personally. May the stories and essays you read give you 2020 vision, helping us to lead Zeta into a new and exciting era. This is indeed an awesome time to be a Zeta!

Special thanks to all of the Sorors across the world who generously dedicated their time and talents to this historical project, with special thanks to Grand Basileus Wright and our Centennial Chair and 20th International Grand Basileus Dr. Jylla Moore Tearte for believing in and supporting this project. I also thank Soror Doris M. Stokes for not only co-editing this anthology, but sharing her experience and patience with me as we brought this project to fruition. Additionally, kudos to Soror Malica Fleming for designing such a fabulous cover, and Soror Melissa Barnes for compiling the submissions from our Zeta Doves. None of this would have been possible without you! I now invite you to enjoy this anthology as I wipe away my tears of joy.

Sisterly submitted,
Rhonda M. Lawson
Keeping it Finer
Centennial Project Visionary and Acquisitions Editor

Grand Expectations: Thoughts on Finer Womanhood

Mary Breaux Wright
International President

On occasion, a Soror will ask, "What is Finer Womanhood?" I want to answer, "You probably don't have it!"

However, Zeta will nurture the Finer Woman in each of us so that we can eventually know and exemplify this founding principle of our Sorority. Finer Womanhood distinguishes and defines Zeta Phi Beta Sorority, Inc., and its members in all aspects of our lives.

The essence of this ideal, Finer Womanhood, has been a fundamental precept of Zeta Phi Beta Sorority, Inc., since its founding in 1920. While many have attempted to define or redefine it through the decades of our existence, this ideal is grounded in the fact that our Founders and other women modeled it as the example for us to follow. Many have wondered about its origin and how it was formed and articulated. Perhaps Brother Charles Robert Taylor left us a clue in his *Crescent* article published in the Fall of 1977:

"My vision is clear as I turn back the curtain of the years. I remember how I wondered about our organization of Phi Beta Sigma. I wondered what would give it new life and inspiration. Sisters, of course! I recall how I thought of a sincere and enthusiastic young woman, who for me was the embodiment of our brotherhood in the sisterhood of which I dreamed. She had character and gifts. She had a beautiful spirit and intellectual effectiveness. She had appeal in her personality and words. I knew that if I won her, she would not give up until she had perfected a nucleus of a sisterhood for Phi Beta Sigma.

*And then I strolled across the campus of Howard University with Arizona Cleaver (my campus date). With fear and trembling, I gave her my secret. I risked all upon my ability to inspire her to become the first sister of Phi Beta Sigma and to begin with herself in establishing a sisterhood of **finer** and stronger women that would make all men proud."*

Perhaps our beloved Founders fully embraced Brother Taylor's heartfelt declaration and vision for Finer and stronger women, as the caliber of woman he desired for his sisters, and incorporated them in the ideals of Zeta Phi Beta Sorority. We may never know their exact thoughts, but we can certainly conclude that Finer Women embody all the qualities that Brother Taylor described.

Lullelia Walker Harrison, Zeta's 12th Grand Basileus from 1943 – 48, was my mentor, and she exemplified those qualities that Brother Taylor envisioned to me and those she led through the years. In the *1920 – 65 History of Zeta Phi Beta Sorority,* author Ola Adams described Soror Harrison as "stately of bearings, refined in mannerisms, distinctly vocal, positive in approach, firm—yet dispensing "mercy"—in business affairs. Adept in human relations, she seemed to know every Soror and had a knack for making each feel special."

Her strong voice of reason while standing firm in her beliefs demonstrated the many aspects of Finer Womanhood that molded my way. She formed my expectations, my Grand Expectations, of Finer Womanhood. When I joined Zeta at Grambling State University, Psi Beta chapter on Friday, April 18, 1969, I noted that these were characteristics I wanted to replicate on my Zeta journey.

Collectively, those tenets have been a roadmap that guides me even today as I lead the remarkable women of Zeta who serve in communities around the world. This unique ideal sustains us in our work and provides a standard for us to follow. Yes, I think that Finer Womanhood must be observable in what we wear, how we speak, and when we wear our letters and the name of our Sisterhood. And yes, Finer Womanhood is an ideal to be celebrated and commemorated annually in all chapters.

I count my blessings daily for my early embellishment of Finer Womanhood. This ideal set the foundation for my marriage to my husband James. I uplifted it as I taught our son Randall

what to look for in the woman that would eventually become his wife and the mother of my grandchildren. I am grateful that James and Randall, both men of Phi Beta Sigma Fraternity, Incorporated, have allowed me to appreciate the inseparable bond of Zeta and Sigma. Randall was born on January 9, Phi Beta Sigma's Founders' Day, and I have always associated Sigma and Finer Womanhood in a very special way as I have navigated the bond of motherhood and sisterhood. His birth certainly called me to a higher existence as a woman, wife, mother and Zeta.

I believe that every member of Zeta Phi Beta Sorority should have goals and approaches to life that are inspired by and grounded in the ideal to "be finer." While it is a self-defining goal and its achievement is in the eyes of the beholder, the journey to and attainment of Finer

Womanhood is observable. Therefore, we must each aspire to "Grand Expectations" of how we exhibit to others and acknowledge to ourselves our representation of the ideal of Finer Womanhood.

As this journey continues, I will stay steady on the course and committed to challenging myself and members of our Sisterhood to hold this ideal in a special place as we achieve our Grand Expectations.

Remembering Finer Womanhood: Stories from a Founder's Daughter

Denise Marie Snow

As we journey toward Zeta Phi Beta's Centennial Celebration, the Sorority is blessed to have Soror Frances Faithful, daughter of Founder Myrtle Tyler Faithful, actively serving in the Sisterhood. A veteran educator for 34 years, Soror Faithful is one of the charter members of Zeta Beta Zeta Chapter in Flint, MI. Her personal accounts about her mother and aunt (Viola Tyler Goings), and the impact Finer Womanhood had on her life are important to capture. The stories Soror Faithful shares about growing up as a legacy and going the Zeta way provide the basis for why celebrating 100 years is such a monumental moment in history.

REPRESENT!

From the very beginning Finer Womanhood was an instrumental component of Sorority expansion. Soror Faithful remembers vividly why the principle of Finer Womanhood was so precious to the Founders, and a prerequisite for being a Zeta. Soror Faithful said, "They saw the other sororities and realized they looked for finer women whenever new Sorors came in."

Remembering the elegance and style of Founder Myrtle Tyler Faithful is a sacred place for Soror Faithful, as watching her mother provided the example for how she would represent herself. She said, "Mom always carried herself as a lady. She always dressed and looked the part. I remember that she did not curse, didn't drink, or smoke. She was very graceful and she never got tired."

Never tiring in her efforts, Founder Faithful traveled the country visiting chapters and regions at conferences and other Sorority functions. Soror Faithful remembers the great things she

always heard about Zeta. "Mom was very pleased," she said. "She enjoyed meeting new Sorors, and they were always so nice to her and wanted to do things for her. These women represented."

In addition to style, Finer Women embody the spirit of sisterly love in how members care for their sisters. Soror Faithful spoke in amazement recalling how Sorors treated her wherever she traveled. "I am so humbled by the way Sorors treat me. It's really some-thing," Soror Faithful said. "Sorors treat me like I am one of the Founders!"

Frances Faithful and Sister, Geraldine Desbournes at 75th Anniversary event of Zeta Phi Beta Sorority, Incorporated

TORCHBEARERS OF A LEGACY

Creating a legacy that can withstand 100 years of mountains and valleys is no easy task. To build the foundation upon which thousands of women have joined came at a great sacrifice. Soror Faithful remembers those sacrificial times well. She said, "Mom would leave for long periods of time. It would get lonely without her." Time together with her mother and the Founders are treasured memories. Soror Faithful gushes as she remembered moments shared with all of the Founders together. She said, "The Founders were very close and so much fun to be around. They kept you laughing."

Having the value of Finer Womanhood instilled and nurtured over time left an indelible mark on Soror Faithful early on. The influence on her decision to become a Zeta was "natural," but she recalls feeling like she didn't fit in with the other sororities. Of course, her mother and aunt were both there when she crossed the burning sands into Zeta!

In less than five years, Zeta will commemorate 100 years of Scholarship, Service, Sisterhood, and Finer Womanhood. The future of Zeta will rest in how new members and youth aux-iliary group members carry the torch of Finer Womanhood. Soror Faithful said, "I would hope [the youth] would continue to carry themselves as the older Sorors and Founders did. Representing Zeta in grace, class, and sisterly love will be the torch all members carry to ensure Zeta's legacy for the next hundred years."

Past International Presidents

Finer Memories

Edith V. Francis, EdD
18th International President

On Sunday, December 13, 2009, Edith V. Francis, EdD, 18th International President, participated in the inaugural Zeta Online Sunday Conversation entitled, **Zeta Sigma Love**. These are excerpts from the interview conducted by Jylla Moore Tearte and Carter D. Womack.

What are some of your memories of the Founders?

Gil and I got married on August 1, 1970. The next day, we left to attend Zeta's 50th Anniversary Boulé. A day or two after that, Gil and I were walking through the gardens at the Shoreham Hotel in Washington, D.C. and we came upon six people who were laughing and talking and they invited the two of us over.

We had been walking hand in hand, and we walked over and WOW! There were the Five Pearls and Brother Charles Taylor, the originator of the idea of Sigma and Zeta being a family organization and who was instrumental in the founding of Zeta. We sat with them and they talked about their walks by the reservoir and we talked about experiences that they had as collegians as they moved up within the organization. They talked about how they had seen the organization grow. We were fortunate enough that after we met those individuals, we also had the opportunity to visit three of them in their homes.

We knew all of the Founders, and we were privileged to have them in our home. But at one point, we had everyone – the three of the five at our house in New Jersey when we first moved in. So, it was a wonderful experience because we actually knew them as individuals and they were a fun-loving group. They were telling some really cute jokes on each other as well as, you know, things that they would share with us. That's always been a very fond memory for both Gil and myself.

We also had the opportunity to meet Soror Gladys Warrington, who was the first initiate for Zeta. Soror Warrington gave us a copy of the 1920 Constitution. It said "Phi Beta Sigma and Zeta Phi Beta do hereby," and it was a joint constitution. She had a copy and she gave it to us and we turned it over to the national office because we didn't feel that it was something that we should hold on to. So, that was at Soror Warrington's home.

Who were some of your Zeta role models?

I'll comment on that in terms of my experiences when I first met Lullelia Harrison. My first impression was "boy, she is a powerhouse and very dictatorial" [laughs]. And I was, you know, an undergraduate and very much in awe of her. As I got to know her, I realized that part of her appeal was the fact that she was an organizer. She was a professional. She was a businesswoman and she wanted things done basically her way. But now that I've had a chance to think about her, it was a good way to be. I learned to work with her and she was a source of inspiration to me in many ways in terms of organizational skills. You couldn't beat her for that. With paperwork, getting details and getting the facts, she was exemplary.

The person who had the most influence in my life was Deborah Partridge Wolfe because I got to know her first as an undergraduate. I then had the pleasure of getting to know her in terms of the educational circle, bumping into her several times at various educational conferences. I was so proud of her because she was a brilliant woman and she would invariably take over most of the meetings. What she had to say was good. She had a point and she worked very hard to see that it went through.

I have to give her credit because when times were getting rough when I was working for my doctorate, she was an inspiration. She would call me and ask, "Well, what chapter are you on now? What are you doing now?" And we got to be very good personal friends. She stayed with me until she made sure I got my doctorate.

Pearls and Pins

Jylla Moore Tearte, PhD
20th International President
2020 Centennial Commission Chair

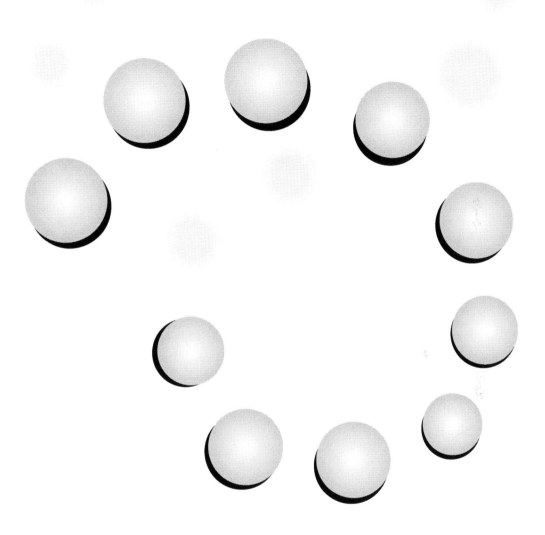

At a very early age, I was fascinated with women I observed wearing pearls and pins. My Grandmother Ethel started my affair with pearls and pins as accessories. Though not a member of a sorority, she had a regal presence that she thoughtfully exhibited with dresses, hats, gloves and pins that she wore with such dignity and pride. Always dressed impeccably, she was one of my early models of a "Finer Woman." I now possess one of her many pins in my personal collection, and I cherish it knowing that at some point in her life, on a special occasion or Sunday morning, she wore this pin, initiating my interest in and collection of pins.

Vera Moore, my mother who was also my Soror, served as the Eastern Regional Director from 1986-1992. The women of Zeta Phi Beta Sorority in my community were always adorned in fine attire and accessories that grabbed my eye, often pearl necklaces or pins. When I think about Finer Womanhood, I visualize pearls and pins, and the relationship I have had with them in the defining moments of my Sorority membership and at each intersection of my life's journey. My mother was a huge influence on my thinking about Finer Womanhood.

In 1971, Alpha Alpha Zeta chapter in Salisbury, N.C., sponsored a debutante ball at which more than 20 other young ladies and I were introduced to society. I was crowned queen, thanks to the efforts of my mother and her Zeta sister, Soror Augusta White. They raised more than $10,000 for me to claim this prestigious title. Each debutante was given a string of pearls, a gift I still love to bestow to young ladies today to mark a milestone in their lives.

Pearls have been called the queen of gemstones. Natural pearls, once rare and highly valued, were reserved for the wealthy. Since the 1920's however, when cultured pearls were produced, women around the world, including our Founders, embraced them as symbols of elegance and refinement. A gift of a string of pearls, a set of pearl earrings, a pin with a pearl prominently set in it, or a simple pearl bracelet will always convey the giver's heartfelt interest in and hopes for the recipient's future and are sure to be treasured accessories for years to come.

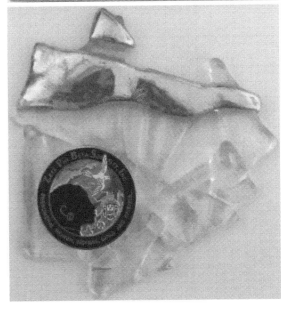

When I became a member of Zeta Phi Beta Sorority (Sigma chapter, 1973), my relationship with pins and pearls was further deepened. My mother was present at the ceremony and pinned me with my first Zeta pin. This pin, with our Greek letters and five pearls, has always felt extra special because I remember how special it was to be pinned by my mother. It visually symbolized my connection with thousands of other women in the Sorority.

In 1992 I received the pin only worn by the Grand Basileus, following my election. It is a silver pin with the Greek letter monogram, ZΦB, with five diamonds encircled by laurel branches. It was an honor and special blessing to wear this pin as the leader of this extraordinary Sorority. When my term ended, I transferred the pin to the newly elected Grand Basileus and was gifted with a gold pin with a guard. This pin has the Greek letter monogram, ZΦB, with fifteen diamonds on the letter Φ and the letters PGB at the bottom. It is encircled by laurel branches and the guard is a number 20, representing my sequence of service as Grand Basileus.

During my "World Class Service" administration, from 1992 – 96, I often gifted members with pins. I initiated the tradition of providing a souvenir pin for Sorors attending Boulés. This gifting of a Boulé pin has survived through many administrations since, and Sorors collect and wear their pins with pride with the first one given at the 1994 Boulé.

I had a very special pin designed in 1994 by Vivian Shimoyama, an entrepreneur in California, for the regional directors serving with me. I also extended it as a gift to Sorority members who made special contributions to the Sisterhood, and gift the few that remain to current day members who do amazing work. The pin was avant-garde in style with the World Class service logo mounted on polished, iridescent glass under a gold bar. It remains one of the most striking and original pins I own.

When I pinned my daughter, Soror Anjylla Foster, as a member of Zeta in 2011, I was touched that not only did she embrace the ideals and values of the Sorority, but that she represented generations of Zetas who are connected throughout our sisterhood, believing in what one pin and five pearls stand for. Celebrating the induction of a Legacy member is such a special, never to be forgotten moment.

As a Legacy member too, I felt special when my Mother, daughter, or sister, Soror Maxine Moore-Allen, Charter Basileus of Omega Delta Zeta chapter, dressed up and accessorized with pearls. Sharing a history of pearls and pins kept us connected and always added a bit of class to whatever outfit we wore. In the back of our minds, we knew that it symbolized "being on our 'finest'" behavior. There is just something special about sharing the wearing of pearls with those we love. I have often wondered what exactly it is about pearls and pins that intrigues and inspires me.

I have shared my thoughts about pearls with other Legacy Sorors, and was surprised how pearls have played similar roles in their lives, too. Doris M. Stokes received her first string of pearls (which she still has) from her godfather at birth. This gift was so special, her mom did not give them to her until she was 16 years old. When her Zeta mom, Soror Doris L. McAdams passed in 2011, she left more than 10 strings of pearls of various sizes and lengths, some of which were passed on to her mom's Zeta daughters.

Pins have been part of fashion across the world for years, and have evolved as the go-to accessory for dressing up an outfit, particularly for

professional women. To this day, the Queen of England is seldom seen without a string of pearls and a brooch or pin complementing her attire. Women at all social levels can now acquire and wear these affordable and stylish jewelry accessories.

In her book, *Read My Pins*, Madeline Albright, the former Secretary of State, writes about how pins may be worn to express moods and opinions, or even convey non-verbal messages. Her personal collection of pins numbers more than 200, and have been exhibited in major museums. Many of her pins are gifts, while others were purchased at flea markets, museum shops or dime stores.

Today's fraternal pins, symbols of brotherhood or sisterhood, have evolved from the standard pin, and are now collectible items in all shapes and sizes. Our Zeta pin is one such item. The early Zeta pins were small, about a quarter-inch wide by half an inch long, with the owner's initials engraved on its back. Today's Zeta pin is double that size (and easier to handle), with no initials on the back. Some Legacy members remember too that to receive their mom's pin when they became Zetas, special permission had to be obtained from the National Secretary to transfer a pin from one Soror to another.

In 1995, I represented Zeta in the United States delegation to the Fourth United Nations Conference for Women in Beijing, China. It was a tradition similar to the Olympics to exchange pins. The pin that I kept as a reminder of this amazing gathering of women from across the world was a replica of the United States' flag with the image of a woman. It is a special pin that carries the hopes and dreams of women across the globe.

At the1998 Boulé in Atlanta, The National Educational Foundation secured two pins for a silent auction that had belonged to Founder Myrtle Tyler Faithful. I won the bid, and they are now cherished pins in my collection. I try to imagine her when she wore them, what she wore them on and how she placed them on her chest. What event she was attending? I wonder how often she wore them. When I see photographs of her, I look to see if she is wearing one of "our" pins.

My passion for pins and pearls is a pastime I enjoy. I organize my personal collection of pins frequently: they chronicle my life. From travel around the world to memorable events, I trace my life story through my collection of pins, hoping that they represent, in a special way, my life of exploration, engagement and enjoyment.

It was a privilege to pin Soror Frances Faithful at the 2014 Boulé with her Life Member pin. With this recognition, the sisterhood applauded her years of service in Zeta and her unique place in the Sisterhood as the only living child of a Zeta Founder. Pinning Soror Faithful was truly an honor.

Some of my favorite pins are constant companions when I travel. I always include a pin from my husband, Curtis Tearte. Whether it is his Omega Centennial pin or an IBM pin, his pins have a special significance and keep him close to my heart when we find ourselves in different locations. I am particularly partial to the diamond dove pin that he gave me that celebrates so many special moments and confluences of thoughts. Whenever I wear this special pin, I am reminded of the love and care that we share. The dove is a magnificent symbol of inseparable love and peace.

Another set of pins that I cherish recognizes my sales success in IBM. I received "100 Percent Club" pins when I achieved the quota assigned for my sales territory and was awarded the 'Golden Circle" pin on three occasions for being one of the top sales leaders in IBM. These pins

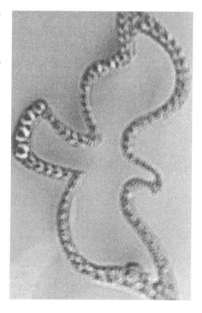

remind me of those achievements and the teams that worked together to accomplish very challenging goals. The pins remind me of the moments when plans and hard work aligned with the result being yet another "pinning" event.

The 2014 Phi Beta Sigma Fraternity, Inc. Centennial Celebration in Washington, D.C., was just the right occasion to wear pearls and pins. Even Brother Jonathan Mason, 34th National President of Phi Beta Sigma, pictured with Soror Anjylla and me, was wearing a pin when we greeted him at a Centennial reception.

The July 2014 Zeta Boulé included a joint Zeta-Sigma Reaffirmation Ceremony, which occurred during Phi Beta Sigma's 100-year celebration. It was a privilege to "pen" this ceremony with Brother William E. Stanley, 28th National President of Phi Beta Sigma Fraternity, in 1995 to celebrate Zeta's 75th Anniversary. The ceremony establishes the ideal ambiance to wear pearls and pins. Thus, in deepening the bonding experience of this ceremony, a special pin was designed by Brother Chris and Soror Malica Fleming for this auspicious occasion. This talented Sigma-Zeta husband and wife team captured the moment with the collectible souvenir pin that was gifted to all attendees. Their use of the infinity symbol in the design perfectly depicted the unbreakable bond of Zeta and Sigma and the infinity symbol is rapidly proliferating as the symbol to represent the bond.

After the Zeta's Launch to Centennial in Houston, Texas on January 9, 2014, I received another special pin. At the "5 for the Founders' Zeta Centennial Launch Weekend", Jan. 14-18, 2015, in Baltimore, Md., Brother Carter Womack, 27th and 29th Past President of Phi Beta Sigma, gifted me with his Centennial President's pin. It was another extremely special addition to my collection that will always remind me of the unique and special bond that Carter and I share. The Zeta-Sigma bond… truly unbreakable.

Pearls and pins invoke and commemorate special moments. Pearls and pins are silent testimonies to the rich histories of women who wear them. The wearing of a string of pearls indelibly links generations of women. The March 2015 induction ceremony for Soror Jasmine Towns included her mother, Soror Karen Boykin Towns, and her grandmother, Soror Gwen Towns. What a memorable and priceless moment of welcoming and pinning a Legacy member into the Sorority. Pins and pearls create a legacy of moments to remember for Finer Women.

Zetas wear pins with pride. Zetas wear pearls with a sassy air of "Finer Womanhood." Zetas give pins with deep meaning. Zetas honor our Founders with reverence, as the Pearls of our sisterhood. Zetas give pins with heartfelt messages. Zetas give pearls with deep emotion and expressions of love. Zetas hold pearls and pins dear.

Without a doubt, I am looking forward to adding the 2020 Visionary Pins to my collection. The Base Pin will be awarded to all Sorors who contribute to the Official Fund Raising Campaign. The "Circle of Pearls" pin, our Official Centennial logo, and the Founder's Society Pin will be a very special collectible to celebrate and support Zeta's Journey to the 2020 Centennial. It is only fitting that these pins be a tangible commemoration of the journey.

Pearls and pins will forever distinguish the extraordinary Finer Women of Zeta Phi Beta Sorority, Incorporated.

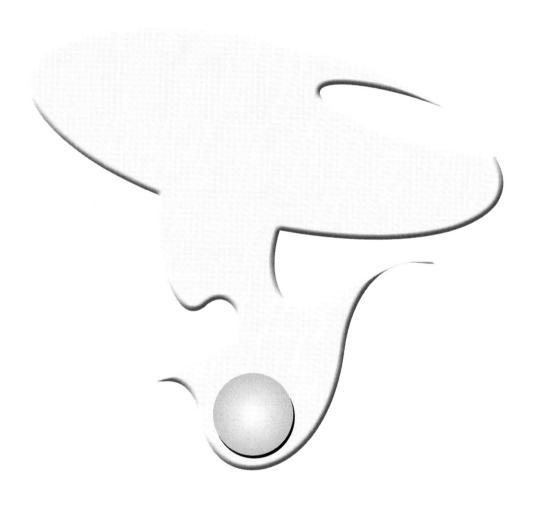

Shaping My Values and Beliefs

Barbara West Carpenter, PhD
21st International President

Throughout my lifetime, I can name many people who have left an indelible impact on helping me to be who I am. Some of those people are Zeta women, and others are not. As I reflect on my life and what impact these women have had on me, I must start with my very first teacher (though not a member of a sorority), my grandmother Tillie Cross West. As a primary school teacher who retired when I was born, her love of books and her teaching me to value the printed word formed the basis of my insatiable thirst for knowledge. It was this beginning that ultimately led to my desire to become an educator like several generations in my family before me.

As I grew up, I learned the workings of Zeta from my closest friend and confidante, my mother Mildred Spicer West, who was initiated into Zeta seven months before I was born. My mother was well known for her speaking ability, which came naturally through her educational training. This was a skill that I worked hard to perfect in my adult life. Her elegant style of dress, her ability to work with people, and her calm demeanor are traits that I have tried to emulate. As a child, my first real introduction to what it means to be a Zeta woman, came from the volunteering efforts that my mother was known for throughout the Baton Rouge, La., community. Those same volunteering skills have stayed with me throughout my lifetime, as I have used them to value and appreciate people of different races and cultures in my everyday working environment.

There are Zeta women to whom I shall always be grateful. One such woman was the 19th International Grand Basileus, Eunice S. Thomas, who had a wealth of knowledge about the inner workings of the Sorority. She was a guiding force in my career as a leader in Zeta. Her ability to recall facts verbatim and her political savvy led to my being elected to the highest office in the Sorority. I developed negotiation and collaboration skills through serving in her administration, and that has allowed me to maintain an effective leadership style in many settings.

Throughout my years as a young child and into adulthood, there had always been a constant figure in my life: the 16th International Grand Basileus, Isabel Morgan Herson, whom I adored. Her diplomatic, gracious and loving manner taught me humility and diplomacy. Unlike many Zetas, I had the privilege of being tutored by Grand Basileus Herson, as we were members of the same graduate chapter in the Sorority. So, learning from her was automatic and totally natural.

No story about my beliefs and values would be complete without mentioning my beloved daughter, Erin Danyelle Carpenter. No, she is not a member of our great Sorority (though she thinks she is), nor is she a college graduate. However, I believe she has had the greatest impact on helping me to become who I really am. Erin is now an adult living with a high functioning level of Autism.

As a parent of a special needs child, I learned early on in our child-rearing life that nothing matters more than caring for someone for whom you are totally responsible. While it was important for my husband and me to be sure that Erin had everything she needed to be successful in life, I learned many valuable lessons from her. The first realization is that "things are not always what they seem to be". Even when medical specialists, teachers, religious figures, and others had an opinion, there were always options and other ways of accomplishing a goal. Erin taught me patience as I searched for educational programs to improve her social skills. She taught me to "go with the flow," as there are no cookie cutter plans for Autistic individuals. All of them are different. My daughter taught me how to love an individual in ways that are totally unimaginable. Finally, my sense of humor comes directly from spending many precious moments with her as she has grown into a beautiful, smart and an accomplished young women in her own right.

It is true that people come into your life for a reason. I have always believed that God places each person in one's life at just the right time for specific purposes. This is what happened to me, and I shall always be thankful for each of them.

As we in Zeta embark on this magnificent journey of preparing to celebrate the 100th year of existence, let us remember that being a Finer Woman is more than just words. We must carry the ideals of character, integrity, perseverance, and caring for others in our everyday lives. We stand on the shoulders of many members of the Sorority who sacrificed much and gave of themselves to make Zeta be what she is today. Keep focusing forward with a positive vision so in the next 100 years, there will still be women who will be proud to say that they joined the greatest sorority in the world.

Thoughts on Finer Womanhood

Barbara Crockett Moore
22nd International President

The concept of Finer Womanhood has been discussed for centuries by both men and women. One of the wisest thinkers of all times, King Solomon, the son of David, wrote about a Virtuous Woman in the 31st Proverb of the Old Testament more than 2,000 years ago. In that beautiful narrative, King Solomon described the characteristics of a fine woman. Of course, the description captures the signs of that time in history. It gives us a glimpse of what a female's role was during that era.

When King Soloman reigned, a woman's place was in the home. The best example of that model is portrayed in his proverb, The Virtuous Wife. It is really immaterial in today's society if one is married or single, but the noble attributes that King Solomon outlined hold true regardless of marital status.

A woman who is thought of as possessing qualities of Finer Womanhood should have the same qualities as the virtuous wife. She is trustworthy, good, not evil, and seeks the best for her household and others. She is industrious and not lazy. She feeds those who need nourishment, whether it is food or simple kindness. The fine woman is concerned about the less fortunate, and shares her resources with them. She is generous and never stingy. She is strong and honorable in all her transactions. Such a woman speaks only good, and becomes wise as she matures.

If the Finer Woman has children, they will want to emulate her and praise her for her example. If she has a husband, he too will give her praise for being his helpmate. Should she lead a single life, she must find her purpose for being. Perhaps she is ordained to be a blessing for those who need her in the role of teacher, physician, or foster parent. Whatever she finds that is her life's work, she will be comfortable in her own skin and be acceptable in the sight of God.

Times When Finer Womanhood Resonated

Sheryl Underwood
23rd International President

The founding principles of Zeta Phi Beta Sorority, Inc., are *Scholarship, Service, Sisterhood* and *Finer Womanhood*. She is Finer when she seeks *Scholarship,* as 2 Timothy 2:15 says: *"Study to show yourself approved to God, a workman that needs not to be ashamed, rightly dividing the word of truth."*

A Finer Woman puts God first in order to be of good *Service*. A Finer Woman recognizes that God is at the head of everything, and that her steps are ordered by the Lord, but if she stumbles, she goes to her quiet place and gets on her knees and asks God, "How can I be of better service?"

At my first Boulé, I had the chance to meet one of our Zeta Founders, Founder Myrtle Tyler Faithful. In her presence, I could really feel Sisterhood and Finer Womanhood. That feeling washed over me and renewed my commitment to upholding the principles of Zeta. There is one thing that a Finer Woman knows, and that is the only way you can be a good leader is to have learned how to follow.

A Finer Woman answers Zeta's call and is steadfast in her service. The accompanying photo was taken at my first Boulé as International Grand Basileus. In it you see five living Grands standing together with the current Grand, and the 2009 and 2010 Miss Zetas. The establishment of the Miss Zeta Pageant was to let people know that Finer Women do not let anyone dictate who we are; we define who we are. Whether you are a one-day Zeta or a Zeta Dove, Finer Womanhood is within you, because to me, Finer Womanhood is the way a woman carries herself. It enhances what she has done, what she will do, and what she will achieve.

Even if your mother, your sister, your aunt, or your cousins are not Zetas YET, you have seen Finer Womanhood within them, because it is within you as a Zeta. Finer Womanhood is a quality that you know when you see it. It is the thing that makes people wonder how you are doing what you are doing. A Finer Woman is not bully, because she defends what is right, just and fair. A Finer Woman is not cynical, because she is supportive and optimistic. A Finer Woman is not oppressive, because she knows that oppression could cause the loss of faith, and according to James 2:17, *"faith without works is dead."* When a Finer Woman walks into the room, everyone knows it is going to be all right.

A Finer Woman prepares herself for success, gain and triumph and she steadies herself in extreme pain and loss and, as Proverbs 31:25, 28, 31, proclaims, *"She is clothed with strength and dignity;... She speaks with wisdom... Honor her for all that her hands have done, and let her works bring her praise at the city gate."*

ANTHOLOGY

Zeta Doves

Zeta Dove Perspectives

Compiled by Melissa Barnes

When asked by International Grand Basileus Mary Breaux Wright to serve as the National Director for Zeta Doves and by Past International Grand Basileus Jylla Moore Tearte to serve as the Centennial Zeta Doves Coordinator, I could have never imagined getting to know so many Sorors who possess wisdom, charisma, and a genuine love and commitment to our Sisterhood.

As I began to read the many "Finer Womanhood" perspectives from our Zeta Doves, I am reminded of my own perspective of Finer Womanhood. Finer Womanhood means more than being a member of Zeta Phi Beta Sorority, Inc. It means being a "fine" woman who possesses characteristics of the very oath that each of us took. Zeta women carry themselves in "such a manner as will not bring reproach upon our sisters." Finer Womanhood is the very essence that we as Zeta women should forever uphold in our principles and in every rule and regulation of our Sorority as we serve as change agents in our communities.

As each of us reflects upon our own perspective of "Finer Womanhood," we should be committed to maintaining high standards of academic excellence (Scholarship). We should strive to put our best foot forward in all we do by continuing our efforts in serving as change agents in our communities (Service). We must strive to uphold the ideals and concepts of the epitome of a finer woman (Finer Womanhood). And, we must foster a sisterly love among all members of Zeta (Sisterhood).

This section of the Centennial Anthology is devoted to virtuous sorors who have dedicated more than 2,476 combined years of service to Zeta. Read the words of wisdom and be encouraged by our Zeta Doves. Enjoy reading their thoughts and viewing the pictures of pride!

Soror Melissa J. Barnes,
Centennial Zeta Doves Coordinator

Marjay D. Anderson, PhD

**Initiated December 8, 1963 into Nu Alpha Chapter (Texas Southern University)
while attending Prairie View A&M University
Current Region: Eastern**

In this, the second decade of the third millennium, it is appropriate to pause and, in awe, reflect on the stellar axiomatic records of the Sorority. As a highly revered principle, Finer Womanhood engenders a myriad of high quality characteristics that have withstood the test of time.

Antiquity reveals that the Creator wisely established the Universe and all that is therein. The origin of the human genome has been scientifically traced to Tanzania (East Africa). The etiological evidence documents the evolution of pre-historic human forms "Lucy" (Australopithecus africanus) – 3.2 million years old; and the non-Genesis "Eve" (Homo neanderthalensis) – 250,000 years old. These fossilar relics represent forebears of human women/womanhood. It then reasons that the beginnings of womanhood belong to distinctive and beautiful ancestors of color. Descendants have proliferated throughout the world from historical to contemporary times.

Humanity moves forward.

The Founders of our beloved Sorority euphorically envisioned everlasting precepts dedicated to Scholarship, Service, Sisterhood, and Finer Womanhood. The Founders were trailblazers who set the high standards that prevail. Sorors strive to emulate the resolve and determination of the Founders. The two perpetual torches of light on the Sorority shield illuminate the pathways for Finer Womanhood. The Greek-lettered inscription (πάντα ἐργασία νίκα) on the shield translates *Omnia vincit labore* (All is conquered through work/labor). These, symbols along with the dove of peace, exemplify the foundation principles of the Sorority and stage the platform for activities.

Time impressively has chronicled the virtues of Finer Womanhood that contribute to successful lives. Specifically noted are self-respect, respect for others, courage, ethics, compassion, honesty, trust-worthiness, tolerance, and above all, infinite and unconditional agape love. The inimitable Women of Zeta exhibit Finer Womanhood, and have demonstrated their prowess throughout the decades by embracing the capacity to harness finite materials to develop and implement meaningful strategies for solutions to problems. Women of Zeta are confident and competent, and significantly contribute to the cultural enrichment of society.

Sorors are compelled to render, through Finer Womanhood, domestic and international service projects; intellectual leadership, philanthropic generosity, scholastic achievements, multiple charitable endeavors, and acts of good will. In environments of harmony and tranquility the sine qua non of Finer Womanhood prevails and flourishes.

All of these efforts result in a powerful force that facilitates efforts to remove those obstacles that impede progress for all humanity. Thus ensuring posterity and prosperity.

It is imperative that the ideal of Finer Womanhood continues to exist. Finer Womanhood transcends time immemorial; global boundaries; human generations; cosmic aberrations in the Universe; the rise and fall of nations; successes and defeats; civic, social, and political-economic conditions. As the Sorority approaches its Centennial year, it behooves all Sorors to become even more committed to principles that bind everyone within the organization and move forward with power and prestige.

The Coda: The Spirit of Finer Womanhood . . . Forever to Behold

Eva Board

Initiated in 1960 in Beta Alpha Chapter - Southern University
Current Region: Great Lakes

Finer Womanhood denotes a woman who is highly regarded, religious, and excels in whatever she does not only as a wife and mother, but as a career woman carrying out her duties and rendering service to mankind. A Finer Woman carries herself in such a manner that inspires others and uplifts both herself and the image of this great Sisterhood. A Finer Woman portrays Christian character traits of humility, love, kindness and patience. She renders service to God's people who are in need, and promotes unity of spirit for bonding, obedience, and perseverance during hardships and suffering. A Finer Woman displaying the above Christian qualities serves as a good example to prospective members wishing to join this great Sisterhood. A Finer Woman tries to keep happiness in her home, her chapter, and her sisterhood and is valued by God, her husband, her children, and those who come in contact with her.

Arbrie Griffin Bradley

Initiated in 1963 in Pi Alpha Chapter – LeMoyne College
Current Region: Great Lakes

Finer Womanhood means treating others with kindness, consideration, and most of all respect. Respect should permeate in all that we do. It means thinking before one acts. It means avoiding those deeds that would reflect poorly on family, race, community, religion, and Sorority – Zeta Phi Beta Sorority, Inc. When one keeps the light of Zeta foremost in her mind, it shines on the path that leads to Finer Womanhood.

Joan Bridges

Initiated in 1959 in Omega Chapter – Winston-Salem State University
Current Region: Eastern

Finer Womanhood…If you have to define it, you may not be living it.   However, to understand it from my perspective, one needs to understand my Zeta lineage.

In my 50-plus years as a Zeta, Finer Womanhood came in the persons of Corinne "Aunt Co" Thomas, Nonie Johnson, Ida Duncan, Matroy Ezell and Pauline Morton, just to name a few. These Sorors from Alpha Alpha Zeta in Salisbury, N.C., were stellar examples of how to be a lady. They invested in me and saw something in me that they nurtured, molded and groomed from Debutante to Soror. Supportive in all that I did, they made sure that I learned through their example. They took me under their wings until I was able to stand on my own in Zeta.

Then add the likes of Vera Moore and Myrt Stevenson.   Anything set before them, they just got it done, and done with excellence. We all lived, moved and breathed the precepts of Zeta, and this engrained in me an ethic of commitment and a heart to serve.

As with a baby bird, it will fly from the nest that has been home for so long in order to create new journeys. My journey took me to Greensboro and eventually to Beta Nu Zeta chapter, where I continued to faithfully and actively serve. It is here that I had the great fortune to serve with some wonderful Zetas such as Mary Guy, Ruth Dailey, Olive Lee, Lillian Harris, Classie Jarman and still serve with Mamie Turner, again just to name a few.

These were further examples of dedication to successfully carrying out Service, Scholarship, Sisterhood and Finer Womanhood. AAZ and BNZ Sorors prepared me for further works in Zeta on higher levels. Crossing paths with these Sorors and countless others on the local, state, regional and national levels groomed me to be an example for my three birth daughters/ Sorors and many others whom I consider daughters, birthed through Zeta. The legacy will continue on through them.

So to summarize, Finer Womanhood is a way of life that is lived with effortless style, amazing grace, a heart to serve, teaching by example, and having care and concern for others. It is living a balanced life, being supportive of efforts, and being committed and dedicated to getting things done against all odds by setting goals and surpassing expectations. Finer Womanhood is a way of being! These are the traits I saw in the Finer Women before me. They are the traits I've lived as a Finer Woman, and will pass to the younger generation of Zetas who are and will be Finer Women.

Marilyn A. Brooks

Initiated on December 6, 1963 in Nu Chapter – Virginia Union University
Current Region: Eastern

The concept of Finer Womanhood places an enormous weight on the shoulders of Zeta Women. It speaks to standards that are high in all activities where Zetas are involved. Zetas are to be governed by those standards. There must be strength of character, an understanding of values, depth of judgment, and firmness of conviction for what is right.

Having been a member of this prestigious organization for more than 50 years has given me an indelible perspective that has permeated all facets of my life.

Life is filled with challenges, many of which can be met either with ugliness or with actions which exemplify Finer Womanhood. When these questions or confrontations come, as they often do, I am continually reminded, "What would a Finer Woman do?" As I approach the solution, several mentors and scriptural references come to mind.

One of the greatest mentors in my life was my mother, who always thought there was a scripture for every occasion and if her children studied scripture, an appropriate one would surely come to mind when needed.

Fortunately, as Zetas, we have the Finer Woman painted for us in the last chapter of the Book of Proverbs where the question is asked "Who can find a virtuous woman?" That scripture describes many of her virtues, and I shall paraphrase a few of them to further refine my perspective:

> *Faith* – A Finer Woman serves God with all of her heart, mind and soul.
>
> *Service* – A Finer Woman renders serve to humankind through her many deeds in her community and the world.
>
> *Charity* – A Finer Woman stretcheth out her hand to the poor; yea, she reacheth forth her hands to the needy."
>
> *Loyalty* – A Finer Woman is loyal to her God first and then the rules and regulations of Zeta Phi Beta Sorority.
>
> *Time* – A Finer Woman uses her time wisely and works diligently to complete her assigned tasks.
>
> *Beauty* – A Finer Woman has beauty of speech – "The law of kindness is on her tongue."
>
> *Character* – A Finer Woman has Godly character – "A woman that feareth the Lord, she shall be praised."

Following this blue print will ensure that we live a Finer life.

Bertha Brown

Initiated in 1957 in Zeta Chapter – Alcorn A & M University
Current Region: Southern

Finer Womanhood denotes a woman with high moral character who has compassion for others. A Finer Woman would not refuse to assist and aid the least of these if there is anything possible that she can do. Finer Womanhood denotes a woman that is looked up to in the community, in her church or wherever she is because of the way she carries herself. A Finer Woman would not say or do anything that would be detrimental to or put a bad reflection on the Sorority. Zeta women are the epitome of Finer Womanhood. Finer women are willing to serve, promote sisterly love, and be loyal and committed to the cause. To be a Zeta is to be a Finer Woman. A Finer Woman is likened to a virtuous woman: she is a crown jewel in her surroundings and is gracious and elegant.

Mary Louise Brown

Initiated in 1960 in Gamma Chapter – Morgan State University
Current Region: Atlantic

Zeta built a foundation for me to grow and develop into the woman that I have become by instilling the ideals of Finer Womanhood and service in my professional community and spiritual experiences. In addition to my spiritual values that I have gained through my relationship with God, I have been able to identify and define my purpose for living by modeling those values and ideals I learned from being a Zeta Lady!

Frances O. Cal

Initiated in 1956 in Beta Alpha Chapter – Southern University
Current Region: Pacific

A Finer Woman possesses class, dignity, and proper etiquette skills, but she is not snobby or stuck up.

A Finer Woman is considerate of others and reaches out to help when there is a need or void.

A Finer Woman is respectable and keeps her word, she is dependable.

A Finer Woman uses appropriate language. She is never vulgar. She speaks with authority, but is always gracious.

A Finer Woman always searches for the truth, even when it is not the majority opinion.

A Finer Woman dresses appropriately at all time. She dresses with dignity.

A Finer Woman walks with God. He is her guide, and teacher. She is in constant prayer.

A Finer Woman inspires others to do good deeds and services for the community.

A Finer Woman expresses sincere gratitude to those who help her or her cause. She knows,

"No one achieves success without the help of others"

Alfreda Brown Collins

Initiated in 1961 in Zeta Alpha Chapter – North Carolina A&T State College
Current Region: Eastern

The words "Finer Womanhood" bring back lots of pleasant memories. One of the drawing cards that attracted me to Zeta Phi Beta Sorority, Inc. was the "Finer Womanhood" component. I saw a group of serious sophisticated young women, well-dressed (suits/dresses and gloves) who walked with such pride and a sense of dignity that made an impression in my spirit. I wanted to be just like those women who portrayed "Finer Womanhood" on A & T College's campus.

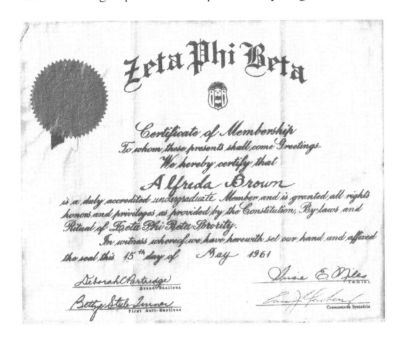

Even though changes have occurred in the last 50 years, Finer Womanhood to me has remained constant. Finer Womanhood denotes women who possess attributes that will make them acceptable to mankind and society as a whole. I see women who are not afraid to take on any given assignment or challenge in obtaining their goals while maintaining a sense of femininity. I am happy to witness Finer Womanhood as embellished, in my mind, making it more resilient than in the distant past. There is a strong need for Zeta Women to be more courageous, especially when faced with adversity. There is a reason for Zeta Women to stand firm on all the principles Zeta Phi Beta Sorority since the environment is changing at an alarming rate.

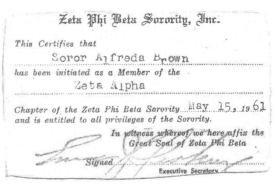

I am a strong advocate for Finer Womanhood. I will always believe that Finer Womanhood will, and should always, uphold the values of honesty, trust, self-control, and self-respect.

Betty S. Corbett

Initiated in 1957 in Delta Epsilon Zeta Chapter – West Palm Beach, FL
Current Region: Southeastern

Finer Womanhood to me means an exceptional woman who stands tall and makes a difference in the community. Finer Womanhood embraces phenomenal women that lift each other up in all their activities. A Finer Woman has a rich heritage that is shared with others.

Ida Mae Moore Croom

Initiated in 1955 in Sigma Beta Chapter – Alabama A&M University
Current Region: South Central

Finer Womanhood means to possess the ability to be free to pursue your own goals. A Finer Woman sees herself rich in wisdom and in wealth. She is successful and loved.

A Finer Woman embodies a positive self-image that is motivated by achievement. She puts God first and herself next because she understands self-actualization—the need to achieve what she wants in life after securing her basic needs to survive. A Finer Woman knows that she cannot make her husband, children, education and business a priority if she does not value responsibility and prioritize her relation with God above all else.

Therefore, a Finer Woman earns success, status, power, honor, love, happiness and fulfillment because she is the founder of her destiny. She understands that her creator is her source who provides all of her resources. As a vessel of honor, a Finer Woman is the essence of a virtuous woman.

Addie R. Faulk

Initiated in 1953 in Epsilon Beta Chapter – Alabama State University
Current Region: Great Lakes

When I became a Zeta, I thought I had something to offer to Zeta Phi Beta Sorority, Inc. I have a lot of experience with Zeta through all of the activities that I participated in on the campus of Alabama State University. Finer Womanhood means helping others whenever and however you can.

Willa J. Monroe Godley

Initiated in 1962 in Phi Beta Chapter – St. Augustine's University
Current Region: Eastern

As I reminisce about the words "Finer Womanhood," I recall two outstanding Zetas who started me on my love for Zeta. I was impressed by these outstanding Sorors like Millie Veasey and Grand Basileus Deborah P. Wolfe. The Rev. Dr. Wolfe left a lasting impression on my life.

Soror Veasey was an outstanding leader who groomed me. She took me in her arms and led me to the 54th Eastern Regional Leadership Conference in Hampton, Va. There, I learned about the many things Zetas do. I saw all the many things my Sorors did. This made an impression on my life. This conference started me on my way to developing a love that I wanted to share with others. Over the years, I have experienced a desire to help others by providing, developing, and sharing the Sorority's principles by living the characteristics of Zeta that each Soror has to share. The words Finer Womanhood showed many outstanding things that make women stand out and set benchmarks. One expression that stands out in Zeta is "they are trailblazers."

Carrie E. R. Grady

Initiated in 1957 in Lambda Chapter – Allen University
Current Region: Southeastern

My perspective of "Finer Womanhood" is that a Finer Woman should be all that she can be, whether the times are good or bad. She should exemplify love, care, respect and concern for humankind regardless of race, age, gender or station in life. She should carry herself in such a manner that all who come in contact with her will recognize that inner peace, grace, strength, love, compassion, courage and determination that emanates from her being or countenance.

A Finer Woman should be well prepared educationally and be willing to share her expertise with others, especially the youth of today. She is socially conscious and aware of the needs of others around her as well as the needs of others abroad because we are a global community.

A Finer Woman embraces her history because it is only when we understand and appreciate our history that we will not repeat the mistakes of the past. Understanding and celebrating our history helps us to give of ourselves in the present, to prepare for the future. Finer Womanhood is the essence of living life to the fullest, which embodies the physical, mental, social, and spiritual aspects of life. Finer Womanhood encompasses enriching the lives of others and seizing every opportunity to make the world a better place for all people.

Marian Anderson Hairston

Initiated in 1963 in Omega Chapter – Winston-Salem State University
Current Region: Eastern

If I were to make an acrostic for the letters in Finer Womanhood, it would read: **F**aithful, **I**nnovative, **N**oble, **E**ngaging, **R**eliable, **W**orthy, **O**bjective, **M**eticulous, **A**mbitious, **N**eighborly, **H**onorable, **O**bservant, **O**rderly, and **D**ependable.

As a student at WSSU, I observed that the Zetas were the most lady-like of the Greek women at that time. They appeared to be serious women who displayed Christian principles. This was a perfect fit for me because I possessed those characteristics as well. I liked the fact also that the Zetas required a strong GPA in order to join their Sisterhood. This led me to believe that they were more about academics than socializing.

Finer Womanhood appeared to be in the forefront of everything I learned while pledging. I came to know that our five Founders were Finer Women; and that the Sorority's chosen scripture from Proverbs was about a Finer Woman.

Finer Womanhood means being faithful to commitments; innovative in one's thinking; and, exhibiting a noble quality of life, taking the "high road" at all times. It means engaging in worthwhile activities at home and abroad, as well as being a reliable person who never waivers in her support of worthy projects. Finer Womanhood means being objective in evaluating others without bias and prejudice. It means having a meticulous nature that motivates one to carefully attend to details.

A Finer Woman has an ambitious drive that creates an inward belief that one should set obtainable goals and fiercely pursue them. Finer Womanhood means being neighborly, embracing those in need wherever they are found. A Finer Woman is honorable because she is highly respected and has a good reputation. She possesses an observant nature that causes her to take seriously rules and regulations set before her. Not only is she observant, she is also orderly in her home, on her job, and in her Sorority. Orderly people are generally dependable people; you can count on them to keep their word.

Fifty-two years have gone by since I was inducted into Omega chapter; but, I still feel strongly that Finer Womanhood should have a similar meaning to every Soror. These qualities are forever!

Rosa Swinney Harding

**Initiated in 1950 in Eta Alpha –
Kentucky State University
Current Region: Great Lakes**

A Finer Woman puts God first in her life and strives to follow His example in relating to people and helping others. I am thankful for the many blessed attributes God has bestowed on us, many of which can be identified through the spelling of Finer Womanhood.

F - Faithful, friendly and fair with others

I - Intelligent and improvising

N - Neighborly

E - Eyes and ears attuned to the needy

R - Reliable and ready to share responsibility

W - Willing to help others

O - Open to opportunities to render service

M - Mannerly and merciful with a forgiving heart

A - Attitude of acceptance and love

N - Nurturing and nudging with encouragement

H - Happy to be of service

O - Obedient to God's plan

O - Open to different opinions

D - Demonstrates by example what Finer Womanhood means

Grace Ausby Houchins

Initiated in 1964 - Beta Theta Zeta - Norfolk, VA
Current Region: Eastern

We know the story of the Five Pearls: Arizona Cleaver Stemons, Pearl Anna Neal, Myrtle Tyler Faithful, Viola Tyler Goings, and Fannie Pettie Watts.

We know the famous place: Howard University.

We know the popular date: 1920.

What we know for sure, with pride, that these were the world's finest.

These women were the world's best.

Since the world is our stage, Zeta Phi Beta deserves my praise.

She acts with dignity and grace; with the sign of nobility on her face.

We live with hearts of compassion and love for humanity.

Zeta's Finer Women are made for charity.

Community service is our ultimate goal.

In the life of a Zeta lady, the story of trailblazing strength is boldly told.

Zelda Hutcherson

Initiated in 1961 in Alpha Chapter - Howard University
Current Region: Pacific

My concept of Finer Womanhood far exceeds the application to members of Zeta Phi Beta Sorority. The concept applies to each of us as a complete person. A Finer Woman keeps her commitments. She keeps balance in her life. She has a sense of humor and is not afraid to laugh and enjoy life with other people. A Finer Woman spreads joys and warmth. She is a person people like to be around. She is friendly and welcomes new members to the Sorority.

A Finer Woman is a friend and confidante. She keeps information to herself that is shared with her in confidence. She does not judge other people's motives or their actions. She lets God be the judge, realizing that He is better qualified.

A Finer Woman maintains her values and remains true to her principles. She is willing to fill in where help is needed without expecting special recognition. A Finer Woman has the maturity to realize that hurt feelings are not fatal.

A Finer Woman is willing to encourage and share her knowledge with other less experienced members of the Sorority. Finer Womanhood teaches us that in spite of how much expertise we have in any particular area, we can perform any task for the first time. A Finer Woman gives generous praise and limited criticism.

The Finer Womanhood program gives Zeta chapter members the opportunity to recognize the accomplishments of others who have made a significant contributions to our communities.

The recognition of the values of Finer Womanhood can be displayed by planning and presenting a timely and professionally presented program that recognizes Scholarship, Service, and Sisterhood that culminates with the overall presentation of Finer Womanhood.

E. Fran Johnson

**Initiated in 1947 in Gamma Chapter -
Morgan State University
Current Region: Atlantic**

God has ushered me through a powerful 86 years of life's experiences—68 of which have included being a part of the Zeta Phi Beta Sorority way of life. These years have defined for me that if you genuinely carry out the ideals of Sisterhood, Scholarship, and Service, then you are well on your way to achieving the ideal of Finer Womanhood. These years have given me a perspective on what it means to be "Finer," although not perfect.

When I think of Finer Womanhood, I picture a woman who:

- is comfortable with who she is;
- is aware of her strengths and weaknesses;
- can acknowledge her mistakes and say "I'm sorry,"
- knows the value of laughter and tears;
- has a happy, pleasant attitude; and
- makes a difference simply by the way she lives and carries herself.

A Finer Woman is someone who exemplifies the characteristics that testify to her growth by overcoming obstacles and hardships in her life; and who has grown intellectually, emotionally, mentally, and physically as a result. She has developed courage by going through obstacles, and yet still has a positive mindset, and is able to share the testimony of her life with others without shame.

She is independent because she does not rely on anyone or anything to satisfy her needs, wants, desires, and dreams. She shows respect for others by having compassion for them. Others respect her because of the values she holds true, her behavior, her dress, her speech, her display of common sense and wisdom, her reputation, and her sincerity, dependability, reliability, and sensitivity.

When I think of Finer Womanhood, I see a picture of a strong woman who is educated, excels beyond her peers, is intellectual, professional, caring, has good manners, listens, and is articulate. A Finer Woman is God-fearing. She gives back to others because she realizes how fortunate she is and tries to be a blessing to others.

Finer Womanhood is a way of life and purposeful. A Finer Woman is special; she takes center stage through her lifetime. She acts like a lady; thinks like a man; works like a dog; and has the patience of Job.

A Finer Woman is a woman of Zeta!

Velma Keller

Initiated in 1964 in Psi Beta Chapter - Grambling State University
Current Region: Southern

Finer Womanhood

- Displaying self-confidence in yourself
- Knowing that one is a part of a sisterhood and a Sorority
- Holding true to all the principles that have been instilled in us from our Five Founders
- Enhancing the usefulness and advance the standards, ideals and general welfare of the community through service by extending activities
- Always ready when Zeta calls and to be a sister to fellow Sorors
- Always representing Zeta to the finest, no matter where you are
- Showing your Finer Womanhood throughout the community and helping others, i.e. setting an example for young ladies
- Always being true to yourself as well as to other Sorors.

Juanita B. King

Initiated in 1954 in Sigma Chapter – Livingstone College
Current Region: Eastern

As a Zeta into my 61st year, Finer Womanhood is a very important principle of this great Sisterhood. One should be able to look at a Zeta and see in the way she carries herself both publically and privately, the qualities of a woman with class and dignity. She does not have to be razor-thin or breathtakingly beautiful. She needs to be one who adheres to her pledge, "I will conduct myself at all times in such a manner as will not bring reproach upon my sisters." To me, internalizing this part of our pledge and living by it exudes Finer Womanhood whether a neophyte, an in-between, or a seasoned Dove. It is my personal belief that our five Founders, were they living, would expect no less than this for all ladies in this great Sisterhood.

Joanne Harvey Lottie, PhD

Initiated in 1964 in Psi Chapter – Clark College
Current Region: Southeastern

Finer Womanhood means

Loving the Lord

Kindness

Appropriate attire, demeanor, and attitude

Helping the poor

Loving and teaching our children

Serving the community and others

Advocating scholarship and being scholarly

Finer womanhood means

Answering the call always

Accepting criticism from a sister

Praying and reaching out to sisters in need

Standing up for the "all Zetas" when they know not.

Conducting ourselves appropriately at all times.

Setting an example for others to follow.

Who's Who—Joann Harve

Edna Metoyer

Initiated in 1950 in Nu Chapter – Virginia Union University
Current Region: Great Lakes

Finer Womanhood to me is much more than two words. Fine Women exemplify upstanding morals, good moral values. Fine Women do not put themselves above others, but walk side by side. Fine Women are able to listen, understand and make fair criticisms. In other words, constructive criticism. Fine Women must exemplify sisterly love in a sisterhood which radiates where other women can feel good about being a finer woman in the sisterhood of Zeta Phi Beta Sorority, Inc. Every Soror should exemplify Sisterly Love in more than just words.

Lizzie G. Miller

Initiated in 1946 in Louisville Municipal College:
Black Division of the University Of Louisville
Current Region: Great Lakes

My perspective of Finer Womanhood grew out of a relationship that the teacher and students at the Louisville Municipal College shared, reminding us that we must SUCCEED in life. The words Finer Womanhood mean to me what it should mean to every Soror. I am a firm "practicing believer" that we are our sister's keeper, but I sometime feel that as African Americans, we have lost the bond that we once shared in a segregated environment.

When I think of Finer Womanhood and what it means to me, I am a believer that Finer Womanhood means seeking out people whom we can assist as mentors or role models to help them attain their goals in life. It does not matter whether the individuals are members of our Sorority, seeking employment, or if they are in need, we should not miss an opportunity to reach others as we climb.

My parents taught us children, "Be careful as you climb the ladder of success," and to not be haughty, but to help others as we climb because we never know whom we will meet if we fall back down. I can remember as a student in college, the Zetas were known as those women who excelled in school. It was known throughout the campus that we were concerned about our fellow man and wanted them to succeed. We were blessed with teachers who were Zetas, who taught us by example as they monitored our grades, our friends and our behavior.

I knew that I had aced all of my college exams when I was called into the office of the librarian (a Zeta Soror), and questioned as to why I had failed my English one. Mind you, I was an English major, and my goal was to teach in the public schools of Louisville. The librarian, who was friends with my English teacher, questioned her privately about a possible reason for my failure. They both knew that I could do better. On the true and false part of the test, I had reversed the answers, and completely had them all wrong. I was at a loss for why I had incorrectly answered the questions. The librarian asked my teacher to give me another chance because she was sure that something was wrong. He agreed to do this if it could be kept between the three of us. The librarian and my teacher put their jobs in jeopardy for me.

To me, the librarian exhibited Finer Womanhood by putting her job on the line to reach out to me. And from that day until now, I consider "Finer Womanhood" as being willing to put your life on the line to help someone who is need of a second chance. I was grateful that someone cared enough for me to give me a second chance. I believe that Finer Womanhood is giving others a "second chance."

I am blessed to have so many women in my life who served as examples of Finer Womanhood, beginning with my mother, "a stay-at-home mom" who emphasized the importance of getting an education and becoming gainfully employed. I was blessed that in high school and college, I was surrounded by the women of Zeta Phi Beta Sorority whose guidance and support prepared me and other women to reach for the stars, not just to be recognized for fame or fortune, but to lift others as we climb. These women of noble character had reached their goals in life, but were not satisfied until others too, had reached theirs.

One such Zeta was my sister-in law, Frances Halsell Gilliam, who inspired me to become a Zeta and reminded me that we do not live in this world alone, that we should reach out to others and share "sisterly love in thought, word and deed." Frances was and is one of the countless women who are responsible for my reaching out to others, and inspiring me lift up those who are oppressed; comfort those who are in need; and, never look for praise from men or women for whatever we do as members of an organization that exhibits "Finer Womanhood, Sisterly Love, Scholarship, and Service.

When I became Director of the Great Lakes Region, Soror Ida B. King was my mentor, friend and midnight caller who taught me by example what was required of me as a leader in our beloved Sorority. Each day that I live, I try to touch someone's life through my church, my Sorority and in my neighborhood. I practice the concept of Finer Womanhood, believing that we are all sisters, with no big "I's, and little u's." I take our oath seriously, to be a protection one for the other, and carry out the mandates of our beloved Sorority at all times.

Elizabeth S. Munnings

Initiated in 1949 in Mu Beta Chapter – Bethune-Cookman University
Current Region: Southeastern

The term "Finer Womanhood" challenges us to be the best that we can be. It elevates our minds and our actions to higher heights. It makes Zeta soar! We must always be willing to hold our standards high for Zeta and for ourselves.

Bettye Allen Murchison

Initiated in 1955 in Omega Beta Chapter – Fayetteville State University
Current Region: Eastern

As we journey to the 2020 Centennial, it is an awesome opportunity to share my perspective of the noble concept of "Finer Womanhood."

As I think about Finer Womanhood, my thoughts go back to our Founders: Sorors Arizona Cleaver-Stemons, Myrtle Tyler-Faithful, Viola Tyler Goings, Fannie Pettie-Watts, and Pearl Neal who set a standard 95 years ago for women of their belief and blazed trails we follow today. The unique heritage the Founders built on the principles of Scholarship, Service, Sisterly Love and Finer Womanhood have stood the test of time, touching many lives through service to others around the world. Therefore, to me, Finer Womanhood is a way of life. It expresses a woman's core values and beliefs. A woman who exhibits courage and endurance, and demonstrates with confidence a commitment to help make the world a better place for mankind.

Other people respect women I consider Finer Women because she is compassionate and values friendships. A Finer Woman knows life has a purpose, and she focuses her attention on that purpose throughout her life. As described in Proverbs 31:10-31, she is strong and kind and truly "a virtuous woman whose price is far above rubies." She commits and exposes herself to activities that nurture hope and a sense of belonging. She exhibits courage and endurance, and transcends the limited thinking of other people, refusing to be satisfied with the status quo.

It is difficult to separate being a Zeta and being a Finer Woman. Once you are a Zeta, everything you say and do must embrace the meaning of Finer Womanhood because we will always be associated with the image people have of Zeta and our commitment to Service, Scholarship, Sisterhood and Finer Womanhood.

Vera Hall Paul

Initiated in 1960 in Beta Alpha Chapter – Southern University
Current Region: Great Lakes

Women: They are individuals who love God, themselves, and people. They have a sense of humor. They are women who are esteemed in their communities, who have unselfishly given of themselves, their time and talents. They have an unwavering commitment to help others. They are women who reflect what it means to not just talk the talk, but also walk the walk for their race. They are extremely positive and do not believe in complaining about life, which should be viewed as a tremendous gift.

Finer Womanhood also means you have a commitment to bring about a better society wherein men, women and children shall have a better opportunity to enjoy their blessings.

Finer Womanhood means a community who believes in a community conscious, action-oriented organization, with a holistic approach with a sincere heart and desire to touch the pulse of the people.

Finer Womanhood means democracy, justice and love for Zeta, the women it represents.

Beatrice H. Pearson

Initiated in 1950 in Epsilon Beta Chapter – Alabama State University
Current Region: South Central

"Finer Womanhood" is a term that represents women who aspire to be builders in the Sorority, or at church, or community. As a member of the Sorority, we should work as a cooperative group to maintain the ideals of Finer Womanhood and Sisterly Love. One should strive to maintain the highest ideals in every endeavor, be it scholarship, a positive relationship in the Sorority, as well as the community. We are role models that others should want to emulate. We are known in the community as builders on the job, supporting community programs and the church. As builders, we are not notorious as we make contributions. As we work in all areas we are not full of arrogance when contributing to self-esteem programs. We strive not to be judgmental, but calm in our ideas, and roles as members of a group. We are open to opinions and ideas rather than taking sides with individuals. We must have patience and understanding of others whether they are in a sorority, educated, poor or homeless. Live by the spirit and treat others as we want to be treated.

Finer Womanhood means working to improve society.

Dorothy Adams Peck, EdD

Initiated in 1948 in Beta Chapter – Morris Brown College
Current Region: Southeastern

The circumstances of my birth—my family constellation with its strong spiritual, educational, cultural and social orientation—serve to undergird my perspective of Finer Womanhood. That perspective is based on the concept of LOVE in its broadest sense: *vertically, internally and horizontally* – love of God, self, and others.

"God created man and woman in His Own image." This is what I was taught and believe. For me this means that from the time I was conceived by my parents and delivered at birth by my "midwife-grandmother," a love affair with God and Christian principles preceded and played key roles in the fervency of love and devotion among family members, as well as with other involved in the varied personal, social, occupational and professional pursuits I experienced.

At birth and throughout their developmental stages, women are blessed by God with degrees of *Fine-ness.* The paraphrased Biblical quotation attributed to Solomon is a description of *Finer Womanhood* qualities of Zeta Phi Beta initiates:

> *They are noble character worth far more than rubies…*
>
> *They set about their work vigorously and are effective in all accepted tasks…*
>
> *They open their arms and heart generously to any and all who seek their help…*
>
> *They are fully clad with integrity, strength and dignity;*
>
> *Wisdom is apparent in all their instruction and counsel.*
>
> *Many do noble things, but these women surpass them all.*
>
> *Their attributes deserve and earn rich rewards for*
>
> *their praiseworthy work in all assignments.*
>
> --Proverbs 1:10-31 (Excerpted/Paraphrased)

Rather than being content with the *status quo,* I concur with Ronnie Oldham that **more excellence in Finer Womanhood should be pursued by:**

> **Caring** more than others think is **Wise,**
>
> **Risking** more than other think is **Safe,**
>
> **Dreaming** more than others think is **Practical**, and
>
> **Expecting** more than others think is **Possible.**

Wanda Perry Poole

Initiated in 1947 in Omicron Chapter – Shaw University
Current Region: Eastern

My perspective of Finer Womanhood is synonymous with the term, "servant to a higher calling." If you are a servant to a higher calling, then you are very mindful of the way you carry and portray yourself in all situations. You understand that you must be willing to help others. This can be done in many forms or fashion. I have chosen to reach back and help the next generation; mentor new and seasoned Sorors; and, support our illustrious Royal Blue and White Sisterhood by serving wherever there is a need.

Clair Floyd Porter

Initiated in 1964 in Lambda Chapter – Allen University
Current Region: Southeastern

FINER WOMANHOOD

F – Firm (and) Fair (Steadfast) (Resolve) (Competent) (Flexible) Factual

I – Impressionable, Illustrative, Imaginable, Intense

N – Natural, Neat, Needed

E – Endurance, Eagerness, Educated, Effective, Efficient

R – Respectful, Reasonable, Reliable

W – Warrior, Watchful, Well-Informed, Whole-Hearted, Willing, Worthy

O – Obedient, Objectively, Obliging, Open-Minded

M – Magnetic, Magnificent, Memorable, Mental Agility

A – Ability, Accessible, Aptitude

N – Nobly, No-Nonsense, Nonpartisan, Noticeable

H – Hard-Core, (Steadfast), Helpful, Honest, Honorable

O – Obligation (Responsibility), Outlook (Possibility – Chances)

O – Observant, Official, Oversee (Supervise)

D – Dauntless, Dedicated, Drive, Duress, Dutiful

Juanita M. Robinson

Initiated in 1952 in Tau Chapter - Philander Smith College
Current Region: Atlantic

Celebrating the Finer Woman we are is always a big part of Zeta Phi Beta Sorority, Inc.- Eta Pi Zeta chapter's activities. Our yearly planning always includes space and time for planning a celebration. We make sure Zeta is shining throughout the community. To me, Finer Womanhood means that Zetas exhibit a sisterly love and special glow among each other and throughout the community.

Bernice Sanders

Initiated in 1955 in Mu Chapter – Claflin University
Current Region: Southeastern Region

I joined Zeta 60 years ago because of the love, care and compassion we felt for each other and others. If we have love, real love for self and others, the world would be a better place for everyone. Finer Womanhood is caring and compassion.

Mary S. Simpson

Initiated in 1952 in Epsilon Chapter
Current Region: Great Lakes

The meaning of Finer Womanhood to me (and should be to all Sorors) is that one is a woman who is distinguished in character and appearance. She exemplifies quality and excellence and does things in a proper and satisfactory way.

Her goals are to be the best she can be and to mentor other women so that they will be the best, too. Since "Finer Women Don't Haze" is one of our mottos, it should be kept uppermost in our minds and hearts. Hazing can be committed in many ways, and a Finer Woman should be cognizant of those ways. A Finer Woman should discourage any type of disruptive behavior. If the behavior continues, steps should be taken to report the behavior to the proper Sorority officers.

We, SORORS, should be implementing the objectives of our five Founders – Service, Scholarship, Sisterhood, and Finer Womanhood – and keep these objectives uppermost in our minds. I hope that Sorors became Zetas for the RIGHT reasons and not just to wear Royal Blue and White and the ZΦB symbols. We, Zetas, should also encourage our Phi Beta Sigma brothers to exemplify Finer Manhood.

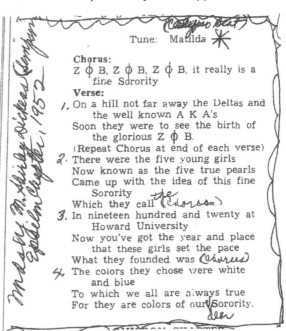

Laura M.A. Smith

**Initiated in 1950 in Lambda Beta Chapter –
Jackson State College (now Jackson State University)
Current Region: Great Lakes**

When I was a child, I thought as a child. I played with my dolls, playhouse, etc. I was born in Jackson, MS to parents who could not read or write. I always had great faith and believed in God.

I grew up very poor, but I was blessed by God to graduate from Jackson State College with a B.S. Degree in Home Economics in 1951. I was one of the charter members of Zeta Phi Beta, Lambda Beta chapter on the campus of Jackson State University. In later years, I received a Master of Science Degree in Education from Indiana University.

I believed in being a good woman so that one day, I could be a good mother. I married Oscar C. Smith, and we were blessed with two lovely girls, Beverly and Evelyn. We were blessed to have a double wedding for them. We were blessed with two sons-in-law, Jesse L. Craig and Winfred T. Shelton, and each family was blessed with one child, Jesse L.S. Craig and LaJoi L.L. Shelton. Now, I have a great-grand baby, Grace Evelyn.

I retired from Indianapolis Public Schools in 1989. My husband passed away on Dec. 10, 2010 after 57 years of marriage. I am a member of Emmanuel Missionary Baptist Church, where I work with the Women's Missionary and Bereavement ministries. My goal in life is to never stop praising God.

My mother, Laura M. A. Smith, is a tremendous woman. Her key characteristics include kindness, warmth, energy and wisdom. She leads her life by keeping God first in everything she does.

My mom raised me to be a respected, upstanding and independent woman, and has always taken time for me. When I'm feeling low, she lifts my spirit with encouraging words and prayer. When I've achieved a significant milestone, my mom is my strongest cheerleader! There are not enough words to describe how much I look up to my mother – she's one of a kind and I feel privileged to be her daughter.

The positive attributes of Finer Womanhood encompass the loving characteristics that Laura Smith exhibited in the past and to the present:

Standards: Choosing to dress and step professionally. That's my Mom.

Morals: Guided by God's Word and submitting to God's will. That's my Mom.

Customs: Baking candied sweet potatoes or preparing to honor a loved one. That's my Mom.

Service: When tirelessly visiting the sick or comforting Sisters/Brothers (by blood or love) in distress. That's my Mom!

Mary Smith

Initiated in 1963 in Psi Beta Chapter – Grambling College
Current Region: Great Lakes

Finer Womanhood to me means that our Sorority practices what it preaches about Finer Womanhood.

Frances Oxner Stephens

Initiated in 1950 in Lambda Chapter – Allen University
Current Region: Southeastern

A Finer Woman is a woman who has respect and love for God and self, and shows this love toward those around her and those she meets. She works to improve self, family and the community where she lives. When she respects herself, she will respect others. A Finer Woman has high moral character and expects the same of her associates. A Finer Woman thinks before she acts, and considers all options before deciding. A Finer Woman acknowledges her errors and moves forward. She is indeed a special woman.

Althea Taylor-Jones, PhD

Initiated in 1965 in Epsilon Alpha Chapter – Tennessee State University
Current Region: Eastern

Finer Womanhood is a principle unique to Zeta Phi Beta Sorority, Inc., and is a part of my life on a daily basis. A Finer Woman embodies a loving and compassionate persona (personality, image). Some characteristics and/or qualities are listed below:

1. She is a God-fearing woman (reverencing-showing respect). This is the most important quality/characteristic/image.

2. She is family-oriented – family comes first (biological, Sorority and mankind).

3. She is community-oriented through the provision of service to and advocacy for the less fortunate, to include those in a state of poverty, homelessness or other misfortune.

4. She is intelligent – displays/uses knowledge in a rational and judicious manner. She is not afraid, rather enthusiastic to share her scholarly experiences with those with whom she comes into contact.

5. She is never closed-minded, rather, open to new challenges and exhibits innovative tendencies to move the Sisterhood forward. Additionally, she employs strategies for the good of humankind, to move her family, community and world forward.

The qualities listed above, as well as others, are essentials to Finer Womanhood. Finer Women are positive women. Therefore, they do not engage in any behavior that is negative, such as intimidation/bullying or hazing.

A Finer Woman is the epitome of the following:

F – Faith, fortitude; forward-thinking; fabulous

I – Intelligence; intuition; industriousness; innovation

N – Nobility; neatness; negotiable; notable

E – Efficiency; effectiveness; enthusiasm; elegance; excellence; extraordinary

R – Reliable; restrained; refined; responsible; remarkable; resourceful

Juanita Williams Toatley

Initiated in 1948 in Psi Alpha Chapter – South Carolina State College
Current Region: Southeastern

Finer Womanhood speaks to a woman who is true to herself with no pretense. It is a woman who believes all things are possible. When she sets out to achieve her goals, it is done with the upmost integrity. A Finer Woman lives a life that sets an example of positivity and service.

Ernestine Turner

Initiated in 1956 in Beta Alpha Chapter – Southern University
Current Region: Pacific

Demonstrating loyalty, honesty and having the ability to show sisterly love without stipulations is what Finer Womanhood means. She should also have a heart to forgive, and high moral standards that reflect character and integrity. It is maintaining a positive attitude with class and elegance and being a woman of faith with the fortitude to rise above difficult circumstances. It is respecting ones' self as well as others and being graceful, carrying yourself in a dignified manner at all times. Having these qualities will allow you to be an example for others, and put you in a position to lead others and give back to future generations.

Bernice Golson Wilson

Initiated in 1950 in Epsilon Beta Chapter – Alabama State University
Current Region: South Central

This photo of Alpha Sigma Zeta 2012 Finer Womanhood Celebration. Back in the day, black attire with hat and white gloves was the signature of fine ladies – Zetas.

The founding principle "Finer Womanhood" encompasses scholarship, sisterly love and service, qualities uniquely identified in Zetas.

I became a Zeta in1950 at Alabama State University with two line sisters – Mary Jackson and Dorothy Richardson. Our first official attendance at a Finer Womanhood observance was with Alpha Rho Zeta and Epsilon Beta Chapters in Montgomery. This was an auspicious celebration for me because I was in an audience of former teachers and family friends (Zetas), who were my role models from early childhood.

Having been recognized as Alpha Sigma Zeta Chapter's "Zeta of the Year," with the prerequisite of a demonstrating qualities of Finer Womanhood – wholeness in mind, body, and spirit – and being an active, productive asset to family, church and community, has kept me focused on its true meaning as one of our founding principles. The Sisterhood, at the time of my induction, was identified as "ladies with class," scholarship, talent and culture. We were Zetas. To be a part of this journey since the spring of 1950 to Centennial preparation has been an awesome experience.

Millie Dunn Veasey

Initiated in 1952 in Phi Beta Chapter, St. Augustine's University
Current Region: Eastern

As I began to reminisce about the words Finer Womanhood, my thoughts carried me back to the beginning of my journey into Zetadom. The Bible—Proverbs 31:10: "Who can find a virtuous woman …."

A Finer Woman indeed, I reminded myself. We all know this reference to women and womanhood too well. Therefore, I needed to think further.

Again, to the Bible—Proverbs 31:15-18: "She is more precious than rubies; and all the things thou canst desire are not to be compared unto her. Length of days is in her right hand, and in her left hand riches and honor, her ways are ways of pleasantness, and all her paths are peace. She is a tree of life to them that lay hold upon her; and happy is every one that retaineth her."

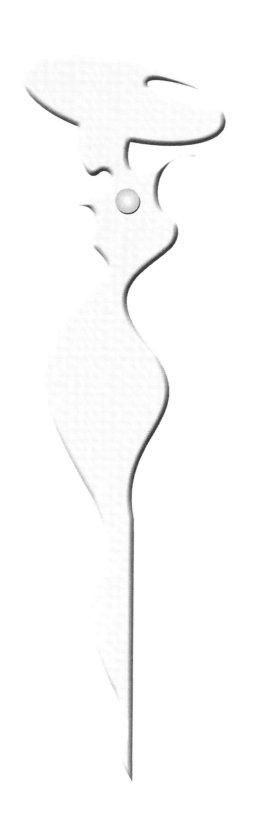

Zeta Legacy to Zeta Dove

Brenda R. Gibson Reed

My 'journey' through Zeta began on August 2, 1939 when I was born to Soror Ione Margrite Hartley Gibson. Mother and her biological sister Soror Thelma Louise Hartley Fisher were initiated into Epsilon Alpha Chapter at Tennessee State University in 1936.

Aunt Thelma served Zeta as Executive Secretary (now Executive Director), and National Trustee Board Chair. Mother, whose footsteps I've been attempting to follow, served her beloved Zeta as: Basileus of Beta Omicron Zeta Chapter for five years; Michigan State Director (when they were called Associate Director); Great Lakes Regional Director for seven years; National Trustee; National Executive Board Chair; Organizer/ Basileus Emeritus of Kappa Rho Zeta Chapter; and, Resident Agent of Birch Haven for 12 years.

Mother was blessed with four Zeta daughters, two of whom—myself included—are still financial and active in Kappa Rho Zeta. Mother had the opportunity to beam with pride when our picture was taken at Boulé 1976 in Atlanta when all four of her Zeta daughters were present. When mother and Aunt Thelma were still with us, they traveled to Regionals and Boulés together and shared the same room. My sister Michele and I also travel together and share the same room.

Michele and I have been ZOL certified, MIP certified, served as undergrad advisors, held top positions in the chapter, region, state; and, I on the National level. I'm sure if Mom were still here, she'd be smiling. I always feel she's smiling down on me every day because I'm doing what she would have wanted—serving God and Zeta.

Our 'family' legacy is as follows:

- Soror Ione H. Gibson, Mother, 1936*
- Soror Thelma H. Fisher, Aunt, 1936*
- Soror Brenda R. Gibson Reed, 1959
- Soror Estrellita O. Gibson, Sister, 1962
- Soror Phyllis C. Gibson, Sister, 1967
- Soror Michele Y. Gibson Whitted, Sister 1976
- Soror Jacqueline M. Whitted Jones, Niece, 2000
- Soror Johnetta P. Morrow, Cousin, 1954*
  *(Deceased)

I was an IZ (Interested in Zeta) and Archonian in the early 1950's, and began 'pledging' in Lambda Chapter, Allen University, Columbia, S.C., where Aunt Thelma was Dean of Women. I transferred to Tennessee State University in 1959, where I was initiated into Epsilon Alpha Chapter in October 1959 during the administration of Past International Grand Basileus Dr. Deborah Cannon Partridge Wolfe.

I was the first Grammateus of Kappa Rho Zeta Chapter after it was chartered in 1981 during the administration of PIGB Dr. Edith V. Francis. I was later elected National, Great Lakes Region, and State of Wisconsin Phylacter in 1992 when Dr. Jylla Moore Tearte was elected Grand Basileus, and in 1996 was appointed Wisconsin and Minnesota State Director during Dr. Barbara West Carpenter's administration. I was also elected Organizer/Basileus Emeritus of Sigma Alpha Zeta Chapter, which was chartered during Soror Carpenter's administration, and later served as Basileus from 2000-2007 and 2010-2012. In 2009, I was awarded "Ms. Finer Womanhood" at the first Ms. Zeta Pageant, which was held during the Zeta Organizational Leadership conference in Washington D.C., and in 2010 received my Zeta Dove pin in 2010 under Soror Underwood. Later, in 2012, I was appointed Resident Agent - Birch Haven following the election of Soror Mary Breaux Wright as International Grand Basileus.

Additionally, I served as Great Lakes Region Representative to the National Nominating Committee in 2009 during Soror Cheryl P. Underwood's administration; Phylacter of Kappa Rho Zeta Chapter in 2013; and National Trustee in 2014 during Grand Wright's administration.

Serving as the Great Lakes Region Grammateus was an honor, privilege and great learning experience for me because Soror Ida B. King was still with us. When she spoke, I had to capture every word because she would ask for it to be read back. If I missed a word, she would give it to me so that whatever she had said would be correct and complete. Soror Lizzie G. Miller was Regional Director during my years as Grammateus, and if something was said during discussion that she didn't think should appear in the minutes, she would tell me "don't put that in the minutes."

I have met many Sorors who exemplify Finer Womanhood in their demeanor, dress, and actions, including Soror Ida B. King (she's the reason I wear 'big' hats); my mom - Soror Ione H. Gibson who walked, talked, lived and breathed Zeta all of my life; and the Founders I had the privilege of meeting and talking to at several Boulés, the sisters Sorors Myrtle Tyler Faithful and Viola Tyler Goings. Whenever I saw Soror Faithful, I would say to her "You don't know who I am," and she'd reply, "Yes I do. You're Ione Gibson's daughter," and, we'd laugh together. Sorors Isabel M. Herson, Luellia W. Harrison, Annye P. Roberts, M. Ann Prendergast, Doris M. Stokes, Mary Breaux Wright, Aunt Thelma, Jylla M. Tearte; and, so many more have also exemplified Finer Womanhood.

It has been a wonderful, inspiring journey on this Zeta road, which has been filled with its ups and downs—thankfully more ups than downs. We were taught the meaning of Finer Womanhood by our mother, who led by example. She and Aunt Thelma were the epitome of Finer Women.

I have served this wonderful sisterhood on all levels; am still serving; and will continue to serve until the Good Lord, God Almighty calls me home to be with Him.

Finer at the Knee of Our Doves

Fighter   **Intelligent**   **Never Giving Up**   **Encouragers**   **Relationships**

Doves Edna Metoyer and Mary Simpson

Rosalind Walker-Lewis

Over the last 17 years as I have worked, played and served in Eta Upsilon Zeta Chapter, Fort Wayne, Ind., I have had the opportunity to grow and to make an impact through work, church and my Sorority. As I have spent time with my Sorors at home or out and about, I think back on some of my most precious moments and realize they have usually been matched with something our Doves have said or done.

Each Dove, Sorors Edna Metoyer and Mary Simpson, now has 60+ years of service to the Sisterhood. They are two of our chapter's charter members and the only ones who have remained actively engaged in the chapter affairs. Soror Metoyer is also a charter member of Lambda Rho Zeta in Michigan. Their Fighters' determination to remain actively engaged in Zeta at all levels often amazes me. During 2013-2015, Soror Metoyer has been the Great Lakes Regional Dove Coordinator, and Soror Simpson, the Indiana State Dove Coordinator. Their minds remain sharp as they share their wit and intelligence at every turn with whomever is willing to patiently listen and learn. They provide clarity to ensure we are performing at the highest levels of excellence.

Although their physical bodies are not always as cooperative as they would prefer, they continue to show by example the importance of Never Giving Up. Through the years, both of them, 30+ years my senior, have been the Zeta Energizer Bunnies. Soror Simpson can dance many of us under the table, and is on the road more than the average person half her age. She is known for her attendance at every NPHC event held in the city, and always represents Zeta in a Finer Fashion.

She works to share her gifts of the English language, as she is the designated proof-reader for our chapter and will "red ink" your paper with the best teachers and professors. Another of her passions is "Table Etiquette." With her travelling table set, Soror Simpson has performed many etiquette workshops around Fort Wayne both for the chapter and for other organizations supporting youth as well. It has also been very interesting to see Soror Simpson grow. Speaking in front of groups was a major challenge for her, but now she is both willing and eager to share with comedic flare.

Soror Metoyer has a grace and charm that draws you to her. This has been seen on many instances when we travel and meet the Sigma Brothers. With all of younger Sorors present, Soror Metoyer would receive the attention and recognition of the brothers, as they seemed to always flock around her as the rest of us stood in awe. We always wondered what was in her recipe!

She continues to remain engaged with the chapter as the Finer Womanhood Program event co-chair, Protocol expert, and other areas of expertise. Additionally, until recently, Soror Metoyer has been taking care of her son, TC, who is wheelchair bound, and her 104-year-old blind mother. She continues to display a tenacity that demands recognition and respect.

Our Doves have been Encouragers to any member of the Blue and White who has had needed a kind word or guidance to deal with either a personal, professional or Zeta Challenge. They have always been trustworthy with secrets of many, and they are wise, reflective of their years. As I have shared my desires of entrepreneurship, in their own way, they have provided words of encouragement and accountability, each with their own style. They have both been mother figures to many inside and outside of the chapter.

As I have traveled over the years with these ladies, one is able to see the lasting Relationships that have been established, as other Sorors are constantly seeking them out and checking on them. Their phone time offers a wide range of telephone numbers called and extensive minutes clocked from around the Sisterhood. The same is recognized when we attend sorority events. It is wonderful to watch Sorors from around the region seeking them out, checking on them, and loving on them. This includes some of the past international presidents. Additionally, when they are not present, I am asked, "Where are your travel buddies?" I know I am in good company.

During my two years as Indiana State Director, I drew upon our Doves on many occasions, taking full advantage of their wisdom. They were always willing to answer any question that I may have had. Also, both are willing to hold a strong discussion or debate with Sisterly Love to ensure their points were clearly understood. Looking back, I realize that I have become a Finer Zeta because I was able to sit at the knees of our Eta Upsilon Zeta Doves, Sorors Edna Metoyer and Mary Simpson. They continue to offer their all to the Sisterhood. I salute them for their gifts of love for Zeta, legacy of imparted knowledge, and kindness of heart that they continue to share with me over these many years.

They are Finer and are committed to passing it along! How many others of us are Finer because we have sat at the knees of our Doves? As is our responsibility, "To Whom Much is Given, Much is Required."

How are we passing it on to those coming behind us?

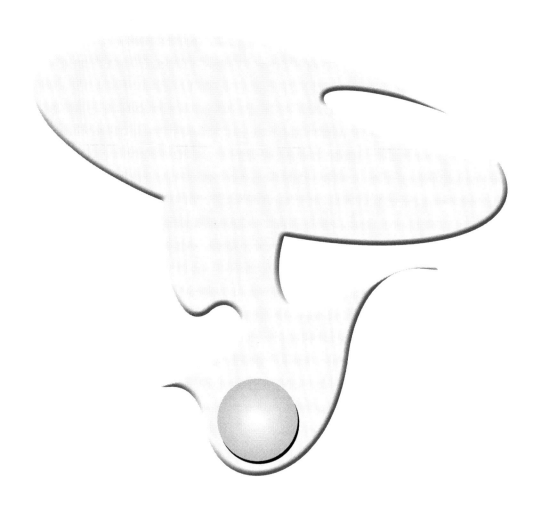

Sitting With Sarah

Cheryl A. B. Christie and Janet Y. Bivins, Esq.

Soror Sarah Mae Felton Bivins has exemplified Finer Womanhood every day of her life prior to, and since, her initiation into Zeta Phi Beta Sorority, Inc., in 1950. She not only has a legacy of service, but has legacies in Zeta.

Zeta Dove Sarah Felton Bivins, now 86 years old, was initiated in Spring 1950 with Theta Beta Chapter, Tuskegee Institute. She has held membership in not only the South Central Region, but also the Atlantic, Eastern, Midwestern, and Southeastern Regions. Soror Bivins has a Zeta Legacy comprised of two daughters (Cheryl A. B. Christie and Janet Y. Bivins, Esq.), one granddaughter (Angela M. Christie), one sister (Patricia A. Felton), one niece (Cannesta Y. Felton), and one triumphant cousin (Melanie Anderson).

She has served Zeta in numerous appointed positions, and has been elected to office at the chapter, state, regional, and national levels, including Chapter Basileus, Missouri State Director, National Trustee. Soror Bivins had the opportunity to work with Past Grands Kissner, Francis, Thomas, Tearte, Carpenter, and Moore. She has been a dedicated member of Zeta for 64 years, and whether in college; graduate school; during her student teaching; as a teaching professional; or retired, she has always maintained her membership in the local chapter. Her longest chapter membership has been with Eta Zeta Zeta Chapter in Kansas City, Mo. from 1969 through 2014. She recently relocated, and is now a member of Beta Delta Zeta Chapter in Philadelphia, PA.

On this occasion, all of her surviving legacies submitted questions for her to answer. The interview was conducted by her daughters, Cheryl and Jan. Here's what she had to say:

This photo of Tuskegee Institute and Tuskegee grad chapter Zetas was taken between 1950 and 1952. Undergraduate Soror Sarah Felton is on Row 2, 4th from the left.

1. Identify two things that attracted you to Zeta when you were a student at Tuskegee Institute in 1950.

I went to a Rush Party where you met sorority members of the different sororities. I was impressed by three Zetas in the chapter, as well as one Zeta professor and one Zeta administrator. I liked their personalities and I liked the fact that scholarship was a big deal.

2. Let's go all the way back to your introduction to Zeta. Who is responsible and how did you know this great Sorority was the perfect fit for you?

The Teacher Educator for Home Economics was a Zeta. She was responsible for student teaching. We had high regard and great respect for her. She was so well-read. She told five of us in the Home Economics Education major who were pledging: "You are pledging Zeta Phi Beta, and I expect more of you than I do the others."

3. How have you seen Zeta affecting the community at large?

Zeta affects the at-large community through her programs. Every Grand adopts some national community service program with which we can readily identify, and our communities have been impacted by our national program-matic thrusts.

4. What changes have you observed in Zeta since the time you became a member to the times your daughters became members, to the time your granddaughter became a member?

When I became a member, Zeta had three ideals. We wrote poems and songs about them when I was pledging. The Founders defined these ideals as Sisterhood, Scholarship, *and* Service *because they felt they were important, in that order. Also, the tune for the hymn used to be different.*

5. Being the first of three generations of Zetas, how important to you was it to instill into your family the passion for the organization?

I hoped from the beginning and certainly when my daughters were ready for college that each would want to be a Zeta. I remained active, wanting them both to see how much I enjoyed being a part of the Sorority. Cheryl being a Zetalite and Jan being an Archonette was a part of that vision.

6. What does *Finer Womanhood* mean to you? Has it changed since your initiation into the sisterhood?

If you think about the various oaths—the Opening Prayer, or our Ritual, for instance—they outline the characteristics of what Finer Womanhood embodies and, therefore, what Finer Womanhood means to me. Defining Finer Womanhood in this fashion hasn't changed for me, and we should all strive to exhibit these characteristics.

7. If there is one gem you could pass on to the next generation of Finer Women, what would it be?

Keep your membership active and current. When you join a new chapter, pay your dues and learn the "lay of the land" before you start offering ideas to change the chapter's culture.

8. Having seen growth in Zeta for over several decades, what is the one thing of which you're most proud?

I'm most proud of the different kinds of community service programs we have defined--from Stork's Nest to Z-HOPE to Elder Care and the St. Jude's initiative. Stork's Nest was initially aimed at teen pregnancy prevention, and with the workshops we offered and gifts we gave people for attending, these strategies helped us address this issue.

9. Successful leaders, I feel, are visionaries. Please share some of the ideas that became realities under some of the strong leadership you experienced.

When we think of strong leadership, one usually refers to different administrations and having an exciting time to be a Zeta. The Kissner years were an exciting time for me. Soror Kissner was quite the leader; I was a State Director and Basileus during her tenure as Grand. Most recently, I said to our current Grand, "This is going to be an exciting time to be a Zeta." Soror Wright has come in at a time when we had serious problems, and she is providing leadership to get us on solid financial footing.

10. What's your favorite thing about being a Zeta?

My favorite thing is the bond we share--everywhere I have affiliated (Tuskegee Institute; Tuskegee; Tallahassee; Durham; Savannah; Philadelphia; and Kansas City, MO). Zeta has meant a lot to me. In Savannah, when I was on maternity leave, the chapter paid for my babysitter so that I could work on chapter tasks during the day.

11. What's your least favorite thing about being a Zeta?

One of the things that has caused me concern is all the politics. Sometimes it is particularly ugly.

12. Do you still keep in touch with your Line Sisters?

Yes. There were five of us—Connie Harper, Mildred Hall, Stella Deloney and Eunice Jones. Over the years I've been in touch with all but one, and that's Stella. She did not return after her sophomore year. I understand that Eunice is now deceased. I enjoy catching up with Connie and Mildred.

13. Other reminisces:

"Sororities and fraternities came to my campus in 1948, my freshman year. You began pledging in the fall (had to be at least a sophomore), and in the Spring you became an "active" pledgee" and then were initiated. We had a strong relationship with Phi Beta Sigma—they were so good to us. We always had a Zeta-Sigma Formal in the Spring. They would pay the bulk of the expenses because they had more members. State meetings were organized after I was out of school. I was the first Secretary for the State of Georgia."

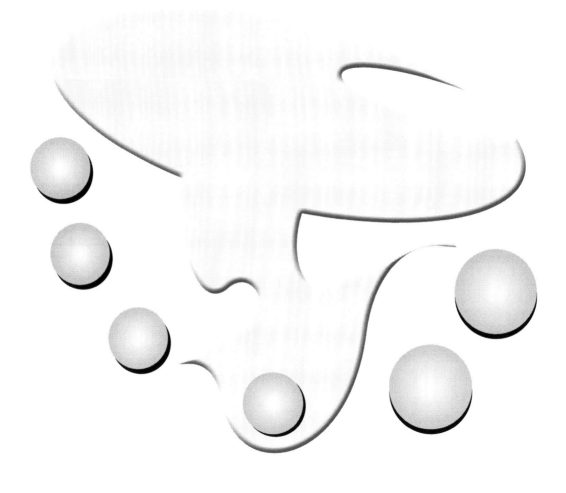

Project Finer Womanhood: A Mother - Daughter Tale

Doris Elizabeth McAdams Stokes

On that June 16th morning, in Raleigh, N.C., when I bounced into the world, it was preordained that I would become a member of Zeta Phi Beta Sorority, Inc. If you knew my mother, you understood this without question. My mother had wanted a son first, but she proceeded to name me after her and added a middle name of Elizabeth, for my great-grandmother, a great aunt and the Queen of England. This tale is about us and how she shaped me in accordance with Zeta Phi Beta Sorority's ideal, Finer Womanhood.

Born in 1920 in the Jim Crow south, Doris Louise Larkin was the daughter of an itinerant preacher and a stay-at-home mother. Hers was a strict home, frugal, with rules that were meant to be followed. Times were hard. My grandfather, a college graduate who believed that education was the key to his success and survival as an African American man, wore a suit and tie every day of his entire adult life, even when gardening. He believed in hard work and self-discipline, traits he passed on to his four children. He was demanding, and the only acceptable grades his children could earn were A's. Anything less meant they needed to apply themselves to their studies more.

My grandmother's life was typical. She cooked and baked, canned food, made her own soap and sewed all of her own and her daughters' clothes. She could wring a chicken's neck with one hand, a superwoman feat to me as a child. She never drove a car and seldom left home until Sunday when she went to church. On these days, she donned one of her lace dresses, put on her white gloves and sensible hat and shoes, and was a lady. She always carried a pencil, a fan, a handkerchief and peppermints in her purse. She wanted my mother and her other two daughters to achieve more in life than she had, and encouraged them to be successful in their studies. This was perfect for my mom, as she wanted no part of a stay-at-home, behind-the-scenes life.

My mother was at the top of her high school class and set her sights on attending college and the life of a professional woman. Even though segregation was a way of life, she was second to no one. She cleaned other's homes to earn extra money, but she too wore her best Sunday clothes out of the house, to town or school. When she applied for and received a $25 scholarship from Omicron Zeta chapter, in Raleigh, NC, she was off to Shaw University. Doris L. never looked back. Earning a master's degree at New York University and returning to Raleigh to be a first grade teacher, my mother had mapped a successful route for continued achievements.

By the time she became Doris L. McAdams, she was a proud member of Zeta Phi Beta Sorority, Inc. She was pledged and branded by Omicron chapter, at Shaw and completed the circle by becoming a member of Omicron Zeta chapter. There were very few examples of professional African American women in the 1940's and the women she met in the chapter, Sorors Nora Lockhart, Blanche Rivers, Janie Anderson, Louise Flagg, Pearl Thompson and Augusta White, were professional women who became her role models and mentors. She was driven to succeed and was fully committed to the Sorority's ideals.

My mother was short, barely five feet, two inches tall and petite. She was fashionable, always having the latest styled clothes and she loved jewelry, pearls and brooches specifically. What she lacked in height, she replaced with personality and substance. The oldest of three girls, she was naturally bossy and a born instigator. My aunts looked up to her and followed her lead in everything. My mom was a fierce competitor, always playing to win or be the best at whatever she did. She had a no nonsense, calm and cool demeanor and rarely displayed her emotions. Mom was ambitious and was often found at the frontline of all of her endeavors, be they at work, church or the Sorority because she was a hard worker and completed all of her tasks to perfection. She was a faithful, loyal, trustworthy friend and sister to a fault.

Behind the scenes, at home, she was a little general. She spent countless hours planning and making lists and schedules. She maintained a neat and clean home that was always ready for the unexpected guest. She kept her family on task, too. What she demanded of herself, she demanded of others. Mom was a woman of few words, preferring to communicate with her eyes or her hand. She accepted no excuses and did not like to repeat herself.

My mother kept boxes of note paper, all occasion cards and stamps on hand. At night, she would sit at her desk and write, never missing an opportunity to remember someone's birthday, anniversary or to offer a condolence. Or, she would spend the entire night on the telephone checking up on people or following up on committee work.

My mother, the professional educator, expected no problems in rearing her own child. I was slated to be raised by the book, according to her schedule, but this did not work out as planned. I was quickly labeled a fast, willful, precocious and hard-headed child, one who would act out, just to see what would happen. Mom did not miss a beat on responding. Trained as a teacher, she believed that children were best seen and not heard. Through her training, she knew that the human brain required a minimum of 18 years to develop, and in her role as mother, her job was to develop that brain. She had rules and she was unrelenting in their application. She believed that if you set the expectation, the appropriate behaviors would follow.

She stated her expectations as rules, and there were rules for every situation in life: rules for being at home; rules being at home with company; rules when at other people's houses; rules for being in a store; rules for riding in the car. There were rules for eating, dressing, walking and talking. I quickly learned the rule, and then broke it. Often. This may be due to the fact that I started drinking coffee at age 3!

I loved to run until I was sweaty and my pressed and curled hair reverted to its natural state; I chased chickens, climbed trees and adored playing in the mud. I hated dresses, and preferred being barefoot. I cut off other girls' hair if theirs was longer than mine. I mimicked the walk, using a stick for a cane, of elderly ladies in public. I used the "for white only" water fountains and restrooms. I rolled and cut my eyes with precision. I broke dishes and glasses on purpose, trying to eliminate that chore. I did all these things because I knew my mother would react to them, and she did not disappoint me. I became an expert in selecting switches for whippings.

After my brother was born, I entered into a new phase of misbehavior. As the first grand-child, I did not want or like him. Now, I had to share everything with him. I told him he was adopted and not really my parents' child. I tried to give him away. I almost dropped him down a well. I led him into all manner of compromising situations, but stopped only when it dawned on me that my mother knew I was the perpetrator and I got the punishment.

Mom started early with the mantra, "You are not acting ladylike." Unknown to me, mom had embraced Zeta's ideal of Finer Womanhood as the ideal to define how women should act and behave. I learned about Zeta Phi Beta Sorority at an early age and associated the behaviors of its members with it. I wanted no part of being a lady; ladies had no fun, were prim and proper and always acted like they were in church. These Zeta ladies came regularly to our home for Omicron Zeta chapter meetings. In the 40's, 50's and 60's, chapters had monthly meetings at members' homes. I was always trotted out for introductions when they arrived. They called themselves "Sorors" and in short order, I addressed every woman as "Soror," too. The Zeta ladies would be dressed up, acting very dignified and then just sit and talk very quietly. They had no fun!

Mom served refreshments from a linen covered table on her "good china" and these ladies drank punch, daintily, in little glass cups. Given all this effort, I knew they were special and important ladies, meaningful to my mom. Sometimes they met at night and all wore white. Although they thought they were acting in secret, I saw it all: the Bibles, candles, flowers, concoctions, and paddles. Then, there would be a group of ladies in blindfolds who would look silly and scared. The entire group would walk around the table in circles and then repeat words after a leader read them. They would sing their hymn and I learned the words and tune too, although I did not understand all that I heard. "What are fer'vered hearts?" I asked one morning. That resulted in my being banished to my grandmother's home when Sorority functions were held at my house.

I attended all the chapter's public programs (under serious threats from my mother about my behavior) and I knew that Zeta Phi Beta Sorority was all about service, scholarship, sisterhood and Finer Womanhood. The first three made sense, but I had no idea what Finer Womanhood meant. I could not associate this yet with their behaviors. I was often referred to as a "future Zeta," which meant to me that one day I was expected to be one of those Zeta ladies. My potential was underscored when I was made to showcase my piano playing and poetry recitation talents. I hated being singled out; it was a ritual I dreaded.

My life as a potential Finer Woman and future Soror took a major turn at age 12. By now, my family had moved to Cincinnati, Ohio which was on another planet as far as I was concerned. I was in integrated schools and all facilities were available to me: libraries, bathrooms, movies, water fountains and amusement parks and I could sit anywhere I wanted to on the bus. I had white teachers and most of my classmates were white, a new phenomenon for me too. I assimilated well, until the day I returned home from school, jubilant that I had won my first fight in defense of my brother. Looking at me with a scratched face, scrapped knees and torn dress, my mom was absolutely traumatized.

"Ladies do not fight on school grounds or anywhere else! You will not act like everyone else. You will not be like everyone else," she ranted and railed for hours and hours. I was scared, given her rare display of emotion.

"You will be a lady, and that is all to that," She vowed.

I had not seen her so upset about anything before. Deciding I had committed a major crime, I thought I would lose my life. I considered my options and decided to change my ways. Besides, I was off to high school, and more important things like boys were on my radar.

Growing older meant there was a new set of new rules about dress and boys that my mother now enforced. She was untiring in her efforts. Red fingernail polish and lipstick, pierced ears, fishnet stockings, black stockings worn during the day, blonde or red hair, tattoos, mini-dresses, plunging necklines, backless dresses, anything see-through, tight skirts that "cupped" my behind, sweaters that stretched across my bust, safety pins in clothes, exposed midriffs, short shorts, bare legs with dresses, wrinkled clothes, exposed underwear, dirty underwear and stiletto heels were forbidden and guaranteed to "bring the family down." Clothes worn to bed, pajamas or night gowns, or clothes worn around the house, robes or slippers, or hair in curlers or hair nets, was not worn when company was present and absolutely not worn out of the house. Women only wore pants to picnics, sports events or to work in the yard, and not to church, school or work. In the 1950's, denim was considered a working class fabric and wearing jeans was unheard of. Ladies dressed up to go to church, go downtown, fly in an airplane or embark on a train trip.

Ladies did not telephone boys, respond to car horns from boys, or stand on corners talking to boys. Ladies made curfew and carried money in their shoes to call home while dating or for emergencies. Young men had to come in the house and meet the parents before going out on a date. This was after the extensive quiz about who he was, how old he was, where he lived and who his parents were. After all, the boy had to be suitable for dating.

Ladies were careful about who they associated with: any male more than 2 years older or in frequent trouble at school or with the law, or known to be a womanizer (or already a father) was taboo. Ladies did not accept gifts from men. A lady did not engage in public displays of affection with men. Ladies certainly did not entertain men in their bedrooms, and the one cardinal rule above all others concerning the opposite sex was that ladies finished college before marrying or having children.

A lady's table manners were impeccable and followed at all times, no matter the hour. All meals were eaten at the table after the food was blessed. Ladies did not eat or drink in the street, in cars or on the go. Ladies did not eat with their fingers. Ladies always used a napkin. Ladies did not leave a store unless their items were all in bags. Ladies corrected sales clerks who referred to them as girls or gals.

When I was old enough to attend regional conferences with my mother, I met other "future Zetas" and we bonded immediately over our shared common experiences with our Zeta mothers. My mother stood proudly with the other Zeta mothers--Ione Gibson, Mary Curtis, Evelyn Robinson, Fannie Harrell and Lottie Kennedy, patting themselves on the back and thanking God they had successfully made it thus far with their daughters. They were growing "future Zetas."

Throughout my childhood, my mom was a wife and mother who worked fulltime. At some point, she returned to school for a second master's degree in library science yet she never missed a Zeta meeting whether at the local, state or regional level. From 1962 – 1969, she served as the State Director of Ohio and shortly after this time, she became a Life Member. She felt it her duty to attend all Boulés, and even managed to be photographed with several of our Founders and many of the Grand Basilei.

In fact, ours was a total Greek home. My dad was an active member of Kappa Alpha Psi Fraternity (I knew this fraternity's hymn by age 5, too), and we traveled to Boulés and Conclaves as a family. By now, my mom had started in on my brother and was demanding of him too. Her mantra to him was, "I will not raise a son who cannot boil an egg, clean a house or wash his drawers." My brother went on to become a successful attorney and Kappa like my dad and to this day, he remains a self-sufficient bachelor.

Mom was active in other professional organizations and was often the first African American woman to hold an office in them. She was forever being honored and recognized by someone. We attended Brown Chapel AME as a family and never missed a Sunday. My mother sang alto in the choir and was in many church organizations also. Even when we were out of town, mom found a church for her family to attend. I too, was required to sing in the church choir and participate in all church activities until I was eighteen years old.

Finally, I was off to college, just two weeks after graduating from high school. My parents, both graduates of predominately black colleges, made it mandatory that I (and my brother) attend one too. My mother was so excited, she personally escorted me to Hampton

University in Virginia. To my great dismay, I discovered that my mom had an on campus spy, Dr. Nancy Bullock McGhee, a Professor of English, who just happened to have been the 13th Grand Basileus of Zeta Phi Beta Sorority, Inc. She kept a close eye on me until her retirement, by employing me in her office.

Freshmen women at Hampton were required to meet with the Dean of Women the first week of school about deportment or how HU women were to behave. My mom was very pleased with this orientation. More rules were presented and I began to understand that they would be a part of my life forever. Now, I had to wear gloves and a hat to town or on Sunday. HU women were allowed to wear pants only on Saturdays, from 1 – 6 pm. It did not become acceptable or fashionable for women to wear pants or trousers until several federal laws were passed and my mother never fully embraced the practice.

All HU ladies were to own a black dress which was considered proper attire for most social occasions. We were not to smoke cigarettes in public or drink anything out of a can or bottle. (It was correct to always request a glass.) Ladies did not stand outside the dorm and talk to men. Young men were not permitted in women's dormitory rooms and under no circumstances was it permissible for a HU lady to visit a men's dormitory. Hampton is surrounded by seven military installations and we were strongly encouraged not to fraternize with any of their members, a rule universally ignored. Missing a class three times in a row or not making the midnight curfew on weekends resulted in a telephone call by the Dean of Women to your home. (There were none to mine.)

During the late 1960s, a major cultural upheaval swept through the nation and behaviors and norms changed radically. Women were free! Upon returning to Hampton my sophomore year, I was amazed that ALL the rules were rescinded forever and for good. There was no dress code and no curfew. The Dean of Women's position was eliminated. Co-ed dorms were instituted as were in-room visits of men. One could skip classes and no one said a word. You could do whatever you wanted and no one ever spoke about being a lady again.

I officially became a member of Zeta Phi Beta Sorority, Inc. on April 29, 1968. Although my mother had not explicitly stated that she wanted me to follow in her footsteps, she was pleased that I had. I had one big sister who told the five of us pledgees that she was graduating that year and she had no time for foolishness. There were just a few rules we had to follow: address her as "Most Honored Big Sister," eat together, walk in a line, dress the same on the weekends and make a scrapbook. To me, pledging was a piece of cake compared to being raised by my mother. Besides, I knew most of what there was to know about Zeta already. My mother could not attend my initiation because of a family funeral but had she been there, her chest would have been stuck out and she would have taken the all the credit for successfully raising a Zeta daughter: I am certain that in her mind, Project Finer Womanhood was complete. She gave me a white Bible and on the inside cover wrote, "Always be a good girl."

Soon thereafter, I was finally on my own, working and living in Los Angeles. I returned home one Christmas, got off the plane and it was revealed that I had cut off all my hair and pierced my ears! I had not had the nerve to tell my mother before I arrived and I was 22 years old at the time. She never said a word. She just took two aspirin and went to bed.

Eventually, I moved back to Cincinnati and transferred to Beta Zeta Zeta chapter, her chapter. Mom was in heaven: she brought a daughter and a Soror to the mix. We did all things Zeta together--chapter meetings, state meetings, regional conferences and Boulés--Soror and Soror, big Doris and little Doris. Ione's daughters, Brenda and Michelle, Evelyn's daughter, Carla, Mary's daughter, Dee, and Fannie's daughter Bernadette, were eventually all active Zetas too. At Boulés, I met more Zeta mothers and daughters, Vera Moore's Jylla and Maxine, and Mildred West's Barbara. The phenomenon of Zeta moms and daughters, was happening throughout the Sorority and would later became the foundation of the Legacy Club that continues to this day.

Mom adopted my friends, Rose, Ramona and Ola, as her Zeta daughters too. After Ramona married, the awesome foursome, mom, me, Rose and Ola, traveled together throughout the Great Lakes Region. Three of us learned another rule: If you are going to associate with Doris L. McAdams, you had to follow her rules. We all deferred to my mother. As the years passed, I watched with great interest other Sorors who were now raising their daughters: Rose and Veronica; Ira and Keisha; Linda and Dawn and Jylla and Anjylla. Based on what these mothers were teaching them, there was little doubt that their daughters would one day become successful women and future Zetas, and they did. My mom was very proud of me as I assumed various leadership roles in the Sorority and later just the two of us traveled to events.

My mom became ill in 2005, just as I retired. After my father passed two years later, my fulltime job became taking care of her. I rose to the occasion, though totally unprepared as I knew nothing about Medicare or senior services. When suddenly, after minor surgery, she could no longer walk, Mom and I had some major hurdles to overcome. Our roles slowly changed as I battled care facilities and physicians and she was dependent on me not just to manage her medical services but her personal business and household too. In time, she was walking again but it was apparent, she would be dependent on someone else to assist her at all times; she could no longer drive, cook or manage her home. My friend and mom's Zeta daughter Ola stepped in to assist us. Those were some of the best years for all three of us. One day, I playfully announced to my mother that I was making the rules now and she agreed, but without missing a beat added, "You do know how to act."

Even though she was semi invalid, my mother insisted on being an active Zeta. When I could get her back to church and chapter meetings, she was happy camper. Our chapter accommodated her and met at her home. After a long absence, we were finally able to attend regional conferences in Indianapolis and Louisville. My mom rode in her wheel chair and like the queen, greeted everyone with a wave.

I made the mistake of suggesting to her that she wear just a white sweater for Anjylla Foster's intake ceremony, to simplify the lengthy process of dressing. Oh my goodness, what a faux pas on my part. She reminded me of the required all white attire and then dressed herself in it. When she passed in 2011, Sorors from all over the region came to pay their respects and as a fitting tribute, her final Zeta service was conducted by Past International Grand Basileus Tearte.

It is said that we learn about life in retrospect: I now realize that all of my mother's rules were just a precursor of being a finer woman and that in many ways, the Zeta pledge was a way of life for her and an example for me to follow. It has served me well. The Sorority ideals were not just to be recited, but instead, they dictated a set of behaviors that were to be lived or acted on.

After African Americans were "freed" again in 1964, I was well prepared to take full advantage of the numerous opportunities that became available. Doors opened not only because I was professionally prepared, but in part, because I was well-mannered and self-disciplined. My mom had set the foundation for me to define my own circumstances years ago and thus I was able to make decisions that proved to be long-term investments that paid off in the future. I profited from her examples of perseverance. I met all my goals and overcame many obstacles.

I admit, I was intrigued by the emergence of the "Be Finer" movement until I realized how many new Sorors were totally underprepared for it. They thought being Finer was just a way of being at a Zeta function and not a way of life. They could look the part but could not integrate it into a lifestyle. Being Finer is a set of behaviors that can be applied to all of life's situations.

I did attend a Be Finer workshop just to find out what it was all about and came away thinking that if Sorors needed to be trained in their "roots" or founding principles, so be it. We find ourselves in a world where just about anything goes, and there are few rules. Celebrities set behavior and appearance standards, many of which are inappropriate for the average, professional woman. Today, many Sorors exhibit behaviors that do not measure up to our Founders' vision and expectations for Finer Womanhood. As an organization, it is more than appropriate to define and teach those expectations and behaviors that delineate us as a group. And, it is more important that we uphold the standard of Finer Womanhood as a group: if it is ever lost, it will be lost forever.

I was so blessed to have had a Zeta mom who not only prepared me for life but also taught me about and groomed me as a Finer Woman. I am beyond grateful. I still hear her voice, reminding me of the rules. I am proud to continue her values. I have had to make some rules of my own too as I have become my mother now, exhibiting many of her traits. Project Finer Womanhood is a work in progress: that will never be complete. Here are more of "our" rules, and you can decide where you stand.

MANNERS

Be well-mannered. Always say "please" and "thank you."

Only written and mailed thank you notes for gifts and other kindnesses count.

Remember birthdays, anniversaries and other special days of others.

If you make a mistake, apologize. Don't laugh at another's mistake.

People do not have to be nice to you: Be kind and gracious to all people you meet.

Do not complain, whine or nag.

Offer to help someone else in need; don't wait to be asked.

Be considerate of and helpful to the elderly, young and disabled.

Visit the sick and bereaved.

When meeting someone for the first time or someone
older than you, stand and shake her hand.

Walk away from confrontations.

Actions speak louder than words.

Often, it is not what you say, but how you say it.

Be interesting to talk to. Expand your mind. Be interested in other people.

DRESS AND GROOMING

Dress professionally and appropriately for the occasion.

Dress like you want to be addressed.

When in doubt, dress up.

Exposed underwear is unacceptable.

Wear clean and pressed clothes that are appropriate for your body size. Just
because something is sold in your size, does not mean it is flattering on you.

Do not place a lot of value on designer clothes and accessories.

Maintain an organized purse and always have something to write with.

MEETINGS AND EVENTS

Be on time; start out early.

If you cannot make an event, let your hostess know.

Don't text other Sorors in chapter meetings with you; everyone can see what you are doing.

Don't talk on the telephone in a meeting. Leave the group.

Keep your commitments. If you say you are going to do something, follow through.

If you cannot follow through, let someone know.

If you become overwhelmed, there is honor in asking for assistance.

Meet your deadlines. Stand behind your word. Be organized.

RSVP on time when requested.

DEPORTMENT

Maintain good posture. Don't slouch when walking or sitting.

Walk purposefully and confidently. Don't drag or shuffle your feet.

Don't run anywhere unless you are jogging.

Always wear a smile, no matter what state you are in.

Bend at the knee (if possible) and not over from the hip.

Don't broadcast your business; maintain a little mystery.

Be the woman a man needs, not the woman that needs a man.

Do not yell or shout.

Act like the Queen who always maintains her composure in public events.

ELECTRONIC COMMUNICATIONS

Don't hit the 'reply all' button unless your response is intended for all.

If you have a response for one person, send an email to that person only.

Ask permission before taking someone's photo or before posting it online.

Do not post your personal business (or anyone else's) on Facebook.
This includes your love life or lack thereof, the alcoholic beverages
you drink, your weight, or your problems with partners.

Your emails or posts should not contain vulgar or profane language.

Always write emails and posts as if they might become public one day.

Don't give out your email address if you do not intend to
check, read or respond to emails regularly.

GROUP MEALS

Avoid saving seats; your group should enter a meal function together.

Eat a small snack before attending a group lunch or banquet.

There will be a 30 minute or longer program <u>before</u> the invocation and it is NEVER acceptable to eat anything on the table before the invocation.

Engage in conversation with others at the table.

Do not talk on the phone or text while eating or sharing a meal with others.

Wait until everyone at your table has been served before eating.

Wait until everyone at your table has been served before attempting to customize your meal or ask for condiments.

If you have specific dietary restrictions, note them on your registration form and be prepared to eat whatever you are served.

Do not be the greedy mega-plate queen when proceeding through the buffet line.

Don't be rude to waiters and servers.

ZETA ETIQUETTE

Finer women ALWAYS pay their dues and maintain an active financial status.

Individually, each one of us represents a member of the whole group.

You are an example of your highest ideal of culture.

Attend all chapter meetings and events.

If you cannot attend a meeting, let your Basileus know.

Support Zeta events with the same (or more) enthusiasm shown for supporting Sigma events.

Correction is best privately given.

Showing too much cleavage or leg is inappropriate for Sorority business functions.

Do not wear white flip flops or house shoes at Zeta rituals.

Do not wear white knee highs and heels with a mini dress.

Finer women invest in professional white or black dresses or suits for Zeta functions.

Sundresses are inappropriate attire for ceremonies.

Wear white underwear under white clothes; any other color will show.

Write your name in your conference bag and book: They all look the same.

Compliment Sorors on jobs well done.

Pearlettes on Finer Womanhood

Voices of Zeta Pearlettes

The idea of the Pearlette Club was presented to International President Jylla Moore Foster by Vondel Smith Sloan, who was appointed National Program Director of Youth Affiliates. Thus, in 1994, at the National Boulé Convention in Orlando, Florida, the national body officially adopted and added to the Zeta structure, the Pearlettes as the third national youth auxiliary of Zeta Phi Beta Sorority, Inc. Pearlettes are a Youth Auxiliary Group for girls ages 4-8.

Finer Womanhood is when you dress and present yourself properly at all times.

– **Laylah Crippen,** Pearlette, Theta Zeta Zeta, Dover, Delaware

Finer Womanhood is being a good friend.

– **Maya Jackson,** Pearlette, Alpha Eta Zeta, Memphis, Tennessee

Finer Womanhood is sitting down and being a pretty Pearlette.

– **Briana Flowers,** Pearlette, Tau Psi Zeta, Alsip, Illinois

Finer Womanhood is to be happy and work very hard to do your best for yourself and for other people too.

– **Jazmin Marrero,** Pearlette, Gamma Nu Zeta, Camden, New Jersey

Finer Womanhood is being fabulous, beautiful, smart and helpful.

– **Justice Hall,** Pearlette, Gamma Nu Zeta, Camden, New Jersey

Finer Womanhood means that you try to be kind, act right, and help people.

– **Najeri Florez,** Pearlette, Tau Psi Zeta, Alsip, Illinois

Finer Womanhood is being proud to be a girl and always doing your best at whatever you do, so that you grow up to be a proud woman.

– **Mei' Calin,** Pearlette, Gamma Nu Zeta, Camden, New Jersey

Finer Womanhood means women that use their strength to help their communities.

– **Kaylyn Johnson,** Pearlette, Gamma Nu Zeta, Camden, New Jersey

Finer Womanhood is like my mommy – she's pretty, kind and does nice things.

– **Mykiah McDowell,** Pearlette, Tau Xi Zeta, Forest Park, Illinois

Finer Womanhood is achieving goals, working hard and taking care of business.

– **Celeste N. Mason,** Pearlette, Sigma Kappa Zeta, Brooklyn, New York

Finer Womanhood is great womanhood.

– **Gianna Shippy,** Pearlette, Gamma Nu Zeta, Camden, New Jersey

Finer Womanhood is the best place a woman can be!

– **Sherita Haskins,** Pearlette, Omicron Beta Zeta, Arlington, Texas

Finer Womanhood is where smart women are helpful and nice to others. And, the women have to be considerate, gentle, polite, and clean.

— **Trinity Haskins,** Pearlette, Omicron Beta Zeta, Arlington, Texas

Finer Womanhood is being awesome in your community by doing community service and being loving and kind.

— **Sana Griffth,** Pearlette, Sigma Kappa Zeta, Brooklyn, New York

Finer Womanhood is being fun and pretty like my mommy.

— **Madison Jack,** Pearlette, Sigma Kappa Zeta, Brooklyn, New York

Finer Womanhood is acting like a little lady and being nice to people.

— **Milana T. West,** Pearlette, Phi Alpha Zeta, Waldorf, Maryland

Finer Womanhood is a woman with class, especially the Zetas!

— **Teri Pridgen,** Pearlette, Delta Zeta, Charlotte, North Carolina

The Sisterhood Speaks

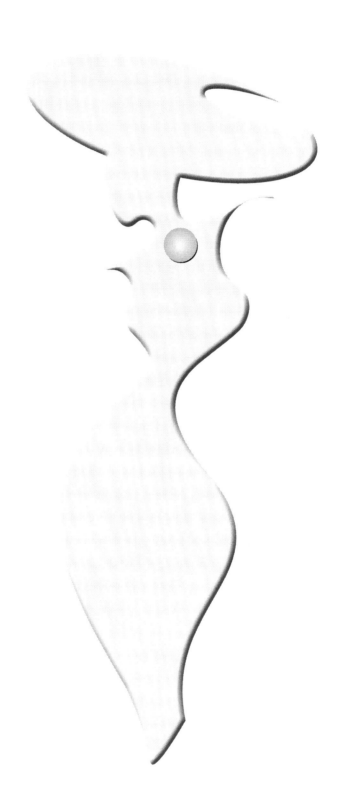

A Finer Woman on Fire

Valerie Hollingsworth

Growing up in Brooklyn, N.Y. doesn't always end in a success story. For some women, it can mean a life of negativity. Thank God that wasn't my story. Thanks to my mother and my grandparents being great influences in my life, there were no options for failure; only options to succeed.

My mother struggled as a single parent and sacrificed for me to have the best that could be offered in terms of a roof over my head, clothes on my back, food in my stomach and the best education that her money would allow. There was nothing my mother would not do for me to make my life better. All she asked in return was to concentrate on my studies and do well in school so I could excel in a career that I would enjoy one day. I took her words to heart and was able to graduate valedictorian from York Institute, a private institution for gifted children, at the age of 14.

I went on to attend Fordham University, where I majored in child psychology with a minor in theater and drama. Because I had started college so young, pledging wasn't an option for me back then. Even if it was, there was no black Greek sorority on my campus at that time.

My opportunity came after college. I had been working for New York Life Insurance Company for several years before I began pursuing the idea of being a Zeta. As a young woman who had graduated from high school at 14 and college at 18, Zeta's ideals of scholarship and Finer Womanhood resonated with me. I was presented with an opportunity for graduate membership in 1982, and haven't looked back since.

One of my most memorable moments during my pledging process was meeting one of our Most Honorable Founders, Fannie Pettie Watts. We actually forged a strong bond of love for each other that shaped not only the way I saw Zeta, but the way I saw the world. Her words, "Be the best you can be, do the best that you can, and give the best of yourself, and you will go far," continue to motivate me, and inspired me to continue being a leader in all that I do.

Today, as the National 1st Vice President of Zeta Phi Beta Sorority, Inc., it is my goal to not only live up to Founder Watts' words, but to spread them to every young woman whom I encounter. My platform is not just membership; it's empowerment. And when a woman feels empowered, there is nothing she can't do!

Someone reading this might think, "Yeah, that sounds all nice and all, but you don't know what I go through at work, in life, etc. I'm tired of standing up, only to get shut down."

Yes, my sister, I know life can be tough. I know that we do not always get what we want, or what we feel we deserve out of life. But we have a choice: we can either accept defeat and surrender, or we can find a new way to overcome our challenges. It's important that we take what we have learned from the defeats or setbacks and use this knowledge to get stronger and come out swinging the next time and stand and say, "I am back so give me your best shot."

The activist Margaret Sanger once said, "Woman must not accept; she must challenge. She must not be awed by that which has been built up around her; she must reverence that woman in her which struggled for expression."

As I read that quote, I think of Mrs. Josephine Groves Holloway, who refused to believe there was no place for African American Girls Scouts in our country. After repeatedly receiving denials to her petitions to allow young African American girls to become "real Girl Scouts," she organized an official club and taught them everything they needed to know about scouting. These young women became so well trained that by 1943, Troop 200 became the first African American troop in Nashville. And by the way, Mrs. Holloway is a Zeta!

I also think of Soror Violette Anderson, who, despite the racial prejudices of the 1920s, became the first African American female attorney admitted to practice before the United States Supreme Court. Soror Anderson later went on to successfully lobby for sharecroppers and tenant farmers, and became the vice president of the Cook County Bar Association. What an awesome example of empowerment!

You might think, "That's history. Times have changed. The world is different." Well, dear sister, I offer you examples of women of today who continue to change the world, even if starting with their own circles. Think about our Sorors serving our country in the U.S. military, or even those serving our cities on the police force. Consider Soror Karen Arrington, who founded the Miss Black USA Pageant, or Soror Jenell B. Stewart, a champion of the natural hair movement. On the political and business fronts, we have Sorors Cynthia Willard-Lewis, Krysta Jones, April Smith, Donna Edwards, Elisabeth Omilami and so many others fighting to effect change each day. These Zetas are on fire!

So how can we carry on these outstanding examples of Finer Women in the 21st Century? A large percentage of that answer depends on how we see ourselves. We must first see ourselves as being worthy of respect and power, and then carry ourselves that way. In order for us to be treated as queens, to be seen as queens, we must first see ourselves as such.

Once we see ourselves as worthy, there is no room for jealousy. No room for hatred. We have now given ourselves permission to respect and celebrate others because we know this is what we expect in return. We are happy with ourselves, and can therefore allow no one else's successes or failures to see ourselves any differently. Just think of our triumphant Soror Zora Neale Hurston, who once jokingly said, "Sometimes, I feel discriminated against, but it does not make me angry. It merely astonishes me. How can any deny themselves the pleasure of my company? It's beyond me."

I know these affirmations may seem easier said than done, but sister, I encourage you to persevere. Take life one step at a time. We don't all get it right the first time. Or even the second, for that matter. I know that I have had to go through the struggle several times to just get it right once. Some of us have lost jobs, which only prepared us for better ones. Some of us begrudgingly left relationships, only to look back and finally recognize the abuse we mistook for love. Some of us have even attempted a project or made a suggestion that wasn't well received. Yet instead of throwing up our hands in frustration, we looked inward, recognized the areas that needed work, reengaged and became stronger!

My advice to you is to cast your cares and troubles onto your God, and pray for direction and purpose. The answer will come. As we grow, we cannot be afraid to make mistakes. Sometimes failure makes us better. It may sound strange, but I treasure the failures as well as the successes in my life because the failures made me stronger and better equipped to get back out there and start afresh. The late Maya Angelou wisely advised, "You may encounter many defeats, but you must not be defeated. In fact, it may be necessary to encounter the defeats, so you can know who you are, what you can rise from, how you can still come out of it."

But Joel Olsteen summed it up for me perfectly. He states, "Loose the sad song and try singing a new song, because when you stop making excuses, God will show up to turn things around for you." Don't let the excuses hold you back. Stop thinking negative thoughts because if you think positively, you will live better. What is most important is to live a positive life, and your blessing will be abundant.

So as we continue developing ourselves into Finer Women who are on fire in the 21st Century, let us use our experiences to become better. Let us work to overcome obstacles while remembering to lend a hand to someone else who may be struggling. Let us never belittle or criticize our sisters, but instead build them up while serving as an inspiration to them. Be professional, yet kind. Stop the back biting and digging a hole for someone else. Lift up your sisters; don't tear them down because no good will come of that type of behavior.

You might notice, that I did not mention physical beauty in my descriptions and affirmations of Finer Women. A Finer Woman is not always beautiful on the outside. Yet, when she is happy with herself, when she grows from her failures as well as her successes, when she shows kindness, her inner beauty enhances her physical appearance. She stands straighter, walks taller, smiles brighter. This is what makes her beautiful.

And you, my dear sister, astounding woman on fire, are truly beautiful, if you just believe it.

My Journey in Zeta Phi Beta Sorority, Incorporated

Scarlet H. Black

Growing up in North Carolina, I was considered a very serious, old soul, and, at times, a very "nerdy" young girl. My parents divorced after my father returned from the Korean Conflict. I had a brother, but did not have a sister, so I found myself being very shy around other girls. I often found escape and solitude through reading books about people and places all over the world.

My mother Mildred Florence Stevenson Harvey's favorite relaxation was to come home from a 60-minute commute from Charlotte each day and sew. Sewing became a life-long hobby of hers, and she was great at it. I did not get many "store bought" dresses, because Mom could make my dresses or suits even better. It was our "thing" together that I would give her a design I wanted, and she could "whip" it up in no time. Ebony Magazine's Fashion Fair or pattern books had nothing on me and Mom. This was also during the Civil Rights era, and my mother was an activist before it became obvious to be an activist. Boycotting stores that did not serve Blacks was also in her thinking. Because of our close mother-daughter relationship, very close friends were few.

My beloved mother was a member of Delta Zeta chapter in Charlotte, N.C. During my formative years, I watched my Zeta mother, her Zeta friends, and women across the spectrum of our Sorority. I wanted to emulate how they carried themselves as women with dignity, grace, and class. These are not easy attributes to achieve, and the journey is always a work in progress. However, the image of a Zeta woman interacting in the world with dignity, grace, and class is a beautiful view to behold, and is something that stayed with me as I made my decision to become a member of Zeta Phi Beta Sorority, Inc. at North Carolina Central University, Gamma Gamma chapter, Durham, North Carolina.

Little did I know that my encounter with Zeta Phi Beta Sorority, Inc. would take me to places I could only read about and to meet people I never thought I would encounter. I found the sisters I never had growing up. Sisters, who are accomplished women and engaging in their own right. Everything you would wish a sister to be, I found in Zeta. Therefore, to be a part of this sorority is amazing and as phenomenal as the women I have encountered along the way. Now, let me give you the rest of my story.

My journey in Zeta Phi Beta Sorority, Inc. really became a destiny I had to keep. I do not know anything else but Zeta. Coming through (what I call) the Zeta system prepared me for much of who I am today in life. Zeta is in my "core being." I was a Zeta youth, debutante, scholarship recipient, and a legacy. Along the journey, I listened, studied the Sorority's structure, policies, etc., and watched phenomenal leaders in our phenomenal Sorority execute the duties they were either assigned, appointed, or elected to do.

To be perceived as a leader, you have to align yourself with practicing leaders. To do this, I had to be present in the moment, participate, and attend meetings, events, activities, and conferences. Often, it was not easy with school, home, church, family and all of the other things that constitute one's life. However, I made a commitment, and I was always taught that when a commitment is made, you follow through, "for to whom much is given, much is required."

There is not a day that goes by when I forget what I have learned by being a member and consequently a leader in Zeta Phi Beta Sorority, Inc. I paid my dues and moved through the ranks. Every "rung on the ladder" counted. Every situation, good or not so good, contributed to my personal growth. Sorors I met along the way have remained precious friends to this very day. You just cannot beat that sisterly love!

My mother always told me, "No one owes you anything, and you are not entitled. Folks want to see hard work and sweat equity. Without hard work, you are just there in name only, and folks know the difference. People are not fooled. With anything that you do in life, always remember, let the work count. But along with the work, folks must also know that you care and that they matter."

These were hard lessons to learn at times. However, looking back, these were valuable lessons to learn. They have become the strands through my journey in Zeta Phi Beta Sorority, Inc., and a life that could not be imagined without Zeta.

Finer...Beyond Measure

Anjylla Y. Foster

When I initially received communication about an anthology on Finer Womanhood, I had no clue what I would say. Yet, I knew that my voice and possibly the voice of others needed to be placed on the record. The ideals that we cherish in Zeta Phi Beta Sorority, Inc. have evolved through time since their establishment by our Founders, and I live in a time that we cannot simply ignore them.

Today, scholarship and service are still self-explanatory for the most part. These are objective principles that can be quantified if debated. Sisterhood can be learned by observation and active participation, and preserved with a hint of common sense. However, the philosophy of being Finer evolves over time. It has a fine line between objective and subjective. It's impacted by outside factors such as trends, social norms, and preferences. And, the world presents us with visual and non-visual cues toward what might be considered Finer, but it is solely our personal discretion on whether or not we agree and follow them.

Some might say that trends, social norms, and preferences should have no impact on being Finer but as a young woman growing up in a time when society is dictated by the media, being Finer requires more discipline and strength than ever before. At times, you need discipline to present yourself as our Founders would desire and the strength to stand convicted to our principle of Finer Womanhood regardless of what is being shown elsewhere.

As a member of Zeta Phi Beta Sorority, Inc., our *finer woman intuition* is the element that makes us different. It is the element that differentiates us from any other woman, that imperceptible quality that sets us apart. We are not the average and should never feel as if we are. It is the principle that distinguishes us from our counterparts. It is the reason why our work is never done and why our work is never easy.

I don't know what being Finer means exactly, but I've learned what it is NOT, thanks to those who have told me to do better. I can consider myself to be Fine, but there is always the implied challenge to be better, to be Finer and for that, my journey toward being Finer beyond measure continues.

My Be Finer Journey

Angellic Ross

I am beyond excited as our Sorority moves to Centennial. I could not have imagined a more thrilling time to be an active member. Throughout the year, I've reflected on our theme of Finer Womanhood. What does it mean to be a Finer Woman? How do I embody these qualities in my daily practices? How do I display this within Zeta?

When I first became a Zeta, Finer Womanhood was the principle that stood out to me the most. This principle compels Sorors to be "different" and stand out in the crowd. Being a Finer Woman means respecting yourself and others, having confidence and determination, and giving unselfishly to others. It provides a standard for each of us to attain success and accept others for who they are.

As I grow in Zeta, I work toward excellence and humility, as only a Finer Woman can do. Each day,

I try to present the "best" version of myself. Professional and competent, I strive to be a woman of quality and purpose and to make a difference, just like our Five Pearls.

I am in awe of the many Sorors I have met who are examples of Finer Womanhood. They are graduates and undergraduates who purposefully embody our ideal as we work to promote and advance our Sorority. They are all different, with their own personal style, but they inspire me to be more. I want to learn from them and share their stories.

Undergrads should remember that Finer Womanhood applies to them, too. It is not some quality that will be bestowed on us when we become graduate members. It is a lifestyle that is enhanced daily. When we become members of the Sorority, we are launched on our individual Be Finer journey. Finer Womanhood is an ideal that should be evidenced in our behavior, dress, speech and the way we conduct business.

Let's Be Finer in 2020! Finer Womanhood is the defining standard of our great Sisterhood.

I Am Zeta Phi Beta Sorority, Incorporated! Monologues

Epsilon Epsilon Zeta Chapter, Orlando, Florida

I Am Scholarship!

I am the eminent expression of wisdom and intelligence.

Lives once touched by my dominant power are changed to become pillars of the community.

I inspire the musicians to play noble sentiments, physicians to heal, lawyers to defend truth and justice, and educators to mold and shape minds.

I convert students into individuals of great worth.

I am ambitious, successful, motivated, and astute.

In fact, I am the University for the Better making of **Finer Women**.

I am Scholarship!

I Am Finer Womanhood!

I am the highest quality of women collectively.

I am not the nester of life. I'm the teacher of how to live successfully, completely, purposely and sweetly.

My mouth is a fragrant hummingbird, fast and smooth—I speak with kindness and wisdom. Though I could sting with each syllable, I chose to be a symbol of peace.

I nurture humanity. I am a beautiful parent, a genuine confidant. I inspired earth to be called by her first name, mmmmm Mother.

Many have aspired to have me, because of my prestige and class. They envy my glory, though they don't know my story.

My love is so dangerous that Sisterhood wouldn't exist without me.

I am Finer Womanhood!

I Am Sisterly Love!

I will not desert you when you have acted out of your normal self and need a friend.

I am sometimes closer than your family.

When you lose your job, car won't work, house is reposed, husband abandons you or your children are sick… I will be the warm meal that you come to.

I have been known to coordinate free weddings, pay increases, and hold you together until you can be properly placed back together.

I am your biggest, most faithful fan.

I am the one that will answer each time you call… I never forget to be in Service.

I am Sisterly Love!

I Am Service!

I work all the hours. I was up early with the sun and I pulled the stars home when my job was complete.

I am that link in between making it and not enough.

I can change your life whether you are completing me or benefiting from my hard work. At either of my extremes, you will never forget me.

I provide housing, shelter, national security, education, food, teaching, relaxation and second chances.

Without me, freedom is dead, purpose is hopeless, though the rich get richer I make their profit seems worthless.

I am not selfish or narrow thinking. I sacrifice for the betterment of other. I make what was once good, turn into Excellence.

I am Service!

I Am Excellence!

I don't "try" to do things; I make them happen.

One time, I saw myself in the mirror and mistook my image for the pursuit of perfection.

I am the most successful attribute that businesses desire.

I am a habit of choice, the result of practice, preparation and purpose.

I am the divine definition of hard work and virtue.

I personally, wouldn't call myself superior, but my qualities call me exalted, eminent and praise worthy. I am one of a kind, Exceptional to the highest degree.

I am Excellence!

I Am Exceptional!

My care is the difference between life and death, poverty and millionaires, dropouts and valedictorians.

I make the right decisions and surpass what can be expected.

I am unusually good and outstanding.

I am held at a higher standard than average. I am intelligence, ability and skill.

You will only associate my name with the most remarkable people you know.

I stand out from everyone that's around me.

Many aspire to be called by my name but very few are Enlightened enough to be me.

I am Exceptional!

I Am Enlightenment!

I accept that I am a divine reflection of a Living Creator.

I polish, calm, heal and restore those that touch me.

My presence allows all those around me to know and love themselves.

I am a spiritual journey, a road with no end. Those that found me, found me from within.

I understand, forgive, love, admire, honor, comprehend, support and truly "get" the ones that seek me.

I am what it feels like to fully live, and live life abundantly.

I am Enlightenment!

You see, **I AM** all these things and so much more.

I AM ZETA PHI BETA SORORITY, Incorporated!

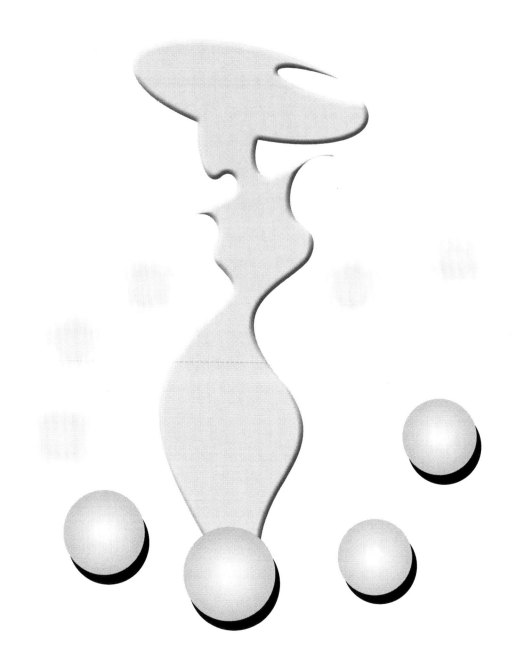

A Finer, Finer Woman Lived, Not Just Defined

Marian Martin

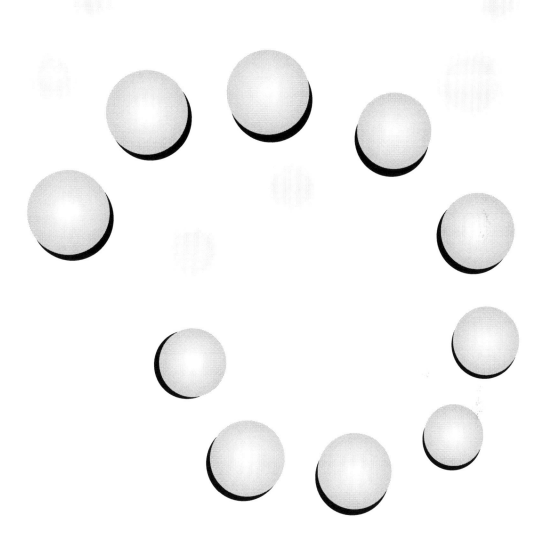

What makes a Finer Woman finer? *Integrity, sincerity, the ability to think logically, enthusiasm, initiative, drive, dependability, communication skills, intelligence, maturity, analytical ability, emotional stability, good judgment, good health, energy, physical appearance, leadership, self-esteem, faith, trust, happiness, goodness, self-confidence, decision making skills, tact, diplomacy, tolerance, adaptability, understanding, a sense of humor, courtesy, neatness (home, self, work), determination, image, poise, bearing, truth, goals, dreams, strong values, realistic ideals, respect, character, humility, faith, compassion, caring, empathy, sisterhood, personality, friendliness or astuteness?*

I have known some finer women, Sorors who exemplify all that Zeta stands for. My story is about my introduction to Zeta Phi Beta Sorority, Inc. and the examples of some of the finer woman, their lives and their actions that I came to know.

The summer of 1959 had not been a great summer for me. Normally a quiet, shy and reserved young lady who loved to read and go to the movies, I worked the first part of the summer as a nanny for a couple of young children, the grandchildren of a well-known oil man and his wife. Their regular nanny became ill just before the family moved to Oklahoma and the children were used to speaking Spanish. I fit that bill and as I had nothing in mind to occupy myself, my mother decided it was the perfect job for me. After all what nanny wouldn't love to be waited on by a housekeeper, gardener, pool man and chauffeur? I was not, at that time, a finer woman.

My mother called and told me I had received an invitation to something called *Rush Week*. For this, I had to arrive at Central State College a week early. I agreed and thought at least I could move on campus and relax before classes started.

I was invited to several tea parties the first two days and noticed that I was the only person of color among the young ladies attending the various events, laughing, chatting and getting acquainted with each other. Finally, I found a friendly soul and asked her the all important question on my mind, "What is going on and why am I here?" Back in the day, teas were the all-important event and one had to observe "the holding the teacup protocol" while balancing a napkin and little plate of cucumber or some other type of bite size sandwich.

The young lady explained that she was with some sorority, ironically with Zeta in its name, and they currently did not have any people of color as members, (I believe at that time we were called Negroes), but she had decided it was time to change that policy. She told me I would receive another invitation from them and that the invitation received on day three meant that group was definitely considering me. I did receive their invitation as well as one from another group. I was shown the sorority house and given all the details about pledging, dues and fees.

While the typical girl faced with this type of decision would be excited and probably interested in expanding her horizons by delving into the Greek world, I considered the cost of a wardrobe and other expenses, and decided it would be a hardship on my mother. I graciously declined the invitation. I truly was not interested in pursuing Greek life and decided to enjoy my freshman year, meet new friends and just work and study. I reflected on my favorite subjects in high school, English, math, science, art, shorthand, typing and accounting, and that they had been taught by teachers who were AKAs, Deltas, and Zetas.

I returned to college after summer break and my friends bombarded me with reasons I should join Zeta Phi Beta Sorority's interest group. Alma Posey Washington, my cousin, talked to me about Zeta at every opportunity. She was a charter member of the newly organized metropolitan chapter, Beta Gamma. I learned too, that my favorite high school math teacher,

Lola Greer, was a charter member of Chi Zeta, the graduate and sponsoring chapter of Beta Gamma.

Miss Greer was a woman of high integrity and her values were above reproach. She was above lying, cheating, or skating inside the guidelines of any set of rules and regulations. She set the standard for not only her Sorors but her students too. She was never known to compromise her integrity. She was always honest and did her best work at all times. She lived in such a manner that when people saw her they said, "No wonder she's a Zeta. See how she carries herself and see her good works." Miss Greer was, in my estimation, a finer woman.

I finally agreed to join my friends and pledged Beta Gamma in the spring of 1961. Soror Lawanna Hackner, a Beta Gamma charter member, was one of the first Sorors I met and got to know well. She had an innate intellectual ability to think logically. Her communication skills and analytical abilities provided a solid foundation for leadership. Problems to her were merely challenges to be analyzed and she could regroup to present the best image of Zeta. She exhibited a maturity far above her years and offered a firm foundation of trust for those younger than her. Soror Hackner went on to be the first undergraduate Soror to hold a National Office in Zeta, that of Third Anti-Basileus from 1961-1965. Even at her young age, Soror Hackner defined and lived as a finer Zeta woman.

Beta Gamma was classed as a metropolitan chapter which meant we had members from various colleges and were not campus-based. We had teas and worked on committees with Chi Zeta chapter members. Soror Greer was our advisor, followed by Soror Sylvia Lewis. Sylvia Lewis never met a stranger. She was out going and could speak knowledgeably on a variety of subjects with diverse groups of people. Her smile reflected interest and her eyes, friendship. Her voice and demeanor reflected caring and empathy during times of trouble and despair, and she often responded with scriptures to provide solace and hope. As a finer woman, she did not resort to pettiness, innuendo and gossip about her sisters or anyone else. She could always find something positive to say. Soror Lewis was indeed a finer woman.

Several Chi Zeta members left an indelible impression on me. I enjoyed working with Soror Opaline Wadkins of the March of Dimes. She was a finer woman who stepped up to a task without being asked. She would see a need and if it was within her physical and experience capabilities, she filled it. She was knowledgeable and could converse with people of diverse ethnicities and creeds.

I also worked with Soror Mayme Jackson at the Urban League and with Soror Clara Luper on her Miss Merry Christmas Pageant, a scholarship fundraiser. Soror Jackson was a finer woman who captivated us, motivated us and enticed us to reach further into ourselves to reach our potential. She offered up little tidbits of praise or snippets of a challenge to lure us into the realm of the unknown such as entering contests, writing poetry or providing gifts. She was interesting to others. She enlightened us, pricked our interest, planted seeds of inquiry and disturbed our psyche to open the doors for discussion and better understanding. She showed us there are still more challenges to probe and more answers to find.

Soror Carol Dunlap Daniels worked hard on the pageant too. She was the very epitome of a finer woman. A quiet, humble person, I never thought of her as a minister. Soror Daniels set her standards and values at the highest peak and her character and ideals shone forth like a beacon of humility and spiritual brightness. She knew that values were the motivating factors in determining goals and that it was essential that she identify, understand, and accept them if she was to use them in consciously directing her life.

Soror Clara Luper was humble when speaking about herself but could be aggressive when necessary. She was not a doormat and did not grovel or curry favor, and did not let pride get in the way of assertiveness when it was needed. Soror Luper is remembered for saying: "Pride is concerned with who is right and humility is concerned with what is right." and *"For whoever exalts himself will be humbled, and he who humbles himself will be exalted."* Luke 14:11. Soror Luper was a wonderful example of Finer Womanhood.

Over a period of time, I was Grammateus, Tamias and then Basileus of Beta Gamma. After graduation, some of us transferred to Chi Zeta chapter. I was elected Third Anti-Basileus and undergraduate advisor to Beta Gamma. By 1972, Soror Wadkins was working with the March of Dimes on their new initiative, a partnership with Zeta Phi Beta Sorority, the Stork's Nest. Beta Gamma chapter discussed this project and decided to hold a series of showers and to support the March for Babies walk.

The first shower was for low-income pregnant women from the "projects" and the second, for low-income pregnant women in the workforce or housewives. We provided transportation, sent out invitations and prepared a low-cost meal. While chapter members prepared the refreshments, the guests played "shower" games and won baby items as prizes. Discussions were held about the importance of prenatal care, the discomforts of pregnancy and proper nutrition during pregnancy. At the end of the evening, we gave each guest a small layette. We enjoyed these showers as much as our guests did.

When Chi Zeta chapter opened its Stork's Nest, it was open on Saturday from 9:00 am to 3:00 pm, and its items were priced from 10¢ to 25¢. Soror Evelyn Lee was such a dedicated worker for her shift, her niece donated $1,000 in her memory after she passed. Dependability is a strong trait of finer women.

The Stork's Nest became my favorite project in the Sorority. Over the years, our Nest had had many homes: a room in a church educational building; a room in an inner city high school; at the YWCA when a chapter member was Director; a rural church near a large medical facility; and, in the trunks of various members' cars. Finally, in 1999, the new priest at Corpus Christi Catholic Church heard about our space dilemma and offered a garage apartment (three rooms and a bath). It was perfect and the director/chair, Soror Bernice Cooksey, accepted it immediately. Soror Cooksey, is a finer, finer woman who lives the definition. She sowed the seeds of friendship, joy, caring, empathy, and sisterhood. Soror Cooksey performed acts of kindness, not for show, but out of sincerity and a true desire to help. Even when she was in the hospital, she worried about Stork's Nest clients.

How can you not be a finer, finer woman when you exhibit traits of courtesy and respect toward all those whom God has made? The finer woman is always truthful, never deceitful. She researches, discusses and tries to find the correct answer so that her responses not only reflect the truth but are supported by fact. She does not seek to deceive with her actions or her words. She does not show hypocrisy or duplicity in her speech or actions. She exhibits earnestness in her communications. Integrity, uprightness and honesty are at the forefront of all her dealings. Her happiness is not dependent on the whims of others. She trusts her faith to see her through hard times. Soror Cooksey is my idea of a finer, finer woman lived and not just defined. In time, she received a Finer Womanhood plaque from Chi Zeta chapter.

In gratitude to the priest for providing a home for the Stork's Nest, I took a class in grant writing and wrote a grant for $15,000 for the church to purchase a vehicle to transport college students and senior citizens to and from church services and activities. My husband had recently died and I was in California when he called to tell me the grant was awarded.

Over time, I was not as active with the chapter but I continued to volunteer at the Stork's Nest while raising my granddaughter and caring for my widowed mother. After my granddaughter moved, to live with her father, and my mother had passed, Soror Washington asked me to consider becoming active with the chapter again. She thought we could reconnect in our sisterhood now as legacy members. I met with Chi Zeta and decided to reunite with the chapter. Soror Washington was the Basileus and she served with poise, gracefulness and bearing, all traits that made her stand out in a crowd and illuminated her facets as a finer woman.

Soror Washington had a bearing which stemmed from her self-confident attitude and assurance that she was indeed projecting the correct image of our Founders' ideology. She took pride in her accomplishments, always striving to do things well. She dressed appropriately and for the occasion, even when she was just running an errand. She offered her legal services to those who could not afford to pay for them and influenced the young men and women in her neighborhood and church to pursue their goals.

Upon returning to the chapter, my first task was to secure 501(c) 3 status for the Stork's Nest. Soror Washington and two former Basilei, Sorors Flora Hamlin and Lillian Marigny worked on this project with me.

Flora Hamlin was a person whose compassion propelled her to offer sympathy, caring, empathy and hope to those in need. Lillian Marigny possessed insight, intelligence, discernment and perception. She was well read and knowledgeable on many subjects. Her astuteness and judgment were praise worthy. She took the time to think before she spoke or wrote because she knew that no matter how much you apologized, once something was spoken or written it could not be retracted. We received 501(c) 3 approval during Chi Zeta's anniversary celebration in December 2004.

My next assignment was to secure funding for our Stork's Nest. I decided on the March of Dimes Community grant. One of the Sorors who worked tirelessly with the *Nest,* Soror

Roland Johnson, had mentioned providing classes at Seeworth Academy, a school on the Corpus Christi Church grounds. Roland Johnson loved to cook and would prepare the most nutritious lunches to serve to the workers at Stork's Nest. She was soft spoken, intelligent and wise.

In 2005, we were awarded a $6,250 grant from the March of Dimes that guaranteed media coverage, prenatal classes, and additional courses that were not available at SeeWorth Academy. Thus began my third task. Soror Washington's intentions became apparent when she nominated me to work as the chapter's Z-HOPE Coordinator. I read the two manuals, drew up a list of activities and courses to be presented for regular students, and used the Stork's Nest Manual to prepare a curriculum for prenatal classes. The Stork's Nest Committee met with the SeeWorth Academy staff, to detail the courses and the type of instructors who would teach them. The curriculum was accepted and I began my search for instructors. Several were found in the chapter and chapter members recommended others.

One potential presenter had last minute contractual changes on her job that would interfere with the proposed schedule. Fortunately a new Zeta, an energetic and enthusiastic young Soror had recently joined our sisterhood and she stepped up to teach after studying the course material. This was Soror Ramona Collins, a former child welfare worker, who was now studying nursing. Full of ideas, she attended NPHC, state, regional and national meetings and engaged in activities with other Greek organizations garnering many "friends." One of her goals was to become Chi Zeta Basileus.

Soror Collins believed in being part of a sisterhood through full participation. She exemplified the characteristics of a finer woman through the unselfish acts she undertook to assist not only her sisters, but her fellow human beings. Her enthusiasm and zeal for life knew no bounds. She was a cheerful giver of her time and talents and worked hard to make every one of her endeavors a success.

Soror Collins took time with younger Sorors who had problems and offered them counseling. She also had advice on using social media, relationships, proper deportment, dress and the behaviors of a finer woman. She was an ardent volunteer and community service worker.

Soror Pearl Fidel, a retired registered nurse also graciously agreed to conduct prenatal classes. She had an exuberant personality which combined with her charm, confidence, and poise, allowed her to make her presence felt as well as known. She was outgoing and delighted to experience new adventures and foods.

Soror Ora Moten, a retired registered dietitian, was a godsend and taught prenatal classes. Soror Moten, in both appearance and speech, was a genteel lady and at all times, she represented the ideals of a Zeta finer woman. She was called to live a life of excellence, to do just a little bit more in all her activities and positions. She aimed for the highest rung on the ladder of success.

When Soror Washington and the new chapter Basileus, Thais Goodwin decided to join us at one of our sexual responsibility classes, they were amazed and quite enthusiastic about what they learned. Thais Goodwin is another Soror who was a finer woman in her bearing. She neither hazed nor bullied and believed one should always be fair in dealing with others. Soror Goodwin was a quiet, unassuming lady, who followed her dream and opened a restaurant.

Our Z-HOPE project won first place at three Boulés, and in 2005, 2006 and 2007, we were the first place winners at the Midwestern Region. In 2008, we received 2nd place and in 2010, we received the Midwestern Region's Distinguished Z-HOPE Chapter award.

The grant and publicity from the March of Dimes generated a lot of interest in Stork's Nest and we received many donations from church groups, individuals and other fraternal groups. The March of Dimes gave us new items from Gymboree, some of which we used in the new baby layettes. When those grant funds were exhausted, I searched for new grant options.

The local Kappa Alpha Psi president had read an article about our classes and was impressed. His chapter gave us $1,000 and suggested Chi Zeta apply for a grant through the Kappa Alpha Psi Foundation. We did and soon received a $2,000 grant. The local chapter of Alpha Kappa Alpha donated car seats and the members of Delta Sigma Sorority donated blankets. The chapter continued to participate in prenatal activities and for two years, Alma, Ramona, Thais and I presented an hour long radio program about the Stork's Nest, premature births and the importance of early and regular prenatal care.

The finer, finer women of Chi Zeta chapter were recognized as the Midwestern Region's Premier Chapter in 2014. The finer women I have described possess many different traits that enable us to complement each other and work together. Decision making skills, tact, diplomacy and adaptability all come into play as the finer, finer woman seeks to achieve her goals. She exhibits tact in her dealings with seasoned Sorors and with Amicae. She does not exhibit impatience when explaining the same thing several times. Rather, she rephrases herself constantly to offer more understandable explanations.

Always there with a ready smile, the finer woman has a keen sense of humor and is able to laugh at herself. She has dabbled in the arts, writing, music and needlework until she masters a particular one, then moves on to conquer a new horizon. She is a good listener and her body language indicates a genuine interest in others. She is a perfect planner and the pressure of a deadline revs her engine and gives her the impetus to move forward.

She maintains her health and energy levels and takes pride in her physical appearance, exhibiting the self-confidence that only these can provide. She sets forth and adheres to an exercise regimen that provides her energy to meet her demanding schedule. She confers with a dietitian about a diet necessary for nutrients as well as snacks and treats. Her beauty regimen is coordinated with her diet and exercise, and take the least amount of time from her busy schedule.

She feels free. She feels she has the courage to live her life the way she wants as long as her choices don't infringe on anyone else's rights. She makes decisions but first seeks to understand how she and others will be impacted.

The finer, finer woman is not a saint. She is humbly aware that "only God can make a tree" and that creating something that perfect and beautiful is not within her power. She is not a prissy know-it-all who thinks she is God's gift to mankind. She is a living, breathing, person, full of the human faults and frailties that others possess.

Like the foundation of a cake, she is two cups of courage, a cup of optimism, a dash of tolerance and a pinch of hope with just a speck of sorrow, and a little pain added in. She is two-thirds of a cup of laughter to sweeten a cloudy day, mixed well. She is baked slowly with warmth and gratitude, topped off with LOVE and served with happiness. No, she is no saint, she just tries harder; works at it constantly; thinks more about self-improvement; and, takes the time for reflection. She thinks before she speaks, ministers to others, and makes sure their needs are taken care of. She remembers that she is a work in progress, and strives daily to be a finer woman.

These finer women not only *embody* and *live* the definition, they *are* the definition of a finer, finer woman and are examples for all Sorors to follow.

A *Pearl* among many, a true *Dove of Peace,* she is a *Finer, Finer Woman.*

She is a *ZETA!*

Friendly; **I**ntelligent; **N**urturing; **E**mpathetic; **R**eligious
Worthy; **O**bservant; **M**ature; **A**stute; **N**oble

Finer Women United

Norma Cox Dartis

My life changed with a newspaper article. While an undergraduate student at Fisk University, a friend in my dorm shared an article with me about Zeta Phi Beta Sorority, Inc.'s upcoming Boulé. The national president at the time had requested that Sorority members "leave their fine jewels and furs behind" if they planned to attend and be prepared to do the work of Zeta. This intrigued me as I had seen a lot of showmanship from other sororities on my campus, but what I read in that article reflected substance. I thought that if you were asked to come ready to address business, then you must intend to effect some change. I remembered my freshman year when 33 Finer Women joined Zeta's Kappa Gamma chapter and had taken the campus by storm. Now, they were talented and respected leaders who enjoyed high academic achievement and a good reputation on campus. These women were aspiring to be special and I knew Zeta was for me.

I was excited beyond compare to join Zeta Phi Beta Sorority, Inc. It sparked a leadership potential in me that increased over time. Our outstanding advisor, Soror Veonie McKinnie, provided the needed encouragement and is still special to me today. Her undergraduate membership in Epsilon Alpha chapter is celebrated on the campus of Tennessee State University. To date, she is a vital part of her community reflecting a Finer Woman's lifelong commitment to service. Our other advising chapter members were noted city leaders and I reveled when I heard their names mentioned on the radio as they charted a course for the city's minority community to challenge the social customs of times. With my parents' teachings, the ground-work was laid for me to believe that I could make a difference by being a Finer Woman too.

I came to understand that a Finer Woman was set apart; she didn't follow the crowd. By being set apart, her goals were not like those of others. She would be known as one who values excellence and therefore would not settle for just the ordinary. Striving to be a vision-ary without regard to what others think is a hallmark of a Finer Woman. As a Finer Woman, I knew I was expected to identify voids and stand in the gap. I carried these thoughts with me as I transitioned to the graduate chapter. They were the impetus I needed to propel me to higher offices within the Sorority and my career. I was called to be creative in my approach yet be effective and this contributed to my growth as a leader. I believe these traits, led to my being asked to serve as the Great Lakes Region's Director in 1996.

Being Finer does not focus solely on appearance, although it does not exclude that, either. Life should never be the same after one encounters a Finer Woman of Zeta. She reasons well and is staunch and unfailing in reaching her goal. A Finer Woman does not rest until she has put her indelible mark on a project. Her thoughts and dreams are forever aligned with the dreams of our five illustrious Founders. I would never jeopardize our Founders' vision.

Collectively, a Finer Woman knows we are strong as a unit, yet she is not afraid to stand alone for a cause she is committed to. There is room for many more women who view elegance, quality, and performance as their calling, and who realize Finer Womanhood is as relevant today as it was in 1920.

A Letter as an Archonian

Bobbie Crudup Qualls

Post Office Box 607
Alcorn College
December 8, 1970

Dear Big Sisters,

This heart of love is dedicated to each of you. I feel the **sisterly love** which is evident in every Zeta's heart.

Thank you for the sisterly love you are showing to my sisters and me as we prepare to enter the Blue and White world into Zetadom. The nightly academic hour keeps me focused on my number 1 reason I am in college (yes, to get a quality education); serving the community is awesome; we are really enjoying reading to young children in the College Nursery. Thank you for modeling through example and teaching us during our Archonians Sessions: 'The Attributes of a Finer Woman, How to remain Scholarly Students, The Power of Sisterhood, and The importance of Serving God and Humanity. Your teaching is filled with Zeal and Enthusiasm!

There is a secret compartment within this heart, where I am placing special treasures: One by one, each treasure serves as remembrance of the Archonian past, and of my future life with Zeta, Dear Sisters.

In a special corner of this heart lies the Founders' vision of Zeta Phi Beta Sorority; the treasure chest is enclosed with Sisterly Love, Scholarship, Service and Finer Womanhood. In the center of this chest is Proverbs 31, for I am striving to become that Virtuous Woman. (Yes, my mom purchased the white bible for me when I told her about this Sisterhood; plus I needed it in my treasure chest). Yes, I am listening as you prepare me for my 'Zeta World'.

Zeta's Love is powerful! It is patient and kind… it does not envy… it is not proud… it is not easily angered… it always protects, always trust, always preserves, always HOPES… Wow, sounds like Mom teaching me about 'The Love Chapter'.

Big Sisters, I love you! This semester as an Archonian has been a challenge of love and refinement; I am now ready to deposit my treasures **of Sisterly Love, Scholarship, Service and Finer Womanhood…**

Your Little Sister,
Archonian Bobbie Nell Crudup
December, 1970

Ingredients for Wholesome Sisterhood

Bobbie Crudup Qualls

Five Cups of Five Pearls' objectives   stirred with Proverbs 31 Virtuous Woman

4-5 servings of Fruit of the Spirit (Joy, Peace, Patience, Kindness, Goodness, Faithfulness, and Self Control) mixed with the Love Chapter: 1 Corinthians 13

Daily 30- 45 minutes of physical activity and/or engage in reducing stress activities (deep breathing exercises, massage, warm bath, visualization moment, mediation, read for plea- sure, singing/listening to music, or participate in a hobby) Have fun!

Sprinkle daily one cup of laughter with productive interactions

Sift through the power of forgiveness and embrace the power of compassion

Add a tablespoon of encouragement and a dash of constructive criticism for progress;

Daily toss a Hershey kiss covered with hugs/compliments/celebrations to humanity

Place all these ingredients in Life's Bowl. Fold gently traits of Finer Womanhood, scholarships for students, and sisterhood attributes. Mix well with prayer and serve God and humanity with humility.

… "and whatever we do on behalf of Zeta Phi Beta Sorority, let's do it in the name of Scholarship, Service, Finer Womanhood, and Sisterly Love; surely, we will be upholding the legacy of our Founders and our National Objectives. What a great celebration!"

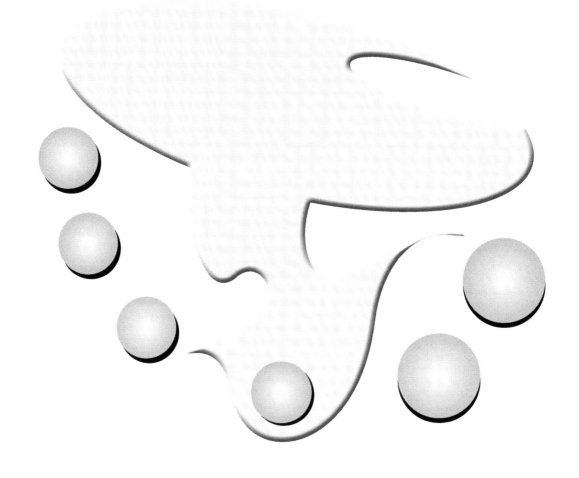

A Spark to an Eternal Flame: My Journey to Finer Womanhood

Papillon Spinks

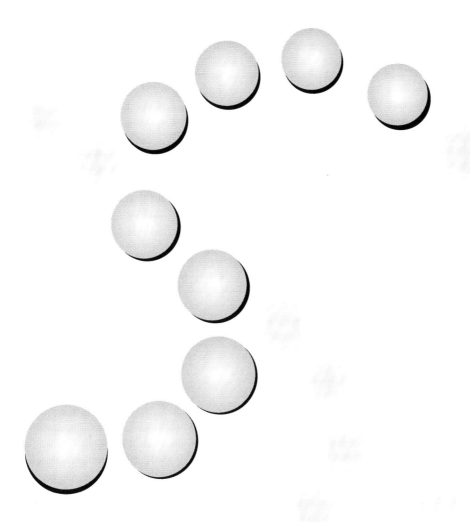

I would like to take you on a journey of my first five years as a member of the greatest Sorority in the world, Zeta Phi Beta Sorority, Incorporated. In my few short years as a member, I have witnessed many things, met many people and received an education that rivals one of a Soror who has been a member for more than a decade. I was blessed with so many Sorors to help me on my journey, and each and every one of them had a hand in making me the Zeta I am today. Each made me confident, knowledgeable and aware of all the talents I had to offer the sisterhood even when I doubted myself. More importantly, I learned about the Zeta ideal, Finer Womanhood as exemplified by these Sorors, their actions and behaviors.

1991

I met a wonderful group of women who were just as much alike as they were different. These ladies exuded confidence, dedication and compassion for those in need. I found out shortly afterwards that they were part of a group known as Zeta Phi Beta Sorority. I was immediately drawn to and interested in being a part of their organization.

I approached Soror Trina Vinson Hayes, Mu Delta Chapter, at Southern Illinois University, in Carbondale, Illinois and expressed my interest in learning about the Sorority and its work in the community. Without hesitation, she asked me to meet her the next day. I thought she would discuss history, purpose and the membership process, but I quickly learned my assumptions were all wrong. Instead, she said, "Let's go for a walk." Our first stop was the student check cashing service where I met Soror Zenetta McDaniels, who today, is the current graduate advisor for Mu Delta. Soror McDaniels spoke about what brought her to Zeta and what she loved most about the organization. She was most passionate about the *sisterhood* and its positive impact on her life. Next we stopped at McDonald's in the Student Center where I met Soror Tuesday Shorty who explained the role Zetas had in the community through their service projects and donations. She told me the chapter was full of women from all backgrounds and different walks of life, yet they were able to come together as one family. Soror Vinson and I then strolled across campus to the library and I was introduced to Soror Nairobi Thomas who was one of the newest members of the Mu Delta Chapter and busting at the seams with excitement. She mentioned that she was the only girl among her siblings and how she had gained more sisters than she ever could have imagined. After meeting Sorors McDaniels, Shorty and Thomas, Soror Vinson asked me to meet her later that day at a local rehabilitation center for patients with brain injuries. I agreed, and met her at the location a few hours later. When I arrived I saw a sea of blue and white. These ladies were playing cards, checkers and even singing and dancing with the patients. I was introduced to all and invited to participate too. When I left, I was more than impressed with the way the ladies worked together and provided a wonderful experience for the patients.

Later that evening, I received a phone call from Soror Vinson who asked, "So what do you think?" I thanked her and asked about Zeta's history and purpose." Her response is one that I will always remember. "You can go to the library and learn all of the information you seek. But what you saw and what you heard from the ladies you met, is what we are all about. What you saw is why we are here. What you heard was what we do to change the lives of young ladies on the verge of beginning the next chapter in their lives. That is what our sisterhood is about. That is Zeta!" At that moment, I knew that Zeta was the one for me. Unfortunately, the opportunity never presented itself during the years I spent at Southern Illinois University but I was determined to change that at some point in my life.

2008

Seventeen years later, well out of college and settled into a successful life with my family and career, I still thought of those women I met in 1991 and the organization I had become so fond of. I reached out to women I knew who were Zetas and expressed my desire for membership. Becoming a member in Michigan, where I had no family and even fewer friends, I immediately felt I was a part of something special. On November 14, 2009, I joined Kappa Rho Zeta Chapter in Highland Park, Michigan and found a family outside my family and a home away from home.

In December, I received an email from Soror Erin Coleman, Upsilon Psi Zeta Chapter, Oak Park, Michigan, about joining the Michigan State Organization (MSO) step team. I was very excited. Soror Coleman was the first MSO Step Team Coordinator and took the challenge head on. The auditions began in January 2010 and when selected, the final team was made up of 18 women from 6 different chapters: Upsilon Psi Zeta, Upsilon Theta Zeta, Kappa Rho Zeta, Lambda Rho Zeta, Beta Omicron Zeta and Pi Gamma Zeta. Our ages ranged from 24 to 38 years old and from 2 months to 16 years in Zeta. Ironically, I was the eldest member of the team yet the youngest member in Zeta. I did not know anyone in the auditorium except for two Sorors from my chapter who I hadn't really gotten the chance to know very well and I felt out of place. Most of these Sorors seemed to have been friends for quite some time and I felt like the new kid at school waiting for my cue to introduce myself. Then Soror Coleman came over and introduced herself. As we talked, she made me feel more comfortable. I had just gone natural with my hair and this was a topic she was very well versed in. She offered to help me with braiding and gave me other helpful tips. Erin was very giving and thoughtful when it came to extending herself to a new Soror. She was as funny as she was down to earth and although she didn't know it, she was exactly the type of person I needed in my life at that very moment. I learned from her that the majority of the Sorors on the step team were from the same chapter, Western Michigan University, and were now, charter members of Upsilon Psi Zeta Chapter. I was very impressed by this and I admired them all, particularly for sticking together for many years. I looked forward to getting to know them better.

At that moment however, Soror Coleman was the Soror I looked to when I needed help and guidance. She gave me my first education on the workings of Zeta and tips on how to fit in. She taught me to be myself and express my creativity no matter how it made me feel. She taught me that being different did not make me different, rather it put me in a class by myself and allowed me the opportunity to show people the real me. I learned that how I choose to dress or wear my hair did not make me a Finer Woman. How I carried myself in my own skin, and being true to myself made me a Finer Woman. Through her kindness, caring and willingness to assist me, a new Soror, in any way possible, she easily became my first mentor in my new Zeta world.

Being a part of the MSO step team was an exhilarating experience. I truly enjoyed being at rehearsals with my Sorors, through the fun, frustration and tears. When we hit Kentucky in May 2010 for the Great Lakes Region's conference, we had our act together and our confidence showed. We stepped on the stage as a team and gave it our all. We won first place. After that, I started spending more time with Upsilon Psi Zeta Chapter members and participated in their community service events. I formed a bond with many of them and began to feel more and more at home in their presence.

After being a Zeta for less than a year, I decided to transfer to Upsilon Psi Zeta Chapter. This chapter was the youngest and fastest growing one in Michigan. It had been chartered on

November 11, 2006, by 13 women determined to make a difference in Zeta: Kim Williams Anderson, Cherise Caldwell, Erin Coleman, Yolanda Dowe, April Groggins, Kimberly Hall, Jackie Jackson, Monica Wallingford, Scheherezade Redmond, Evonne Williams, La'Tia Peete, Monique Pittman and Robyn Wyatt. They were all graduates of Western Michigan University's Tau Delta Chapter. In their years and tutelage in Zeta, they were taught to be trailblazers. They were interested in starting new trends and standing on the forefront to lead Zeta into the future. Interested in being more visible, aside from just attending annual conferences, they wanted to be seen in their communities and recognized as a group of women who continuously upheld the Zeta ideals of Scholarship, Service, Sisterhood and Finer Womanhood. Upon graduation, these Sorors searched for a graduate chapter that shared their passion for new, innovative and out the box thinking. They explored many chapters in the Detroit area, attended meetings and participated in community service projects, but they could not find a chapter they felt would be a perfect fit for them. After much discussion, they decided they would branch out on their own and charter a chapter that they could mold into the perfect fit for all of them. This chapter became Upsilon Psi Zeta.

When making the decision to take this bold and risky move, they had no idea the growth the chapter would encounter over the next 8 years, nor did they anticipate the impact they would have on the community and Zeta as a whole. Today, Upsilon Psi Zeta Chapter, has grown to over 40 members. These amazing Sorors have lived up to the challenge of being true leaders and trailblazers by bringing new ideas to life in the Detroit area and becoming mainstays in their communities.

2010

Although I was a new member of the chapter, I knew and was very familiar with most of the Sorors in the chapter as they were with me. I was ready to work and always knew that I wanted to be heavily involved in new membership. At the time, Soror April Groggins was serving as First Anti-Basileus. Having met her when I first joined Zeta, she was now huge part of my early education in Zeta. I joined the membership committee as her co-chair and shadowed her. I watched her every move as First Anti and took notes. She was a wealth of knowledge and very patient with me when it came to my learning curve. As the sororal year went on, I was very active and whenever there was something that needed to be done, I was there. I got to know many other chapter members and my responsibilities grew. I made it my personal mission to register and attend all state, regional and national Conferences to further my knowledge in Zeta.

September 2011

At the time, Soror Groggins, encouraged me to seek out the position I was interested in and having faith in my own abilities, I took the leap. I ran for the office of First Anti-Basileus and lost. I was heartbroken. I took it personally and felt I lost because I was new to the chapter. It was at that this time that I learned a valuable lesson from Soror Groggins. She told me that chapter members needed to see me in a different light, and that I needed to listen and learn as opposed to thinking I had all the answers. In short, she told me that I needed to humble myself and show that I was prepared to take constructive criticism as well as accolades.

After hearing this, I listened more and learned about the positions I was interested in. Soror Groggins had shown me that while I was capable, I was not a rock star and still had a lot of growing to do. With that, she taught me *humility.*

Soror Groggins appointed me to the position of Z-HOPE Coordinator. Needless to say I was less than enthused. Although my heart was in membership, April assured me that there were so many other ways I could serve Zeta. "I am appointing you Z-HOPE Coordinator and you will excel in whatever position you are in. Once Sorors see your capabilities and your passion, you will quickly become one who is known for going above and beyond the Zeta call. I will do everything I can to get you out front so people can see your talents." I accepted the appointment and in doing so, I put my foot forward on my Zeta journey. April's plan was the beginning of something very special and I now realize that sometimes a person can believe in you more than you do yourself.

March 24, 2012

My first six months in Upsilon Psi Zeta had been full of education, laughter, disappointment and tears but the element of sisterhood was still there. The "togetherness" of the chapter kept my zeal alive and I continued to work hard despite many disappointments and road blocks. I jumped feet first into my position of Z-HOPE Coordinator and worked tirelessly to implement Z-HOPE activities into the very fabric of the chapter. Once we were on track, I started to feel good about the work I was doing and gained a true passion for touching the community. When I delivered donations to the various shelters and group homes I was deeply touched by the gratitude shown by the residents.

Once I delivered items to a women's shelter, a little boy aged 6 or 7 greeted me in the main office and started looking through the bags. "What you got in there?" he asked me. "I have some things that some of your neighbors need," I responded. He asked, "Is there anything in there for me?" I told him some of the things I had in the bag and he said, "That's good. My Mama could use all of that." Hearing him say those words warmed me and I understood the impact Zeta had in communities where people were in need. After that I was hooked. I made it a point to hand deliver every donation. The people in the community were as much a help to me as I was to them.

I also participated in all other chapter activities, scholarship ad and event ticket sales, social events and walks for different causes, and did not give a second thought to the work I was doing. I was having a blast! I never looked for accolades or rewards. Knowing the importance of my work was reward enough. However, in true sisterly fashion, the Sorors of my chapter rewarded my hard work and commitment. On March 24, 2012 at our annual Scholarship Luncheon, I was named "Zeta of the Year." I was taken aback, genuinely surprised and at a loss for words. They made me feel special even though I didn't feel that what I had done was special at all. In just six months, I realized that working hard for Zeta had become my passion. That award, my first Zeta award, will always be the most important one to me no matter what else the future holds. That award gave me the reassurance that I was in fact living up to the words on our shield, OMNI VINCIT LABORE. I was on the right track and I couldn't be happier.

April 2012

Just one month after receiving my award, I attended the Great Lakes Region's conference and was surprised yet again. Upsilon Psi Zeta competed at the regional level of the Z-HOPE competition and when the winners were announced, our chapter won 2nd place! April pulled me aside and whispered, "You know UPZ has never won an award on any level right? Thank you. I knew you could do it."

The next day, at the end of our first business meeting, an older Soror I did not know walked up to me with a purse, a conference bag and a pair of shoes in her hands. She looked me straight in the eye and in a stern motherly tone said, "Soror, these are Soror Frances Faithful's things. Do you know who she is?" I answered, "Yes, Founder Faithful's daughter." "You are to be her escort for the rest of the day. Wherever she goes, you are to remain at her side at all times and tend to her needs. Carry these things and do not set them down. Do you understand?" I am sure I had a deer in the headlights look on my face, but I nodded my head and answered "Yes Ma'am." I had never met Soror Frances Faithful, and I began looking around the room for her. She was not hard to spot, sitting in a chair surrounded by Sorors wanting to take photos with her. I walked over to her and introduced myself. I did not have a clue as to what I was supposed to do besides stay with her. I treated her like Zeta royalty and made general conversation with her. She was sweet and asked me a lot about myself. We ended up having a great day and I was very aware of the privilege I had been given. I couldn't understand why that Soror, whoever she was, had chosen me. With no answers I just chalked it up to pure luck. I would find out later that it was not luck at all. Again, my commitment had not gone unnoticed and again I was rewarded.

July 2012

The Boulé was held in Chicago and I was so excited to attend my first one. This was an election year and I was a delegate. The first day of business meetings was rough; there were many problems and it did not seem that we got much done. I was very disappointed and discouraged. I made the comment that I was never attending a Boulé again if this was how business was conducted. An older Soror heard this and stopped me. "Soror, please do not be discouraged. This is not how we normally do business. Sometimes things may go off track but do not let that be a reason for you to disassociate yourself." I knew this Soror; she was the one who had ordered me to escort Soror Faithful in Detroit. I said, "I never asked you for your name but I am Papillon Spinks." She replied, "Yes Soror Spinks, I know who you are. My name is Jylla Moore Foster *(now Jylla Moore-Tearte),* the 20th International Grand Basileus." I was floored.

I returned the next day with a renewed attitude about the business sessions of Zeta. Over the next few years, I would see Past Grand Tearte at various conferences and when I spoke to her she always remembered who I was. She is an amazing woman who exhibits the finest of Finer Womanhood. She is as stern and intelligent as she is wise. She is steadfast in her work for Zeta and she is giving. Most of all, to our great sisterhood, she is a leader. My chance meeting with Soror Tearte was an unexpected lesson in itself. I first got to see the stern side of her as she gave me a task coupled with specific instructions. The next time I saw her I experienced her kindness, as I thanked her for the previous assignment she had given me and the opportunities that were sure to arise from it. The third time we met, I experienced her words of encouragement as I shared my sheer disappointment about the activities of the day.

I watched her at every conference I attended and got to know her better. The way she moved through the crowd greeting people or the way she spoke and carried herself. When she spoke I listened. She spoke softly but with confidence, easily getting her point across and delivering her message effectively. There was not a dignitary in the room that she did not know and as she greeted them, she treated them with the utmost respect. She had held the highest, most coveted office in our organization, yet she was as humble as one could be. When she addressed the sisterhood as a whole, I could feel the power in voice and her passion for Zeta. She has continuously pushed and given me the confidence I need, to rise to the occasion and excel to the next level. Soror Tearte exhibits every element of Finer Womanhood. Her teachings, known and unknown, coupled with what I learned from countless other Sorors, have blessed me with the recipe to becoming a Finer Woman. She has become my mentor, and gives me honest opinions and feedback when I need them the most.

September 15, 2012

I enlisted my Basileus to travel with me to Flint, Michigan to videotape an interview with Soror Faithful. We pulled up to Applebee's, equipped with nothing but an iPhone, an iPad and some paper. I had gotten to know Soror Faithful a little more over the past year and Soror Groggins had met her twice. We had a list of prepared questions to ask but before we got to those, we realized Soror Faithful was interviewing us! She seemed to want to know as much about us as we did her. Soror Groggins and I were lucky enough to learn some things "off the record." It was a once in a lifetime experience to sit with her and hear about her Mom and Aunt, our Founders, Myrtle Tyler Faithful and Viola Tyler Goings. Stories of her childhood, her first Boulé and what it was like to hang out with women Soror Faithful described as, "Very funny. They loved to laugh together and joke around." She did let us in on a little secret that I am free to share.

For a long time, she did not know that her mom was a Zeta. Neither her mom nor her aunt tried to persuade her to join Zeta and they did not talk about the Sorority much. Soror Frances Faithful chose Zeta on her own and became engaged with her a mother and aunt when she attended her first Boulé. She was Founder Myrtle Tyler Faithful's escort. I couldn't help but display a "cheesy" smile about this. Soror Faithful escorted her Mom, our Founder, and now I was escorting her. No words can explain how both Soror Groggins and I felt as we headed back to Detroit. We were like two children going on about the new toys we had gotten for our birthdays. To top this, we had notes, audio and video, that no one else had. We were on cloud nine!

The very next day, on September 16th, chapter elections were held. This time things would play out differently for me. At the end of the meeting I was installed as the First Anti-Basileus of Upsilon Psi Zeta. I felt like I had arrived, finally getting the position I sought from day one. I was on top of the world. I formed my committee and immediately went to work. In my mind, during my entire time in office, I was doing an excellent job. As it turned out, that was not enough. In fact, that had worked against me. I had watched Soror Groggins so closely I convinced myself I knew all I needed to do the job just as good as, if not better than her. I had stopped learning from others about doing the job because I felt I already knew everything and that I had all the answers.

When my term ended, I asked for feedback from my committee members and some of what I was told was news to me. I had made many, many mistakes. I went to my mentor for guidance and she responded, "The only way to learn to do a job is to do it and make mistakes. If I had told you what you were doing wrong, you would have no mistakes to learn from. I was never going to let you do anything drastic that would hurt Zeta, but I wanted you to find your own way. I was teaching you, just as I was taught; to think on your own and when it's all said and done, do an honest assessment and learn from the experience as a whole. You may have thought you failed but in reality you were successful. You were smart enough to ask for feedback, listen to it, accept it and try to figure out how to improve." She made perfect sense and today, I would give this advice to any Soror.

I received a phone call from the Michigan State Director, Elner Taylor telling me that Soror Faithful had personally requested me for her escort at the upcoming Michigan State Meeting. I couldn't believe she actually requested me to me to escort her again! Soror Taylor said, "Yes, she remembers you, but she cannot pronounce your name. She asked for Pappy." I laughed at that as no one had called me Pappy since I was a little kid. "I would be honored to escort her," I responded. I knew I had to do some research on being an escort so I reached out to some older Sorors to advise me. They gave me tips about the job, which was proof positive that getting out and meeting Sorors who could help me was the right thing to do.

I thanked Soror Faithful for requesting me as her escort and she responded, "Why wouldn't I? You took good care of me and you were very pleasant company." This was once again a privilege and an honor. There was nothing else that could possibly happen in 2012 that could add to the amazing experiences I had already had that year.

April 26, 2013

Since first escorting Soror Faithful, we developed a good relationship and at the 2013 Great Lakes Region Conference in Indianapolis, I was very relaxed. I learned so much that I don't know where to begin or end in sharing the experience. Some of her teachings were funny and some seemed insignificant, but I took every opportunity to listen to what she was saying to me. Some lessons were taught in a funny way, like proper etiquette at the dinner table. One day, after watching me, she told me she was going to teach me proper table etiquette. "Finer Women know the proper way to eat and behave at the dinner table. You need help in this area, and I am going to teach you how a Finer Woman eats!" There was no malice in her words, as she taught me subtleties that most people would not take the time to show me. Other times she was very stern in her teachings.

Before attending a dinner banquet that required after 5 attire, I mentioned that I did not like the "glittery" clothes that most officers and dignitaries wore and that I did not own such clothing and would never buy any. The tone of her response was different from the times before. She sounded like a mother giving a life lesson to a child. "Sometimes you have to do things that you don't want to do because that is the job you chose, Missy! If you want to play the part, you have to dress the part." I sat in silence, like a scolded child. I looked up to Sorors like her, enamored by the way they carry themselves and exhibit Finer Womanhood. They are what I aspire to be like.

On another occasion, in the simplest way possible, she taught me the importance of being patient. I had learned firsthand what it was like for her to be Zeta royalty; we could never walk 3 feet without someone stopping us, asking for her photo or autograph. Many times I became very frustrated as we may have been en route to another event and stopping was going to make us late. I felt that as an escort, my job was to keep her on time. While I was correct in this assumption, I overlooked the fact that I had had the privilege of seeing and talking to her every day and many other Sorors had never seen or met her. They were simply taking advantage of their opportunity to do so.

The Reaffirmation Ceremony at Boulé 2012 was a turning point. We had spent hours standing at a table as she gave autographs and posed for photos. The line of Sorors never seemed to end and it was growing longer and longer. Sorors pushed their way to the front, leaned on the tables and crowded around her. I became very irritated, and although I did not raise my voice, I was very insistent with Sorors that they step away from the table to provide her more space. Soror Faithful sensed my irritation and later, once she was all settled in her room, she brought the subject up. She asked me, "Why are you so mean to Sorors?" I was completely floored by her question and sat in silence.

Before I could answer she began her lesson. "Whenever I traveled with mom as her escort, I always noticed that no matter how many Sorors stopped her, no matter how much time it took for photographs and autographs, she never said no. I have seen her stand for hours to accommodate Sorors and if she did that, then I can do the same. You must learn to understand the reasons behind Sorors' actions and know that there is never any ill intent, even though it may seem to you that they are behaving rudely or being inconsiderate. You have to LEARN TO BE PATIENT." Those last words resonated with me the most. If she could be patient through all of the chaos that comes with being Zeta royalty, then so could I. "One day," she said, "you will be in a position to be constantly stopped for pictures and autographs and when that time comes, you will need to be patient with our Sorors. If you do not, you may be viewed as unapproachable and a Finer Woman is not only approachable, she is dignified in the way that she deals with people." After that, I never grew impatient when she was constantly stopped or had to stand for hours giving autographs and taking pictures. Instead, I learned to be kind to our Sorors and put my energy into creating a system for there to be autographs and pictures without chaos. Once I learned to be "patient," escorting Soror Faithful became easier. Now, I give other Sorors the opportunity to sit and talk with Soror Faithful in the hope that they will ask the right questions and walk away with something more than just a photo on their journey to Finer Womanhood.

Now, when I am unsure of what to do I confide in Soror Faithful for an honest opinion, even if it is one I do not want to hear. She teaches me how to be a "Zeta Grownup." She once said to me, "Sometimes you need to do things that you don't want to do because you have accepted a role and that is the job." I took this advice to heart and have learned to apply it to almost any aspect of life. It is so amazing to sit and talk with her. She is funny and very knowledgeable about the business of Zeta. We have developed a great relationship and I am honored to be in her circle. She is a mentor and a friend and a shining example of Finer Womanhood.

September 2013

At the State Meeting, Director Elner Taylor wanted to give a tribute to the all the past Michigan State Directors. Her program included a portrayal of all of the past directors, performed by various Sorors. Soror Faithful was asked who she would like to portray her and she chose me. When I called to thank her she said "I know you will do a fine job. You know everything you need to know to portray me. I wouldn't have picked anyone else." I took what I learned from the interview with her and began to write. The result was *"Faithful Reflections."* I let her read it before I presented it at State Meeting and she was delighted with it and my delivery.

May 26, 2014

It was Memorial Day and the position of regional Epistoleus was vacant after Soror Tonia Jenkins was appointed State Director. The chair of the Regional Executive Board, Soror Taniqua Carter, asked me if I was interested in the appointment. I accepted without hesitation and had my first regional position.

September 21, 2014

I had served as First Anti-Basileus, Second Anti-Basileus and Z-HOPE Coordinator for my chapter. I had been chosen to fill a vacant seat on the region's Executive Board and now I was looking at a position at the state level as Epistoleus. I had thrown my name into the hat prior to being appointed the regional Epistoleus. On September 27th, I was sworn in as the Michigan State Epistoleus. The blue and white stars seemed aligned for me. My Basileus, mentor and good friend April Groggins, appointed me co-Z-HOPE Coordinator for the second time. I seemed to have come full circle, ending back in the position in which I started, but now with experience and knowledge that many Sorors do not come across in a Zeta lifetime. I am truly blessed. This education has humbled me, the relationships enriched me, and the experiences have changed my life. I want to honor and thank all of the Sorors I encountered.

There are many, many other Sorors that have guided me as I traveled on my five year journey. Often, Soror Faithful and I sit with the nine past Directors of the Great Lakes Region and being with those Sorors has become a highlight of the conference. Watching them, I know why collectively, they were all appointed to that office. I have learned so much from them, and respect them. I keep them and many other Sorors in my heart and thoughts when I reflect upon my first five years in Zeta. There *will* be more stories for me to recount and more journeys to document, in the future.

The Essence of Finer Womanhood

Lavern J. Holyfield, DDS
Inspired by the poem, Trees, by Joyce Kilmer

I think that I shall never see
A Sisterhood more exquisite than Z Phi B.

With women whose services deserve praise,
Women who are magnificent in so many ways.

Women who walk in integrity;
Women whose accomplishments are praiseworthy;

Women who consistently make the right choice;
When one of them speaks, she does so with a voice

That's worthy of respect and majesty.
That lovely woman of Z Phi B,

A woman whose values are exceptionally good,
Zeta, the essence of Finer Womanhood.

My Zeta Village!

Karen Blount

I was 5 days old when I was introduced to the legacy of Zeta Phi Beta Sorority, Inc. My mother, a 1950 charter member of Delta Eta Zeta, Ft. Lauderdale, Fla., chapter, gave birth on Dec. 20, 1959. Being an officer and in the midst of bringing in new members during her pregnancy, she hosted a combination intake and surprise baby shower on Dec. 26, which was also her birthday.

These Sorors established a rare culture of sisterhood by coming together and establishing the first Greek-lettered organization in Broward County. Not only were they former college friends and Sorors of my mother, but they were also the village that raised me. They were my elementary school teachers and our neighbors, as well as church members. The sisterhood was so strong then that they all purchased their first homes in the 1960's in the same

neighborhood, within blocks of each other. They were all educators and worked in the same neighborhood school.

Their female children, though older than me, became my life-long friends. All of us are now Zetas in the same chapter. As we all grew up in Zeta, these ladies continued to support us as Zetarettes, Archonettes, Sub-Debutantes and Debutantes. In 1954, these Sorors established the first Debutante Cotillion in our community for young black women. We were all required to participate as our time approached as seniors in high school. This tradition continues in the chapter. Last year, we celebrated the 60th Debutante Cotillion.

When I became a Zeta in 1978 at Bethune-Cookman University, they were there, ushering me into the Sisterhood. In 1982, I moved back home, and became a member of Delta Eta Zeta, and immediately became the youth advisor for a few years.

It was not long before they entrusted the leadership of the chapter to me a Chapter Basileus. I was the youngest member of the chapter at the time, so I knew I was not really, "in charge." I was there in a position to be trained in the Zeta way. Once the Sorors who raised me realized I had a mind of my own, they "allowed" me to have input as the Basileus of the chapter from 1992-1996. When they finally let go, we were able to transition the generations and make the collaborative effort to become a "Model Chapter" in 1996.

Starting in 2000, as each one of these ladies passed away, over the years, it was like losing a part of my childhood. I learned a life lesson from each one, even when we did not agree, and each one had a story to tell. My mother was the last one to pass away in 2012, which closed the circle. The body that encircled me as an infant, carried and provided support over the years was gone. Several were able to witness the third generation of the legacy begin with the induction of my two daughters in 2006 and 2008.

As I continue my Zeta journey, I am grateful for my Zeta Village of Finer Women, and how they prepared me and made me tough enough. I will continue to "pay it forward" through my work in Zeta and through my daughters whom I hope embrace and appreciate the legacy of Zeta and how strong Zeta Women impacted their lives. Our legacy continues looking forward to 100 years.

The Legacy of Being Finer

Keisha D. Smith

From my beginning, I witnessed Christian values, intelligence, self-determination, dedication and the delivery of quality service and consideration to others. I observed servant leadership demonstrated through acts of kindness and unselfishness. I grew up in with parents who cared about my development and future, parents who were distinguished educators. They led me to believe that I could and would do anything I wanted to pursue. My parents equipped me to be a good citizen and allowed me to decide if I would take their teachings seriously and apply them to my life. My father, the late Willie A. Smith, Past National Grand Keeper of Records and Seal for Omega Psi Phi Fraternity, Incorporated and mother, Ira J. Ebbs, Past Great Lakes Region and Kentucky State Directors, invested in me throughout my life. They surrounded me with positive resources and provided direct tough love. Through my mother, I have a greater perspective of and full appreciation for effective communication and collaboration while serving others. Ira J. Ebbs is an outstanding representative of a Finer Woman in the 21st Century.

"Keeping it Finer" are encouraging words with great accountability. Women who keep it Finer possess wisdom and strength and the ability to serve other people. Women with humility, diverse skill sets, and talents keep it Finer. There are countless women I thank for adding value to Zeta Phi Beta Sorority, Incorporated and my life. Through the support of these women, I am indebted for the experiences I have received while learning from them. Before I began my journey, there were five phenomenal women who laid the foundation as undergraduates: Founder Arizona Stemons, Founder Pearl A. Neal, Founder Myrtle Tyler Faithful, Founder Viola Tyler Goings, and Founder Fannie Pettie Watts. Prior to my undergraduate experience, I sat at the feet of Ira J. Ebbs, Toni Thomas, also a Past Kentucky State Director, Joyce Holliman, Bobbie Qualls, the late Avil Harris, and members of Eta Zeta chapter in Louisville, Kentucky. Notably, I recognize Soror Lizzie G. Miller, Past Great Lakes Region and Kentucky State Directors, for her poise, and the lifelong experience and ongoing Zeta Dove service, she graciously gives to Kentucky and the Sorority. Soror Miller has freely given her spiritual guidance which we have all benefited from and we are forever grateful.

As I grew up, I learned from the Sorors of Eta Zeta chapter. Engagement with local chapter members and leaders was just the beginning. My parents and siblings traveled to Greek leadership conferences for family vacations. My mother and father served as elected and appointed officers at the local, state, regional, and national levels of their fraternal organizations yet they taught their children that God is first, family is second and education is third. Leadership follows the attainment of the other three.

As a student at the University of Kentucky, I majored in elementary education and communications. I learned a great deal about life in my short time away from home and was eager to graduate and begin a career in education. Before I headed into the real world, I attended an informational held by Iota Mu chapter. Celeste (Finch) Harris was the president and Chanty (White) Headspeth was the membership intake coordinator. As undergraduate women, these chapter members were business oriented, professionally dressed, and academically strong. They had a commanding presence on campus. I knew Zeta Phi Beta Sorority was the right organization for me because of what I had learned from the actions and activities of my mother, her Sorors, and the members of the Iota Mu chapter. With nine other undergraduate women: Carolyn Bivens, Tarita (Terrell) Burton, Tanette (Weathers) Hannon, Labron (Wordlow) Horton, Joequetta (Jackson) Shkneil, Monica (Durr) Lowe, Marcia Overstreet, Jamila Packer, and Raina Turner, I applied for membership and, in March 1996, we were inducted into Zeta Phi Beta Sorority.

In April 1996, we registered for and attended the Great Lakes Regional Conference in Cincinnati, OH under the leadership of Dr. Jylla Moore Tearte, 20th International Grand Basileus and Doris M. Stokes, the 17th Great Lakes Region Director. We attended workshops, business sessions, luncheons, and the closing banquet to support our growth and development. After the regional conference, I reflected and celebrated the fact that my mother was my first state director; Soror Stokes was my first regional director; and, Dr. Tearte, my first International Grand Basileus. These Sorors were all very impressive women to me. Moreover, Sorors Tearte and Stokes were legacy members too. They were all Finer Women, who were organized, spoke and carried themselves well, and their love for the Sorority was more than evidenced. This was how I wanted to be.

I began to envision a path that would lead to my holding a Sorority leadership role in the future. In April 1997, I attended the Great Lakes Regional Conference in Fort Wayne, Indiana under the leadership of Dr. Barbara West Carpenter, 21st International Grand Basileus, and Norma C. Dartis, Past Great Lakes Region Director. I was recruited to serve as an escort for Past Grand Carpenter, an opportunity that revealed more insights for me from the First Lady of our esteemed organization. Past Grand Carpenter is an example of a Finer Woman and I noted too, she was a legacy member.

I relocated to Oklahoma and became a student at the University of Oklahoma where I transferred to Theta Mu chapter. Soror Dartis had shared with Soror Lillian Marigny, Past Midwestern Region Director that I was moving and I was extremely excited to make this transition. The members of Theta Mu chapter, Sorors Shannon Byrdsong, LaNytra Fuller and Keisha (Coleman) Driskell, welcomed me into their chapter.

I attended the 1998 Boulé in Atlanta, Georgia and learned many lessons and Zeta tips from Oklahoma State Director, Dr. Zola Drain. I sat next to her as an active listener and absorbed her commanding presence, self-confidence, and knowledge, all qualities of a Finer Woman. With knowledge and tools gained from my previous training, I envisioned being one of those women who possessed confidence and the desire to hold leadership positions in the Sorority and continue the legacy of Zeta.

The women who expressed interest in Theta Mu chapter in the spring of 1999, not only exceeded the membership criteria, but brought a fierce drive of excellence and willpower that was recognized by their peers and campus organizations. The talents of these women, Shavonya (McClarty) Coleman, Kameelah (Wesley) Harris, Destiny (Robinson) Peters, LaTosha Steel, Monica Stephens, and Rashida Wesley, were unmatched. I graduated from the University of Oklahoma with a communications degree and immediately traveled to Philadelphia for the 2000 Grand Boulé and ran for and was elected National Third Anti-Basileus.

My mother's mantra had always been: Stay with the facts. Do the work and remain focused on purpose and I continued to heed her words. Her guidance and wisdom never left me and have been beneficial to my endeavors. While serving on the National Executive Board, I met, worked with and learned from Dr. Shirley J. Bowles, Past National First Anti-Basileus, Dr. Nell Ingram, Past National Second Anti-Basileus, Valerie Hollingsworth, Past Chair of the National Executive Board, and two National Executive Directors: Vickie Robinson and Lois Sylver, all examples of Finer Women. Triumphant Soror and Past Grand Basileus, Dr. Deborah Cannon Partridge Wolfe, was a strong mentor as she taught me key lessons when I served on the National Educational Foundation's Board of Managers. The outstanding leader we know today as our Grand Basileus was serving as the National Director of Protocol at that time and I felt honored to be in her presence as she carried out her position's duties.

I transferred to Chi Zeta chapter and continued to learn from Basileus, Soror Ora Morten. Triumphant Soror Alma F. Posey Washington, Esq., Past National Phylacter, Lillian Marigny, Past Midwestern Region Director, Thais Cox Goodwin, Dr. Mary Tillman, Mary Ann Spicer, Lisa Givens and several phenomenal Chi Zeta women who served as my mentors. I was honored when Theta Mu chapter members created a scholarship in my name in support of the Sorority's founding ideals.

At the 2002 Grand Boulé, I ran for National Graduate Member-At-Large but did not win that office. I was thankful for the experience and the women I met and fellowshipped with through the entire process. A career opportunity found me relocating to Louisville and transferring to Eta Zeta chapter.

My mother, was appointed regional director and from 2002 – 2006, and I served as her assistant. Change is inevitable and I was very fortunate to be among Regional Director Ebbs' Cabinet of State Directors: Michelle Porter Norman (IL), Darling Pleasant and Carrie Harris (IN), Bobbie Qualls (KY), Barbara Hartgrove-Holley (OH), Triumphant Soror Cassandra Bronson (MI), Fannie Harrell (MN), and Jennifer B. Wright (WI). One of the lessons I learned from being with these women was that my mother respected them and they respected her. Furthermore, everyone respected their offices and protocol. Soror Ebbs provided guidance and oversight while ensuring that Past Grand Barbara C. Moore's programs where implemented. highlighted each state which in turn, highlighted the region collectively. She truly has been the model for how I lead today.

After the 2012 Grand Boulé in Chicago, much prayer, and dialog with my family, I decided to apply for the office of Kentucky State Director. On Thursday, August 2, 2012, International Grand Basileus Mary Breaux Wright held her first tele-town hall and announced the regional and state director appointments. I was so appreciative and grateful to hear my name called as the Kentucky State Director. I have now had the pleasure of serving in the Great Lakes Region with Michelle Porter Norman, Director, and my colleagues and fellow State Directors, Connie V. Pugh, (IL); Susan Johnson, PhD, (IN); Elner Taylor (Past Director) and Tonia Jenkins, (MI); Bernadette Harrell, (MN); LaRita Smith, (OH); and, Milika Miller, (WI).

Past National Director of Amicae Affairs and Past Great Lakes Region Director, Annye P. Roberts called me to communicate her support. She provided teachable moments and encouraged me to include the Amicae in all that I planned to do for Kentucky and Zeta. I welcomed her words of wisdom and remembered my positive interactions with dynamic women such as Amica Janice L. Brown, Great Lakes Region Amicae President and the regional and Louisville Amicae. I was appreciative of the encouraging messages and expressions from so many individuals and close friends such as Beverly Cook in Arkansas and Brunhilda Williams-Curington, National Phylacter. Since that day, the Kentucky State Association has been standing tall in collaboration and effective implementation of Grand Wright's initiatives.

I acknowledge that I could not have performed and met the expectations of our dynamic Sorority if the Lord had not already written my journey. My family provides unconditional support and encouragement on a consistent basis too. They give more than I could ever ask for and I would be remiss if I did not share that I wholeheartedly appreciate and love: Damonte (son), Fern (sister), Kingsley (brother and member of Omega Psi Phi Fraternity, Inc.), Shereese (sister-in-law), Brentton (nephew); Branae (niece and Archonette); Baylee (niece and Amicette); Addyson (niece), and Kingsley, Jr. (nephew). My family motivates and strengthens me. They live through these experiences with me and I would not trade them for anything.

To the Kentucky State Association, all 10 graduate chapters and seven undergraduate chapters, the Amicae youth auxiliary members, you have my gratitude for accepting me and allowing me to serve you. My legacy of service is built on the shoulders of many Sorors, all outstanding Zetas and shining examples of Finer Womanhood.

Amicettes on Finer Womanhood

Voices of Zeta Amicettes

In 1955, Hattye Tillett suggested to the Amicae Club of Washington, D.C., that daughters and granddaughters of the Amicae be organized into a social and civic group. Esther C. Peyton of Beta Zeta Chapter of Washington, D.C., sponsored this project and the D.C. Amicettes were the only group for a number of years. They were an excited group of adolescents comprised of daughters and granddaughters of Zeta Amicae, Phi Beta Sigma brothers and Zeta Phi Beta members and other junior high school students who were invited to join. At the 50th Anniversary Boulé in 1970, the Amicettes were added to the Zeta structure as the junior-high auxiliary. Amicettes are a Youth Auxiliary Group for girls 9-13 years of age.

Finer Womanhood is being able to carry yourself with class while upholding a positive mindset and appearance, all the while knowing how to handle your business as needed.

– **Gabriela Jones,** Former Amicette, Kappa Iota Zeta, East Point, Georgia

Finer Womanhood is having respect for yourself, taking care of your responsibilities, being confident, and having good manners.

– **Laela Ware,** Amicette, Alpha Theta Zeta, Savannah, Georgia

Finer Womanhood is having respect for yourself and others, being true to yourself, and knowing your self-worth.

– **Maya Amber Miles,** Amicette, Delta Zeta, Charlotte, North Carolina

Finer Womanhood is realizing when you need to be mature.

– **Alexis Robinson,** Amicette, Omega Mu Zeta, North Brunswick, New Jersey

Finer Womanhood is taking responsibility for your actions.

– **Kaziah Betts,** Amicette, Omega Mu Zeta Chapter, North Brunswick, New Jersey

Finer Womanhood is a better way for a lady to live life.

– **Tori Robinson,** Amicette, Delta Mu Zeta, New York, New York

Finer Womanhood is making life better for yourself and others, and mentoring young ladies in need.

– **Alana Coleman,** Amicette, Delta Mu Zeta, New York, New York

Finer Womanhood is being caring, strong, confident and independent.

– **Nia'lee Thompson,** Amicette, Delta Mu Zeta, New York, New York

Finer Womanhood is being the best woman you can be at all times.

– **McKenzie Landry,** Amicette, Eta Sigma Zeta, North Little Rock, Arkansas

Finer Womanhood is being the female version of Jesus, being a sister to all and spreading love and kindness in all that you do.

– **Tiauna Capel,** Amicette, Epsilon Iota Zeta, Greenville, South Carolina

Finer Womanhood is when you are caring, encouraging and independent.

— **Amaya Davis,** Amicette, Tau Psi Zeta, Alsip, Illinois

Finer Womanhood means sisters forever and the respect and loyalty that Zeta Ladies have.

— **Jaylynne Smith,** Amicette, Omega Mu Zeta, North Brunswick, New Jersey

Finer Womanhood is being kind, caring and saving other people's lives without asking for anything in return.

— **Kariana James,** Amicette, Gamma Nu Zeta, Camden, New Jersey

Finer Womanhood is success.

— **Aleigha Walker,** Amicette, Omicron Epsilon Zeta, Albany, New York

Finer Womanhood is precision, class, and style. It's everything little girls dream to be.

— **Lamaya E. Nelson,** Amicette, Omicron Epsilon Zeta, Albany, New York

Finer Womanhood is the path to becoming a woman.

– **Michelle Montgomery,** Amicette, Xi Mu Zeta, Markham, Illinois

Finer Womanhood characteristics of a woman include community service, high morals and good character.

– **Briana Hunter,** Amicette, Alpha Phi Zeta, Richmond Virginia

Finer Womanhood is always being your best and serving your community.

– **Jasmine Jones,** Amicette, Xi Mu Zeta, Markham, Illinois

Finer Womanhood is having respect for others, being responsible and honest, and always being ladylike.

– **Simone Gilbert,** Amicette, Theta Lambda Zeta, Champaign, Illinois

Finer Womanhood is women being independent, working together, and getting the job done while still looking classy. It is also being positive role model for all young girls.

– **Vivica McBean,** Amicette, Gamma Nu Zeta, Camden, New Jersey

Finer Womanhood is ZETA! It is also a woman who is kind, genuine, and not mean to other people.

– **Kennedy McGruder,** Amicette, Delta Zeta, Charlotte, North Carolina

Finer Womanhood is treating people with respect and exercising the Golden Rule.

– **Chandra Pridgen,** Amicette, Delta Zeta, Charlotte, North Carolina

Finer Womanhood is being excellent and showing responsibility to everything and everyone.

– **Christiana Seabrooks,** Amicette, Delta Zeta, Charlotte, North Carolina

Finer Womanhood is learning to be better than you were before! It is knowing that you are to be a friend to everyone and help where you can.

– **Praize Medley,** Amicette, Delta Zeta, Charlotte, North Carolina

Finer Womanhood is women being examples for young ladies like me.

– **Kymala Banner,** Amicette, Beta Omicron Zeta, Detroit, Michigan

ANTHOLOGY

The Voices of Zetas

The Epitome of a Finer Woman

Undrané C. Tisdale and Venus G. Wilson

Everyone's story is different. All Sorors did not start off with a background of Zeta Phi Beta Sorority in their lives. Some, are just introduced to it during their collegiate years. Here are the two different ways we were introduced to Zeta Phi Beta and some of the moments that influenced our lives.

Venus

I did not grow up in a blue and white household. Both of my parents were Greek, but they were inactive in their organizations and I had no idea that they were even fraternal group members until I was in high school. I knew very little about Greek letter organizations except for what I saw in the media and heard from different people. Later, I discovered that most of my immediate family was Greek but I still had no desire to be Greek myself. It's funny to see what life has in store. Once I started college, my thoughts about Greek life changed drastically and for the best.

My first year at the University of Arkansas, I was focused on my studies and Army ROTC. At that time my main goal was to get an education and possibly get commissioned into the military as an officer. My first year of ROTC was very difficult. I was not used to the structure and physical and mental toughness that was required of service members. Sure, I grew up as an athlete and dancer, so I knew how to push myself, but Army ROTC became a whole new beast that I just had a difficult time conquering. Thankfully one of the junior level cadets saw that I was having a rough time adjusting to the lifestyle, and decided to be my mentor.

Later, I found out that he was a member of Kappa Upsilon chapter, Phi Beta Sigma Fraternity. One day, he invited me to a Blue & White Barbecue at his house and he introduced me to some Zetas. My first thoughts of them were that they were genuine and down to earth. They took time to get to know me and they wanted to know me personally. This led me to want to pursue Zeta.

During my sophomore year, I decided it was the right time to go Greek. I went through the intake process in the spring of 2012. On a very cold night in March, we had our presentation show outside. To this day, I still have no idea how I was able perform a whole entire show in 3 inch stiletto heels on a brick surface. There were three of us, Shantae, Raven, and Ashyle and together, we were known as the "PHInest Four Blu ReactantZ." After a night of fun, joy, and complete bliss, the real work of being a Finer Woman of Zeta began.

Since being a member of Phi Theta chapter, I have learned many different life lessons that have helped me grow into the person that I am today. I have learned what sisterly love and sisterhood really are. I was an only child never knew what it was like to have siblings. I knew I could always rely on my parents whenever I needed anything and they helped me solve a number of different problems and obstacles that I was facing. I also knew that I could always rely on myself as well.

Once I became a Zeta, I finally had another bond that I had yearned for as a child: I finally had sisters. My Sorors have helped me open up and grow in ways that I could never imagine. They have been there when I was at my highest and lowest points. They have given me praise when I have done well and tough love when I was in the wrong. I have learned how to function outside of my comfort zone. During my first full year of being a Zeta, I was on my chapter's executive board. Currently, I have taken on the role of being the Basileus. In hindsight, if someone asked me if I would possibly see myself holding a leadership role in my chapter, I would have honestly said no. Even though it has been a challenge being the Basileus, it has also been very rewarding. I see a bright future not only for myself for my chapter.

Undrane`

Have you ever seen that picture of a little girl wearing a blue and white dress, standing in heels five times too large, looking into a mirror? She is gazing at the mirror looking at herself with the desire to become a member of Zeta Phi Beta Sorority. The little girl in the picture reminds me of myself when I was young. Since the age of 5, I had always been exposed to the royal blue and white of Zeta through my family, family members and friends. However, just one lady inspired me to be the striving, diligent Finer Woman that I am today, and that was my mother. Do you remember growing up? I always wanted to be like my mother and try to look like her because I looked up to her. I tried on her heels and her pearls, and I definitely wanted to try on her Z Phi B.

I had been around Zeta all of my life and that was all I knew. At the University of Arkansas, I was a bit unsure about joining a sorority even though I had dreamed of becoming a Zeta. I thought joining a sorority would lower my grade point average since I was on the Dean's and Chancellor's lists my freshman year. I worked hard at my studies and did not want anything to interfere with that. Yet, somehow Zeta pulled me in.

I had been introduced to other sororities during Convocation. Convocation was a new term for me, one I had to research online. Each year my school introduced the National Pan-Hellenic Greek Council, better known as NPHC, on campus by having a step show called Convocation. I attended this event wearing all neutral colors since my mother told me that to do otherwise, might be offensive, and I wanted to start out with friends, not enemies. I saw the crimson and cream divas holding their pyramid high and the salmon pink and apple green girls indicating their poise with their pinky fingers. They were very good, but Zeta was a better and I appreciated not being able to put them into one single category.

They continuously interacted with me after Convocation. The members of Phi Theta chapter always invited me to events and genuinely appeared to care about me. They constantly called me even though I did not like talking on the phone. They invited me to places even though I was busy. Phi Theta chapter members were real and I liked that. With the Sigmas, it started to feel like family. I took the big step and decided to apply to Zeta Phi Beta, Sorority, Inc.

I will never forget the day I officially became a member in the "Phi-stee" Phi Theta chapter. Now thinking about it, it all seems like a blur. The night before I became a member of the Phi Theta chapter, I was blindfolded and once it was removed, my mother was in front of me dressed in white. I was flabbergasted because for some odd reason, I had not expected her to come. I had literally just talked to her 30 minutes before the ceremony. When I asked her what she was doing there, she replied, "I wouldn't miss this for the world." After a few tears and loving moments, I was led to another room and there was the rest of my immediate family. I cried this time, for they had traveled from another town to be with me. This was very special to me because I did not see them that often. I was excited too, about the gifts and food. I received Zeta paraphernalia of every kind, from pencils and pens, to shirts and jackets.

Since I was inducted as a member late, in spring semester, I did not have the real experience of Zeta until my junior year in 2013. Heat. Scorching heat stung my skin as the three of us stood at attention waiting to practice a step again. I was practicing for my first show in Convocation 2013. We practiced and practiced and practiced and practiced. Then, it was show time. The theme was all about uniqueness in a sorority shop. We presented other sororities as stereotypical and portrayed them as manikins. Yet, Zeta was that different sorority with a diversity of members. We all dressed differently which signified our individuality, but we also were similar since we shared Zeta. On stage, I felt the lights on me, about as hot as it was outside. Nevertheless, we did a good job and many people congratulated us. I later learned that it is not about how other people comprehend you or your sorority. It is all about how sorority members feel about themselves overall.

After some of our chapter members graduated, there was only Venus and I remaining, the only two Zetas on campus. I instantly thought that we were in danger of becoming extinct on the University of Arkansas' campus, then I looked at the bright side: at least 100% of the chapter would always be in attendance at all events.

Throughout the year, we counted on Pi Chi Zeta graduate chapter members who fed us, bought items for us, and just were there when we needed them. We were very thankful for the relationship we had with them.

This was our chance to start anew. We had so many ideas and could not wait to get them implemented. We needed to get ourselves out there. We both broke out of that box and performed a step show. I will never forget the felicitations we received in just an introduction to on campus. We were so proud of ourselves. Sisterhood can be rewarding it is for life.

With any group, no matter if it is a sorority, fraternity, committee, or business, there will be ups and downs. However, I have learned that even though ups and downs come, the bond that binds the members together stays strong. I can compare it to the story of the big bad wolf and the three little pigs. Many groups build their 'houses' with bonds that will not withstand the big bad wolf. In order to withstand them, those bonds need to strong to keep the "house" stable. I enjoy it that my chapter is close-knit and we can act like sisters of the Dove and help each other be Finer Women. We are both so glad to have taken this route in our lives.

*The Kiln Process of Becoming
and Continuing to be
a 21st Century Finer Woman*

Miriam D. Summerville Dufer

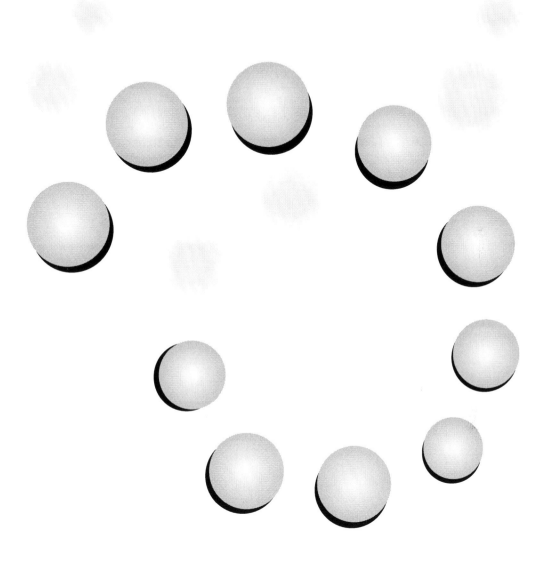

The 21st Century Finer Woman is subjective to every Zeta, yet every Zeta inherently knows and feels what Finer Womanhood feels like and what it is. It is similar to the feeling I had when I knew for sure that Zeta Phi Beta Sorority, Inc. was the only sorority I wanted to be a part of. It is similar to the feeling I have when I feel the presence of The Holy Spirit and know that I am a child of God.

While stationed in Seoul, South Korea, I discovered Zeta Phi Beta Sorority, Inc., after being wooed by another sorority. My Battalion Commander's Administrative

Assistant was a Zeta, and I knew there was something special about her but I couldn't put my finger on it. I told her that I had just had lunch with the president of this other sorority and that it went well. She simply asked me to check out the Zeta homepage. I went back to my office, went to the homepage, and my learning began.

I was blown away that the programs that Zeta was passionate about collectively, I had been supporting individually. My daughter was born premature and I had been working with the March of Dimes on my own. When I saw that Zeta was partnered with them, I was in awe. As I kept reading and clicking links, my mind was made up. I knew then what was so special about her. I ran back to her office and asked how I could become part of this amazing organization and as they say, the rest is history. I was born into Zeta Juneteenth of 2006 with Pi Eta Zeta chapter on a line of five (TNT). I was the quad (4SHO).

For me, finding my life's mission has been paramount in discovering who I am and who I want to be. Every few years, I adjust my personal mission statement to make sure I am on track for focusing on what's important in my life. If you would like to build your own, visit http://www.franklincovey.com/msb/. My new mission statement represents my definition of being a Finer Woman:

> I am at my best when I am doing something I feel passionate about and find fulfilling. I need to be challenged and empowered to think outside the paradigm. I perform best when I have the ability and opportunity to help and empower others. I will try to prevent times when I am micromanaged and feel my skills are being wasted.
>
> I will enjoy my work by finding employment where I can find challenging tasks and the opportunity to discover innovative ways of doing tasks. I prefer to work independently where my skills, education, and experience can be maximized.
>
> I will find enjoyment in my personal life through writing poetry, fiction and screenplays. I love to read. I love movies, especially foreign films. I love spending time with my daughter. I love sharing my experiences with others as a mentor. I love my Catholic faith and attending classes that teach specific subjects about the Bible and the church. I love spending time with family and friends. I love spending time with my Sorors and working with Zeta Phi Beta Sorority, Inc.
>
> I will find opportunities to use my natural talents and gifts such as being a Mother, Writing, Researching, Baton Twirling, Singing, Ballet, Music, Golf, Being a Friend, Being a Mentor, Public Speaking, Decision Making, Being a Leader, Being a Follower, Event Planning, Military Leadership, Strategic Planning, Public Relations, Crisis Planning and Communications, Foreign Languages, and helping others.

I can do anything I set my mind to. I will write full time and be a traveling public speaker around the world. My life's journey has been riddled with many hardships and cruel situations I've had to survive. I believe I must take the lessons I have learned and share with others so that they know they are not alone and that they can survive as well.

I will be a person who will be surrounded by family and dear friends. The tribute statement I would like them to make about my life is that I have a legacy of helping others reach their goals. My most important future contribution to others will be giving of myself and empowering others to follow their bliss and achieve their goals in life.

I will stop procrastinating and start working on:

- Being more politically involved on the local level to institute change whether it be working on a political campaign or seeking office.
- Sharing myself and my story with others, because remaining silent is like being in prison, and sharing is liberating and a learning opportunity for others. Letting them know they are not alone.
- Capitalizing on the gifts God has given me and not being afraid to use them in my life. They are vast, useful, and profitable.

I will constantly renew myself by focusing on the four dimensions of my life:

- Physical: Yoga, Qigong, Krav Maga, Walking, Swimming, Baton Twirling, Ballet, Dancing, Golf, and Tennis.
- Spiritual: Attending Mass, Going to Confession, Bible Study, Meditation, Prayer, Helping others, Tithing, Volunteering, and Ensuring my daughter's Catholic education and milestones are met.
- Mental: Attending MENSA meetings and gatherings, administering MENSA tests, reading, writing, research, lively debates with others, learning new things, using my foreign language skills, and mentoring.
- Social/Emotional: Attending therapy, attending social events like ballet, opera, theater, movies, concerts, Zeta socials, sporting events. Visiting with friends and family. Sharing my thoughts and feelings with people I trust and not holding everything inside. Being open to new experiences and new people. Allowing myself to feel whatever I am feeling and being ok with that.

If I could invite to dinner three people who have influenced me the most—past or present—they would be Antonia "Toi" Baquet Derricotte, Jacqueline Lee Bouvier Kennedy Onasis, and Myrtle Tyler Faithful. From these three people, I will strive to incorporate the following attributes into my life:

- <u>CREATIVITY:</u> Antonia "Toi" Baquet Derricotte, Cave Canem[1] co-founder, was born April 12, 1941 in Hamtramck, Mich. She has published five collections of poetry, including *The Undertaker's Daughter* (University of Pittsburgh Press, 2011). An earlier collection of poems, *Tender,* won the 1998 Paterson Poetry Prize. Her literary memoir, *The Black Notebooks,* published by W.W. Norton, won the 1998 Anisfield-Wolf Book Award for Non-Fiction and was a *New York Times* Notable Book of the Year. Her essay "Beds" was included in *The Best American Essays 2011,* edited by Edwidge Danticat. Recognized as a Distinguished Daughter of Pennsylvania in 2009, her honors include the 2012 Paterson Poetry Prize for Sustained Literary Achievement; the 2012 PEN/Voelcker Award for Poetry for a poet whose distinguished and growing body of work represents a notable presence in American literature; the Lucille Medwick Memorial Award from the Poetry Society of America; two Pushcart Prizes; the Distinguished Pioneering of the Arts Award from the United Black Artists; the Alumni/Alumnae Award from New York University; the Barnes & Noble Writers for Writers Award from Poets & Writers, Inc.; the Elizabeth Kray Award for service to the field of poetry from Poets House; and fellowships from the National Endowment for the Arts, the New Jersey State Council on the Arts, the Rockefeller Foundation, the Guggenheim Foundation and the Maryland State Arts Council. She serves on the Academy of American Poets' Board of Chancellors and for many years was Professor of English at the University of Pittsburgh.[2]

From Toi I have learned to write from a place of freedom and realize that everyone has their own "truth." It is within that truth that writing becomes alive. When one examines their personal truth, own this truth, and feel compelled and brave enough to share this truth, a Finer Woman has no chance but to break out.

Finer Women allow people to tell their own truths through active listening and creating open and honest dialogue. I wrote my first Master's Thesis on Toi: The Image and Identity of the Black Woman in the Poetry and Prose of Toi Derricotte (October 31, 2006). From Toi, I learned and continue to learn to be brave in my writing and to break free of what is expected. Via her guidance and inspiration, I take chances in my writing and feel a freedom to think and write outside the paradigm. One of her books, *The Black Notebooks,* she presents a non-fiction account of her experiences in academia and perhaps in life in general from a fresh yet intimate perspective:

I began writing this book in the middle of a severe depression. My husband and I had just moved into an all-white middle- and upper-class neighborhood ten miles from New York City. I had spent months looking at houses, over eighty, and I had decided not to take my husband with me to the real estate offices because, since he is recognizably black, when I had, we had been shown houses in entirely different neighborhoods, mostly all-black. I had soon found that houses in the "best" neighborhoods, perhaps like the produce and meat in the "best" supermarkets, are comparatively less expensive.

At night, under cover of darkness, I would take him back to circle the houses that I had seen and I would describe the insides.

I began to be conscious that my reaction to hearing a comment in a shoe store or seeing a young black boy on the street was a reaction of fear. My adrenaline would increase, the fight or flight response, as if a part of me wanted to jump out of my skin. A dark man who had been a Marine told me how, after six weeks of boot camp during which time he wasn't allowed to look in a mirror, he came upon himself in an uncovered mirror and was filled with dread and sadness. He had forgotten he was black.

I wanted to get away, not only from that black person who seemed to be the catalyst of my feelings, but, more to the point, to get out of my own mind, from those thoughts and feelings I so loathed in myself. My reactions were not rational, not "thought." They seemed to be as visceral as instinct. James Baldwin said, "The white man needs the nigger because he cannot tolerate the nigger in himself." But does the black man too need the nigger? I sensed that the structures that hold us together as a society and create devastating realities may be built around the most basic instincts for self-preservation.

These structures must originate even before conscious memory because I truly cannot remember the first time I "learned" I am black. It is as if every experience I have had of realizing I am black, all the way back to grade school and before, when I used to wander undetected across Ryan Road to where the Polish people lived, is tainted with that fear of discovery, of being recognized as black.

So many black people spoke of hatred for "them," for those "niggers" who were messing it up for the rest of us. It is self-hating and destructive, but racism is insane, and, surviving it, we have often had to think in desperate ways. "Forget" sounds like such a passive act, but anyone who has experienced the powerful force of repression will know the effort it takes to un-forget, to remember.

I began to be aware of that state of consciousness that so alarmed, that "remembering" of myself as a black person. I began to keep track of it, to write of it in my journals. I believed that my unconsciousness of my blackness, my "forgetting," was symptomatic of some deep refusal of "self," a kind of death wish, and I felt that my symptoms, however much I was alarmed by them, carried some real and essential message which, once acknowledged, I could eventually accept and understand. Of course these writings were private. I told no one. (195-201)

In recent years, I have felt blocked creatively due to my experiences in Iraq and my marriage and subsequent divorce. Amazingly, while I was deployed to Iraq, Toi wrote me an extremely kind letter that I have kept until this day.

- WELL-BRED: Jacqueline Lee Bouvier Kennedy Onasis, former First Lady and Publisher, was was born on July 28, 1929 in Southhampton, New York. Marrying then Senator John Fitzgerald Kennedy, on September 13, 1953 began her journey to becoming the First Lady of the United States. She will always be remembered and admired for her fashion style and grace as she was a true well-bred icon. As with Toi Derricotte, I find similarities between myself and Jacqueline Kennedy.

  According to the John F. Kennedy Presidential Library[3] website, Jackie also enjoyed reading. Before she started school, she had read all of the children's books on her bookshelves. Her heroes were Mowgli from Rudyard Kipling's The Jungle Book, Robin Hood, Little Lord Fauntleroy's grandfather, Scarlett O'Hara from Gone with the Wind, and the poet Byron. Mrs. Bouvier wondered if Jackie might one day be a writer.

  Like Jackie, I was an early reader, beginning at the age of 4, and I became a veracious reader which fed into my love of writing. My love of reading has led me on so many journeys in my imagination as well as in my life. I am what is considered a bibliophile, and have a collection of books that rivals most high school libraries. Mrs. Kennedy Onasis worked as an editor at *Doubleday* and made considerable contributions to the literary world in her work which as a writer and editor, I admire and appreciate immensely. When I think of Finer Womanhood and the life of Jacqueline Bouvier Kennedy Onasis, I see good breeding (or what we Southerners simply call "Home Training"), strength and perseverance, beauty and grace, intelligence and scholarship, and the ability to continually reinvent oneself when life throws you punches so hard that the average person would remain knocked down.

- TRAILBLAZER: Myrtle Tyler Faithful, one of the Founders of Zeta Phi Beta and an English Teacher. As a Zeta, of course, who wouldn't want to share a meal with our Trailblazers, but I find her particularly interesting because we have a few things in common beyond Zeta. Born on November 7, 1901, we're both Scorpios, which would be a wonderful topic of conversation as we compare our traits of which I believe would be many. She taught Math, but she also taught English, and as an English major I can only imagine the academic tête-à-têtes and anecdotes we could share over dinner.

  One of the things I like to think about when reviewing history is the context of the time in which events occurred. Looking at just her birth, she was born only two generations after the abolishment of slavery and probably still during the time of Southern Reconstruction, and grew up during Jim Crow. Although she attended Howard University, the world she saw was so different from the world we see now, and yet so many things are the same. She could have attended Howard, taken her classes, graduated and moved on, but something in her and our other four Pearls would not allow them remain silent and just go with the flow. They had a story to tell, and we are a result of that story. Trailblazers, Finer Women, have stories that they are compelled to share with the world.

As a trailblazer, sharing my story and my challenges have not only been a way of personal healing, but also a way of sharing myself with others and letting them know they are not alone. In a sense, allowing myself to be vulnerable has empowered others to build strength. It is within that vulnerability that a Finer Woman emerges as a Sister, Scholar, and Server of her community (which would be international in my case).

As one can see, the common thread that runs through my personal mission statement is sharing my story, which I will do now. Being a Finer Woman, for me, has been a process. Like the process of making porcelain, the process is difficult, but the result is a masterpiece. The ingredients must be put in a kiln[4] of temperatures between 1,200°C and 1,400 °C (2,200°F and 2,600 °F). The end result is perfection.

Much like the kiln, I have traveled through this intense heat and believe that sharing my story is what makes me a Finer Woman. I am a survivor of domestic abuse. I was a highly educated United States Army Commissioned Officer with an extremely successful career. From the outside, my life was perfect. On paper, my life was perfect. I had multiple academic degrees, attended the right military schools and courses, had the right military assignments and performed exceptional in all of them. I was married and had a beautiful and well behaved daughter. I had fulfilled every officer's dream of commanding in combat by commanding in Iraq, and I actually commanded not one but two military police companies simultaneously, which is unheard of.

However, the man whom I was married to was both emotionally and physically abusive and my life at home, at times, was far worse than being shot at in Baghdad. Nothing is ever all good or all bad. When things were good, they were amazing. When they were bad, well, there are some stories I will take to my grave. What I can tell you is, don't ignore the red flags. They do appear, and I ignored mine from the start. If you don't have personal boundaries or have never been taught about them, learn and implement them in your life and stick to them. If the people in your life are unwilling to respect your boundaries, they have no place in your life. This may even be family members, but in order to live your own truth, boundaries must be set and adhered to.

Inside the kiln, I also found Post Traumatic Stress Disorder as a result of my deployments in the United States Army. I had attended briefings on symptoms and things to look out for in my Soldiers, but was blinded in seeing these things in myself. On one occasion, I'd planned on blowing myself up on a hand grenade range that I was running. On another occasion, I attempted to stab myself in the gut but found the knife too dull to complete my mission. On yet another occasion, I swallowed as many pills as I hid in my home and went to bed to sleep. As I lay there, I told God that I was weary and begged him to deny me to open my eyes in the morning. Needless to say, my eyes opened and I sought help.

As a captain in the United States Army, exhibiting any form of weakness is embarrassing, dangerous, and possibly career ending. I was in so much emotional pain that I knew I had no choice but to seek help. PTSD is not something you just get over, and it does still have a negative stigma associated with it. I was at a crossroads. I could continue to suffer in silence or ask for help and begin to heal.

I chose the latter and as I began to heal, I shared my story with others, which empowered them to seek help. I found that by humbling myself and showing Soldiers that I was human and flawed (something people in the military understand is real, but rarely admitted) I was able to share how far down the proverbial rabbit hole I had plummeted and by seeking help, I was getting emotionally stronger day by day.

Today, I am mentally and physically healthier. I have been happily divorced for almost two years. As a Finer Woman of the 21st Century, I remain in the kiln being perfected, but standing on the shoulders of giants who have come before me and leaning on the shoulders of my Sorors and friends who love me and wish the best for me. I am no longer keeping quiet about my struggles because my voice is helping others come out of their rabbit holes and find their light.

FOOTNOTES

1. https://www.cavecanempoets.org/. Cave Canem is a home for the many voices of African American poetry and is committed to cultivating the artistic and professional growth of African American poets.

2. http://www.cavecanempoets.com/faculty#derricotte

3. http://www.jfklibrary.org/JFK/Life-of-Jacqueline-B-Kennedy.aspx

4. "kiln." *Dictionary.com Unabridged.* Random House, Inc. 10 Apr. 2015. <Dictionary. comhttp://dictionary.reference.com/browse/kiln>.

WORKS CITED

Toi Derricotte. "Introduction: Writing The Black Notebooks." Callaloo 20.1 (1997): 195-201. *Project MUSE.* Web. 12 Apr. 2015. <https://muse.jhu.edu/>.

My Three Finer Mentors

Brunhilda C. Williams-Curington

From my birth, there have been three women—my mentors—who exhibit the characteristics of being Finer Women. Who are these women? They are my mother, Corinne Denny Williams; my godmother, Maxine Gales Bukey and my other godmother, Lizzie Gilliam Miller, whom I fondly call Aunt Liz. Ever since I could put one foot in front of the other, they have been in my life teaching me, molding me, cajoling me, stretching me, working to make me into a Finer Woman just like they have always been.

What makes a Finer Woman? A woman who is caring, possesses tough love, offers advice and constructive criticism, has an abundance of "Mother Wit," is always above reproach, speaks her mind, and is not overly concerned about other people's impressions.

All three of my mentors were, and are, very independent and have all been trailblazers. These mentors have guided me on my journey through puberty, into adulthood and are still available to offer me good thoughts and advice even as I enter my more seasoned years. Even though one of my godmothers, Maxine Bukey, died a number of years ago, I still feel her presence whenever I need to make a serious decision. My mother is now a stroke survivor and Parkinson's patient so I take care of her now like she once did for me. Though she does not do a lot of talking, I still feel her positive thoughts. My aunt Liz is still very much alive and vibrant; she is still a huge part of my life and is my senior advisor. I will not make a serious decision without her counsel.

These trailblazing icons have been very important and very special in my life. They have always been there in one form or another, and have been the "wind beneath my wings," allowing me to soar to great heights while knowing that if I need to correct my course, they will or would offer a quiet course correction.

I feel very honored to have had three women who have made such a large difference in my life. Had I not availed myself of their wisdom, knowledge and intellect I do not believe that my life would have been this full of memories and achievements. To them I say: I love you! Ladies, you rule!!

Growing Into a Finer Woman

Rhonda M. Lawson

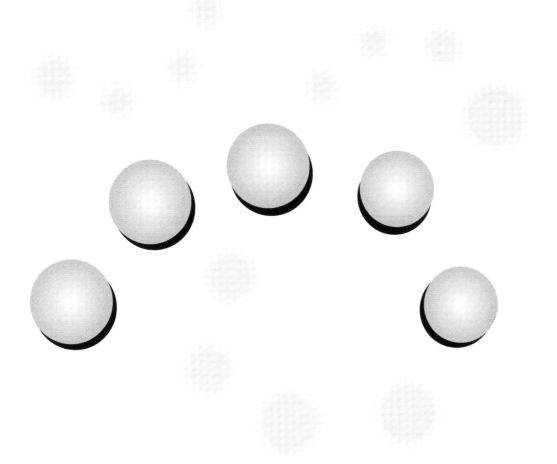

I can't help but feel a mix of surprise and honor when young women tell me they look up to me, or when I'm told that I should take someone under my wing. "Me?" I want to ask. I sometimes wonder if these young women would still see me as such a role model if they knew my story. Who was I to give advice with all the mistakes I've made in life? But then again, maybe I could offer them something *because* of my story.

You see, I was born at Keesler Air Force Base in Biloxi, Miss., the daughter of two Air Force noncommissioned officers. By the time my parents divorced when I was eight, I had already seen Turkey, Italy, and Spain, in addition to several cities in my beloved United States. My mother, Phyllis Jones, went through her own struggles getting used

to being an active duty Airman and the single parent of two girls at the tender ages of 8 and 4 who missed their dad and didn't understand why he was gone. It was a difficult transition, so she sent my sister Renee and me to New Orleans to live with our grandparents, Earl and Helen Randall. Her decision may not have been popular with every mother in her position, but it wound up being one that would shape all of us into the women we are today.

New Orleans was my first experience living outside of a military environment. Not only that, it was my first time living in "the hood." I looked different. I spoke differently. I read faster—too fast, if you ask some people. While some grownups saw me as special because of my "worldly experience," the other kids just saw me as, well, different. I was always seen as smart, but never the girl whom boys found attractive. I was teased mercilessly for my plain clothes, knotty hair, funny speech, and big teeth. In fact, the only time "pretty" and "Rhonda" ended up in the same sentence was when a family member greeted me.

At first, I would give as good as I got. If people talked about me, I would try to talk just as badly about them. I say try because I was never very good at ribbing. The words I would use to cut down my opponent greeted laughter, but it was *at* me, not *with* me. Yet, even when I was losing, I never gave up. I'd keep going until a teacher or some other grown up finally told us the shut it down.

I would even lie awake at night thinking of ways to rib people. I was worst at "ya momma" jokes, so I would constantly try to think of original ways to make the entire class laugh while bringing the pain to my opponent. If people talked about my nappy hair, I'd talk about their greasy face. If they talked about my clothes, I'd talk about their shoes. And if all else failed, I could always rely on the old standby: "Ya Maw." I tried not to use that one because there was always a chance that that could spark a fight, and I'd lost enough battles to know that fighting was not my forte.

I wasn't afraid to admit that the ribbing often got to me. I was tired of being called ugly. I was tired of people making fun of my hair. I was tired of people making fun of the way I talked. I would lament to my family, but they always said what adults were expected to say to girls in my situation.

"The kids at school always call me ugly and laugh at the way I talk," I'd say.

"Don't worry about them," my aunt would tell me. She was only 10 years older than me, and also lived with my grandparents, so she was the one with whom I identified most. "They're just jealous. What you need to tell them is, 'My momma is in the United States Air Force. What does your momma do? Welfare?' But be ready to fight if you say that. That's how *I* was back in school."

Now, you know I never told anyone that. First of all, those words would never roll off of my tongue correctly, and second, I already told you I couldn't fight!

Things didn't change once I moved back in with my mother. I had just turned 13, and my mother had just finished a tour in Korea, and had been reassigned to Fort Worth, Texas. I was happy that my sister Renee and I had been reunited with our mother, but disappointed that still no one saw me as pretty. One night, I sat outside with a friend, depressed because all my guy friends only saw me as just a friend, while they salivated over another girl. I had to admit that the other girl was beautiful.

"She just doesn't realize that she leads the perfect life," I said.

"Yeah," my friend agreed. "She's so pretty."

Little did either of us know what she really did to maintain her popularity. I won't put her business out in this forum, but let's just say she was a little less than virtuous for a 14-year-old. My friend and I also didn't consider the way she treated people whom she felt were not on her level. All we knew was that she was prettier than us, and that must have been enough.

Over the years, Renee and I would bounce between my mother and grandmother, depending on my mother's military assignment. Once I reached the 11th grade, Renee moved to Moreno Valley, California with my mother, while I remained in New Orleans so I could graduate from high school. The ribbing had slowed down, and, thanks to a few very good friends with high self-esteem, I began feeling better about myself. I dressed better, walked with more confidence, and even began dating. But unfortunately, the effects of so many years of name calling remained ingrained in my psyche. Before ever getting to know a person, I automatically felt that they saw me as ugly. I grew defensive, but the fight in me had softened. I would still fight back when teased, but it became obvious that their words affected me more than I cared to admit.

I wouldn't realize the worst effect of the name calling until much later. Not only did I automatically think the worst of people, but I began doing things I wasn't proud of just so I could get them to like me. While I didn't commit crimes, I did things that demonstrated that I loved attention from boys more than I loved myself. All I succeeded in doing was earning a bad reputation, one that I couldn't outlive even after joining the U.S. Army and getting married years later.

With such a troublesome childhood, it might be easy to say that I needed to establish a relationship with God. It would be easy to say that I needed to love myself. Some might even say I needed to find something to do and take my mind off of finding a boyfriend. The funny thing is that I had all of that. I was the president of the youth department at church. I tutored kids every week. I was accepted to Loyola University, one of the most prestigious colleges in New Orleans, where I was active with the Black Student Union and, in 1993, joined Zeta Phi Beta Sorority, Inc., and became a charter member of Iota Omicron Chapter, a city chapter on the campuses of Loyola and Tulane Universities. I joined the Army the following year as a military journalist, winning various writing awards. I also continued to mentor kids, ensuring they didn't go down the same path I had travelled in high school.

The problem was that I had not yet found my value. That value would not be found in the number of men who found me attractive. It would not be found in the amount of compliments I received, or the awards I earned. It would not even be found in the success I found as a published author or the degrees I would earn in my pursuit of education. I would not find that value until I sought it. I needed to *believe* I was worthy of respect and value. It would be years before I sat down and really took to heart all of the lessons my grandmother taught me while growing up.

"If you've got it, flaunt it," Helen had told me. "But there's a difference between classy and trashy."

In other words, wear clothes that fit you well. Baggy clothing often hid a woman's appearance instead of accentuating it, and tight clothes sent the wrong message. She taught me that I didn't have to show a lot of skin to be sexy.

"Always go for the fella who likes you," she'd also said.

It took me a long time to realize what this meant. She wasn't telling me to settle. She was teaching me not to run after someone who didn't have my best interests at heart. If he didn't show me that he wanted to be with me, and refused to show me respect, I shouldn't waste my time.

"Remember, you are Helen's grandchildren," was the punctuation mark that ended every speech and piece of instruction she gave my sister and me.

I always laughed when she said that, but even today I straighten up when I think of those words. I'm sure we've all experienced a moment growing up when someone said, "Aren't you so and so's child?" When we walk into the world, we represent more than just ourselves. People know us, and they know our histories. If I didn't change my path, I would dishonor that history.

Although Helen grew up in the roughest neighborhoods of New Orleans, she was probably the prissiest woman I had ever met. She always looked her best when she left the house, even if she went to the grocery store. She was married at the age of 19 and bore four children to a man who was willing to fight for her love. Earl Randall stayed faithful to their marriage for more than 50 years. Yet, I resisted her words, thinking that she was just old fashioned, and that times had changed since her heyday. Had I had any sense back then, I would have realized that she knew exactly what she was talking about!

Although Helen passed away in 2004, I still hear her voice in my head. She's still talking to me, guiding my decisions. I hear her when I cook dinner. She reminds me to say my prayers. I can't even get dressed in the morning without her yelling at me to dress from the bottom up, because it keeps my clothes neater!

My mother, Phyllis Jones, had her own pieces of advice for me. It's because of her that I am a senior noncommissioned officer in the U.S. Army today. Although I didn't follow her footsteps and join the Air Force, once I finally began heeding the life lessons she taught me, life became just a little bit easier.

It was Phyllis who taught me that "every brother ain't a brother and every sister ain't a sister," meaning that sharing a commonality with someone was not an automatic pass for trust. Every person didn't have my best interests at heart.

It was Phyllis who taught me not to wear my heart on my sleeve. Her words reminded me not to give anyone so much power over me that they determine my emotions.

It was Phyllis who taught Renee and me to go hard for our children. If no one else had our backs, Phyllis did. Although we didn't always agree with our mother, we could never doubt that she loved us. Even when we were separated, Mom showed her love. When we had to sell ads for our debutante ball, Phyllis sold the most ads for us although she was all the way in Korea! Even when she didn't have the money, Phyllis put me through modeling school, knowing it would boost my self esteem. She never let any teacher or friend disrespect us, even after we became adults.

It took me taking three steps back and reflecting on the life lessons Helen and Phyllis taught me to realize my worth. Notice, I said my mother and grandmother. Not Steve Harvey, Tyrese Gibson, or any other man who has capitalized off of women with broken spirits. No shade to those gentlemen because they're great in their own rights, but it always amazed me how many men wrote books that just repeated what our elders taught us years ago.

Besides, there was no book in the world outside of the Holy Bible that could make me stop repeating the same mistakes that I had made most of my young adult life. After a while, they were no longer mistakes. They had become habits, and as many of us know, old habits are hard to break.

So what caused me to reflect on the lessons my mother and grandmother taught me, and finally break my habits? I'd like to say that I had an epiphany, but it was a little more complicated than that. It was actually a series of events.

The first happened a few months after I was married in 1997. A friend had asked me to ride with her to her boyfriend's barracks because she wanted to see if his car was parked outside. Really? Was I ever so stressed out over a relationship that I had to play Private Eye? Of course, I had. Years later, after my divorce had thrust me right back into the dating pool, I would remember that moment and try to ensure that I would never find myself in that same position.

In 1999, I gave birth to my daughter, Beautiful Lawson. Now that I think about it, God truly does have a sense of humor. How was a woman who had such an emotionally tumultuous childhood and was still learning to overcome bad habits going to be equipped enough to raise a girl? I suddenly had to reassess everything I thought I knew. The way I saw it, I would either watch helplessly as she made the same mistakes I did, or I would become overprotective, not allowing her to grow and mature. I was determined not to do either. Instead, I decided to live by example. I didn't just want to *tell* my daughter what a Finer Woman should be. I had to *show* her, especially after the divorce. She needed to see her mother take care of the household, succeed at her job, serve her community, finish school, and still navigate the dating world while remaining a woman of God. It wasn't always easy, nor was it perfect, but it remained a goal that I kept before myself daily.

I often hear a mix of Helen and Phyllis in me as I teach Beautiful to be a Finer Woman in her own right. I smile inside as I gently tug Beautiful's earlobe, reminding her to put on a pair of earrings like my mother used to do to me. I hear Helen's voice as I remind Beautiful to sit with her legs closed while crossing her legs at the ankles instead of her knees. Thoughts of Phyllis come to me when I teach Beautiful how to make and save money, just as Phyllis tried to teach me when I was 15. I've even uttered the words, "Everyone knows you're Rhonda's child," reminding Beautiful that she represents me when she walks around our small community. Helen would sure love to hear me say that!

Watching Beautiful grow has been a lovely medley of pleasure, humor, frustration, and pride. She has become a cheerful teenager who is comfortable in her skin, and is slowly developing her passion in life. While I can only pray that my constant speeches about applying herself, not following the crowd, demanding respect, and being careful about the way she speaks to her peers and teachers are sinking in, I take pride in the fact that my divorce and constant separations due to the military have not stopped her from being a well-adjusted, very respectful teenager. My budding actress continually seeks volunteer opportunities, attracts the love and admiration of the younger children in our community, and has developed a fashion sense that I could have only imagined when I was her age. I thank God that she has not made many of the mistakes of my past, but I work hard to help her live up to the regality that her name implies so she may realize her own value.

As my relationship with God deepened, so deepened my sense of value, as well. It took time, but I finally began believing that I really was fearfully and wonderfully made! I had always had a relationship with God, but over the years, I grew closer to Him, and drew further away from behaviors and thoughts that tore me down. I began recognizing the messages in the Bible stories that I taught in Bible Study and Vacation Bible School. Change slowly took over my life, making me happier inside and outside.

I also began walking around with a smile. People began seeing me as friendly and approachable. I was the person who would not only say hi, but ask how you were doing. I was the one who tried to make the new person in my military unit or the visitor in church feel welcome. Unfortunately, some took it as flirtation and others took it as weakness, but I couldn't shake this new demeanor. And believe me, I tried, but it was important to me that I didn't let people keep me down. My smile had become a permanent part of me. My smile also helped me to exhibit more confidence. Although I hadn't healed all of the wounds from my past, I had learned to overcome them.

God also put people in my path who would ensure that I continued this positive journey. As I grew to be a leader in Zeta, I saw women who demanded respect without ever uttering a word. My big sister from Iota Omicron, Lillian Ebanks, who is still a great friend to this day, was a great example of Finer Womanhood from her dress, to her leadership style, to her demeanor. Our current international president, Mary Breaux Wright, who was my State Director when I became a Zeta, exemplified dedication, knowledge, and grace as she ascended the ranks of our great sisterhood. The moment I saw our then-international president Jylla Moore Foster, now Jylla Moore Tearte, in Ebony Magazine as one of the country's top leaders, I knew she was a woman I would be proud to have as my president. There are so many other Zetas I could mention, but the list would be endless. However, when I see the way our Sorors move about the room with their heads held high during Sorority events and conferences, it reminds of who I represent. When I see the awesome work Zetas do in the community, including feeding the hungry, awarding scholarships, raising awareness of the dangers of premature births, growing Zeta into a viable international organization, and getting engaged in social justice, I know that I have aligned myself with women of substance.

On a personal level, I can also say that it is the encouragement of my Sorors that kept me motivated to finish my bachelor's and master's degrees. It was my Sorors who stayed by my side when I gave birth to Beautiful, and later when my husband and I divorced. It was my Sorors who kept up with my family when I left Baltimore for a two-year tour in Korea in 2007. It was my Sorors who took up a collection to give me the money to move my family to Maryland after they were displaced by Hurricane Katrina in 2005. It was my Sorors who encouraged and advised me when I chartered and led Chi Pi Zeta chapter in Hinesville, Ga., in 2009, and Alpha Alpha Theta Zeta chapter in Belgium in 2014.

My examples of Finer Womanhood don't end with Zeta. I saw powerful women in the Army who were true professionals, leading Soldiers while defying racism and sexism. I will forever look up to Command Sergeants Major Teresa King, Cynthia Howard, Emma Krouser, LaToya Sizer, and so many more women whom I can't possibly attempt to try to name in this essay. I met Christian women who demonstrated each day what true faith really was. If I reached out to these women right now, they would never hesitate to pray with and encourage me, and I thank them for that. All of these women saw the potential in me and thought enough of me to pull me under their wings. I wanted to be like those women, and I knew I had the tools to do it. I just had to believe in myself and work toward it.

However, what really spurred my growth was the other women God placed in my path. I met young women who reminded me of myself in my younger years, and my heart went out to them. Women who felt alone in the world. Women who needed encouragement. Women who hadn't realized their potential. Women who didn't put their best foot forward because they weren't "tryin' to impress nobody." Women who, like me, had given up their power. In order to help these women, I would have to draw on every life lesson I'd ever been given.

Being a Finer Woman in the military isn't always an easy feat. For many women, the military would be the first time they had ever had to truly be responsible for themselves. There was no one to wake them up in the mornings and drive them to work. There were financial services available, but no one to force them to save their money or spend it wisely. And unfortunately, more people would rather talk about a woman disrespecting herself over the hundreds of men on the installation, than pull her to the side and advise her. For women living in the barracks, the community can seem very small, so much so that a woman who didn't have a steady boyfriend could run the risk of earning a bad reputation.

Life wasn't any easier for those who rose through the ranks to become leaders. Female leaders are still confronted with sexism. There are still men who believe that women have no place in the military, causing some women to feel they must work twice as hard to show that they are just as good as their male counterparts. Women who assert themselves are often dismissed and given labels like evil, mean, or bitter. Many are still judged by their looks, being thought of as less of a Soldier if they're too pretty, or "mannish" if they aren't pretty enough. Yet, it has always been my belief that these women are some of the strongest people I have ever met because they take on racism and sexism, while still managing to take care of their families, serve their communities, and still look darn good in the process!

One moment I would never forget was back in 2008 when I was counseling a young rape victim who had become enraged when she saw the man who had assaulted her. I was stationed in Korea at the time, and had still been dealing with the breakdown of a relationship that I was sure would lead to marriage. This particular woman was my second case ever, but proved to be my toughest. She had been raped by people whom she'd considered friends, and she felt that nothing was being done about putting these men behind bars. While it wasn't my job to investigate the crime, it was still my responsibility to provide her the support she needed to get through this terrible ordeal. When it came to her, my failed relationship wasn't nearly as important.

It was a Friday night, and I was in bed watching television in my barracks room. I had talked to my client just less than an hour prior, and she told me she'd felt better about things, and wanted to go to the community club with her friends. When my phone rang again, it was her in a rage telling me that she had seen the perpetrator there. I told her the same words my mother had told me years ago: "You let him have your power every time you get upset when you see him. It's time for you to take back your power. Do not let him control your emotions."

If only I had a dime for every time I should have followed that advice when I was younger. I don't know if my client even followed that advice, but I think back to those words often when times get tough for me. I also continue to share them with the teenagers and young women whom I encounter in my daily walk.

Each woman I encountered in my life taught me something that I could apply to my own life. While most taught me what *to* do, some taught me lessons on what *not* to do. As I matured, I became more aware of how I presented myself to the world. I was no longer the unattractive awkward girl who couldn't relate. Because of the village I encountered throughout my life, I felt more attractive, confident, friendly and helpful. Teenagers had begun calling me their second mom, while young adults have called me their big sister. Beautiful and her friends call me the "cool mom." Young Soldiers have asked me to mentor them. I had been presented with a badge of honor that I was proud to wear.

Today, I share that badge of honor with every woman with whom I come into contact. Because of my past, I have made it my passion to empower women through my books, dissertation, and even my social media posts, sharing with them that their past does not determine their future. I firmly believe that when women come together, powerful things can happen. If we can stop competing with each other, letting division rise between us, and placing ourselves on pedestals above those whom we think are not on our level, we can do things that have yet to be imagined. I just want to do my small part in making that happen.

I won't dare say that I have it all together. I still make mistakes from time to time, and still have a few habits I need to break. But I can honestly say that my journey to becoming a Finer Woman has been fruitful. The lessons I have learned throughout my life have shaped me into a woman who has learned to inspire, motivate, share, and overcome. At the same time, I am still learning.

With all of this in mind, I welcome young women who ask my opinion about a decision they need to make. I take pride in the number of women who were inspired to be Zetas because of something I said or did. I will continue taking time to talk with teenagers and encourage young Soldiers.

The message I strive to pass on to these young women is that their value does not lie in their beauty, nor does it lie in their education. It's even more than being active in the community. Finer Womanhood is an intangible concept, but it is not impossible to reach. However, for me, the true mark of being a Finer Woman is learning from the mistakes of the past and using those lessons to shape the future. Most Finer Women weren't born perfect, neither do they go through life without ever making a mistake. Yet, when we take time to think about our actions, learn from our mistakes, and continue carrying ourselves to a higher standard, that is Finer. We must also share those lessons with others. This is how we love. This is how we grow. This is Finer Womanhood.

Stepping as a Finer Woman

Malica Fleming

I fell in love with stepping during my undergraduate years at the University of Virginia. I have fond memories of performing with my chapter Sorors, traveling to homecoming step shows and road-tripping to Step Correct competitions in New York City and Philadelphia. After moving to the Washington, DC area in 2000, I became frustrated with the lack of Zeta representation in local step shows so I recruited six Sorors to help create the ZPhiDynasty Step Team.

I had the pleasure of coaching and performing with more than 25 Zetas on the team over a period of five years. While we didn't win every show and had our fair share of challenges, we were ultimately successful as a step team because we represented Zeta Phi Beta Sorority, Inc., in the spirit of Finer Womanhood.

It would have been easy for our team to make the fun and excitement of being on stage our main focus, but as Finer Women in the 21st century, ZPhiDynasty understood that our primary responsibility was to represent Zeta Phi Beta Sorority, Inc. in the best possible way. As we cultivated our look and developed our step routines, we constantly questioned ourselves. Does this routine and our look positively represent Zeta Phi Beta? How do we want Zeta Phi Beta to be remembered?

I believe we understood what it meant to look Finer, but did we understand what it meant to be Finer? Our step team was provided with an opportunity to demonstrate what we believed to be true at the Delta Sigma Theta Greeks in Motion for Scholarship Stepshow at Howard University's Cramton auditorium in 2006.

At the time of the Greeks in Motion Stepshow, our team was comprised of six Sorors from Virginia, New York, North Carolina who resided in the DC/MD/VA area. We were mothers, Web designers, real estate agents, dentists, and business owners bound by our love for Zeta Phi Beta and a determination to see our sorority represented in Finer fashion at local step competitions.

We chose a carnival theme for our show because it was different from what step teams in the DC area were doing at the time. Additionally, I had just returned from carnival in Trinidad and had lots of ideas on how to implement the theme authentically. We studied our audience and knew that the excitement and high energy of carnival would have widespread appeal. Lastly, we were careful to choose music and costumes that were Finer in nature and would leave a positive impression of Zeta Phi Beta on the audience.

Shortly after our team arrived at Cramton auditorium, we settled into a small dressing area shared with the competing sorority step team. This particular step team was undefeated and assumed they had the step show on lock – especially since we had stepped against them previously and lost. To further complicate things, the step show was organized by the same sorority as the competing team, so we were in, for lack of a better term, "hostile" territory. It was almost certainly expected by the predominantly crimson crowd that we would not defeat the reigning champions at their own step show. It also didn't help that people who knew we were stepping against this team voiced their own doubts about our ability to beat them. From the outside looking in, the odds were stacked against us.

As we prepared for the show in our dressing room, we were met with rolling eyes and nasty glances from the other team. A short while later, a member from the competing step team smirked at one of our team members and said sarcastically, *"Oh, you're stepping tonight? I'm sooo sorry to hear that."* I felt like I was living a scene from the "Mean Girls" movie. I mean seriously, was this high school or a graduate chapter step show? It took every ounce of strength within me to stay calm and ignore the taunting we received from the other team. But I knew it was more important for me to stay Finer and keep our team focused on the upcoming performance.

The stage assistant arrived to let us know that it was time for us to perform. As the butterflies flew around in my stomach, we moved to our places in the back of the theatre and set the atmosphere by dimming the lights. Next, we blared Machel Montano's "Madder Dan Dat," an infectious soca tune, through the sound system while our flag bearers waved Trinidad and Jamaican flags at the front of the stage. As the crowd focused on the stage, we came down the aisles unexpectedly in our carnival-themed costumes. With three Sorors in the left theatre aisle and three Sorors on the right, the crowd was totally caught off guard as we danced our way to the stage in blue tank tops, white capris, white sneakers, silver-sequined head bands, royal blue feather earrings and body glitter. We had every audience member, young *and* old, on their feet and cheering us on – and this was just the introduction! It was our time and for the next 12 minutes, we ruled the stage. Our team executed every step and transition with the precision, accuracy, confidence and enthusiasm you would expect from a Finer Woman of Zeta Phi Beta Sorority, Inc. It was definitely a first class performance.

At the end of the step show, all teams were called to the stage for announcement of the winners. We were being judged on our theme, intro step, stepping complexity, transitions, appearance, crowd reaction and showmanship. As we waited for the announcement of first place sorority, out of the corner of my eye I noticed a member of the other step team walking forward with camera in hand – presumably to snap her team's victory photos. The look on her face when ZPhiDynasty was announced as the first place winning sorority was priceless!

I was (and still am) proud of ZPhiDynasty for keeping it Finer, not only in how we presented ourselves, but in how we acted and performed in the face of less-than-Finer circumstances. The lesson for that previously undefeated step team? Never underestimate the power of a 21st century Finer Woman.

Keeping It Finer in Every Situation

Katrina M. Ngalle

She was articulate, kind, and spoke with wisdom of women twice her age. She was about 25, and I listened intently as she explained what being a Zeta meant to her. There were three other women on the panel, but she was the focus. Her makeup was flawless, her dress was classy, and her one piece of subtle paraphernalia was perfectly placed.

Afterwards, a group of us waited to speak to her, wanting to know how to become a Zeta. However, what I soon realized is that being Finer was something that she was well before she became a Zeta, and that being a Zeta merely enhanced that. Carla Z. Peeples (may she rest in peace) died at the tender age of 40, but before she died she showed me and others in various chapters throughout Michigan and Illinois that being Finer was essential not only in Zeta, but in life.

My 20 years as a Zeta and working with women from all walks of life have taught me that frustration, anger, and disagreement are a natural part of being in any organization or company, but being able to "Keep it Finer" while doing so is a gift that one develops through various life experiences.

Keeping it Finer Chronicles: My Story

Everyone has a story, even those who were born with silver spoons in their mouths. I am no different. Through all of my setbacks, I've learned that being Finer can optimize your ability to bounce back. As I reminisce on the struggles, I also remember that my reaction and attitude helped me to overcome the obstacles that had the potential to destroy me.

Gunshots Don't Sound Like Firecrackers

Gunshots don't sound like firecrackers, but if you've never heard a gunshot, you would think they do. It was an ordinary September night, a Monday, the day before the first day of school. I was anxious and excited, as this would be another year to prove to my teachers that I was the best, but that day soon changed from ordinary to extraordinary. It altered my life forever. I remember lying in the bed asking myself, "Why are people lighting firecrackers this late in the night? Don't they know we have school tomorrow?"

I didn't hear firecrackers that night. Those were gunshots. My mother had been shot three times in our home. She wasn't a drug addict, an alcoholic, or a prostitute. She didn't even have a boyfriend (she NEVER brought random men to our home). She was a hardworking single mother who had just become a member of the church I had attended with my aunt for years. I never understood how it could happen or why I, at the tender age of 10, was the only child to be awakened by the commotion as my older sister and younger brother slept soundly.

The first gunshot rang out, and I heard a scream, then the second, as creaks on the steps became louder, and then there was a whimper. "Come out of that bathroom, so I can finish you off", a woman's voice yelled in anger. There was a cry and a slam of two doors. I went to my mother's room to investigate. There she was, covered in blood and on the telephone with 911. I was told quietly to return to my room, and I didn't. I just stared and asked if she was okay. This was a dumb question that we both knew the answer to. My mother mustered up all the strength she had, looked me in my eyes and sternly said, with teeth clenched, "Go to your room now."

My first lasting impression of being Finer is when my mother forgave her shooter, who after a few years, called our home as if they were 'friends.' My mother would laugh and say, "I can be nice to her, but I don't know if we can be friends." That was unbelievable to me, and sometimes I still can't comprehend that level of forgiveness, but I strive to have it.

You see, Finer, for many, is a subjective term, but for me it's simple. According to the dictionary, Finer means "of very high quality, very good….high standard, second to none." If I am to use this definition in my mother's situation, it is easy for me to see that only a person of a very high standard can forgive to that degree. It's not to say that people who can't forgive aren't good people, but Finer is special. It's beyond good, it's what most are not.

Homeless and Almost Childless

I walked away.

I walked away with nothing except the clothes on my back. We had a Lexus and were preparing to purchase our white picket fence dream home, but that would be a dream deferred as I had to swallow every bit of my pride and ego. I lived with my mother in another city as a temporary solution. By this time, I was unfamiliar with the life that existed in her neighborhood, but I had no other choice, no other option for my daughter and me. Here I was a college graduate, educated, articulate, and homeless. How would I bounce back from this?

The knocks on the door were louder than normal, but I didn't think it was out of the ordinary, so I continued to braid my 3-year-old's hair. Then there were bangs on the door, and I heard, "Open this door, it's the police!"

I never imagined my ex-husband would resort to such underhanded methods as revenge because I left with our child. My daughter was snatched from my arms by a police officer as she screamed and cried for her mother. I was in pure disbelief. My ex-husband had gone to court and created the most incredible, embellished story that caused them to believe that my daughter was somehow in danger. As chaos quickly engulfed my mother's home, I could only cry in response to my daughter's plea to remain with me.

In the next few weeks, my daughter was returned, and I fought various court battles over the years with my ex, who continued to use custody as a method of expressing his anger with me for choosing to save myself. In every battle and court appearance, I learned to keep calm, although I was angry and frustrated. God helped me to keep my sanity and forgive him. We were even friends before he remarried. Despite everything, I kept it Finer, and that is why I have my daughter today.

Movin' On Up?

A five-star hotel with all of those amenities was quite impressive. I had never done anything like this in my life. Of course I had traveled and learned a bit of French during my visits to Europe, but I'd never done this.

There was applause for us as we entered the hotel, and I certainly felt like a star. As we walked toward the reception area, we were given cool towels and drinks, as the temperature that day was about 110 degrees. It was an exciting moment; no other company had treated me this well. I was now welcoming the good life, and I deserved it. Or so I thought.

I was invited to teach in the United Arab Emirates, and the company hosted the beginning of our stay in this beautiful five-star hotel. I was overwhelmed with joy. My hard work in obtaining my education was finally paying off. My two children absolutely loved the change, especially in the beginning.

In Michigan we lived in a three-bedroom, but now we were confined to a hotel room, which meant more compromise than a 14- and 8-year-old could muster. They fought more than normal. And after a few weeks of paying for dinner for three, along with other necessities, my funds were running low. We had to resort to washing our clothes in the tub and hanging them on the balcony to dry. We ate more than enough during the buffet breakfasts provided by the hotel. We ate small snacks for lunch, and for dinner we began to eat sandwiches. Oh, and the rice cooker in our room provided us with our gourmet meal for the day. Dining out was out of the question. I wanted to go home, but relatives would have said, "We told you not to go in the first place."

I was determined. The company had told me to leave my children at home while they ensured I was settled, but I insisted on bringing them. I should have listened. My children were miserable and waiting for us to begin our lives. The glamorous hotel life was not glamorous at all.

After about four weeks in the hotel, I was given the directions to our new home. I abhorred it. It was a very small, one-floor, three-bedroom nook. It was a shotgun type home, and I almost began to cry. Would my children have to endure more? It was in the middle of nowhere, there was no play area for my son, and it was not the type of community living I was accustomed to. I wanted to pack my bags and return home, but a friend encouraged me and told me to speak with the housing director.

I explained my situation, and he said there was little he could do, but he would try. I thanked him and sadly returned to the hotel room. Again, I went, and he told me to be patient. Two weeks later, I had a notice to vacate the hotel, and again I was told by the housing director that there was nothing he could do to change my housing situation at that moment. I graciously thanked him as I watched others yell, scream, curse, and cry to get improved housing.

"One more time," I said to myself, and went to his office with my children. I watched as people yelled at him while demanding a change of housing. I just waited. One girl cried. I just waited. A man threatened to return to his home country, but I continued to silently wait. The director looked to be fuming and enraged. As he finished with his final customer of the day, he handed me a set of keys.

"You will be moving in a four-and-a-half-bedroom, five-bathroom villa," he said. "Shhhhh, don't tell anyone."

My children and I were ecstatic and I realized that thanking him during the time he really didn't produce anything, never yelling at him, or threatening him was how I earned this beautiful villa. Keeping it Finer was surely in action.

A New Beginnging

Walking the streets of Belgium during the summer months gives me relief from my some-times mundane life. This would be my eighth trip, but my second from my new home in Abu Dhabi. As my daughter and I peered at a map, lost, looking for our favorite waffle eatery, he approached.

"May I help you find something?"

I glanced up from the map and said, "Je ne parle pas l'anglais."

He burst out laughing and said, "You do, I just heard you speak English."

It was awkward, I was with my daughter, yet we were lost, so I humored him. During our short walk, we exchanged a few niceties, and I gave him bits and pieces of general informa-tion about me. I was a visitor to Belgium on multiple occasions, I spoke enough French to converse with locals, and I wasn't married. And the young lady who walked with us was my daughter, not sister. He led us to our destination with ease and as we departed, I shook his hand. He asked if he could have my number as subtly as possible as my 15-year-old watched frowning (she had not experienced a man approaching me). When we finally spoke, I asked him why he wanted my number, as I was a tourist passing through, but he said it was my aura. He watched me from across the street and noticed that even though my daughter and I fumbled with the map, that I was confident. After our first few dates and a week of talking to one another, he said that I would one day be his wife.

In my husband's culture, it is necessary that the woman he presents to his family is not only someone he loves, but someone who embodies the characteristics of a lady. I'm honored that not only he chose me, but he saw in me what I sometimes can't see in myself. I'm not perfect by any stretch of the imagination, but the fact that he chose me because of what he saw prior to even talking to me speaks volumes. Finer is a vibration that emanates. It is more than what you say; it's your aura.

As Black women of the 21st century, we are bombarded with issues that not only affect us individually, but our communities as well. However, we must remember that those who came before us had struggles that can't be recreated within our wildest imaginations. We tend to forget that our foremothers didn't settle and because of them, we have more economic and political power than our Black counterparts in the world. Finer womanhood began with all of those women who endured beatings, rapes, imprisonment, and even death to move our people forward. They were able to accomplish that without losing the characteristics that made them women. They are the beginning of the example of Finer women for Black Women.

My stories are not unique to many other women of the 21st century. We are the continuation of our foremothers' examples. My stories of defeat, devastation, and overcoming are not unheard of for us, but I learned early on that in order to exemplify those traits that are Finer, I'd have to exemplify what I was taught by them.

A Finer Woman never settles for mediocrity because of circumstance. She strives to be the best and uses each experience to improve. She never accepts mediocrity in her life. She pushes herself to greatness, as there is no other option. When she opens her mouth, those around her clearly understand that she is Finer. Above all, she helps others to achieve; she's a giver. She realizes her importance as a mother, an aunt, and a grandmother, and how her influence is irreplaceable. She knows there are people watching her at all times, so she strives to be the example. This does not mean that she is without flaws, or that she is not affected by those life issues that affect us all, but she endures. She is not perfect, as none are, but she strives for perfection in every aspect of her life. She understands how perceptions can perpetuate or mitigate negative stereotypes.

As an educator in Abu Dhabi, I have been afforded the opportunity to impact a new culture while diminishing the world wide stereotypes that don't include an educated bilingual, Black woman who travels the world, despite her past hardships. Overall, my goal is to epitomize Finer Womanhood through my example, my works, and how I am perceived. A woman does not have to be a superstar to have a valuable presence in her community. A Finer Woman understands that. Essentially, Finer Women of the 21st century have limitless opportunities to exhibit the attributes of 'Finer.' We are surrounded by them every day, and it's our choice to ensure that we relish every opportunity as one to demonstrate our Finer Womanhood.

A Letter to My Chapter

Lisa G. Eley

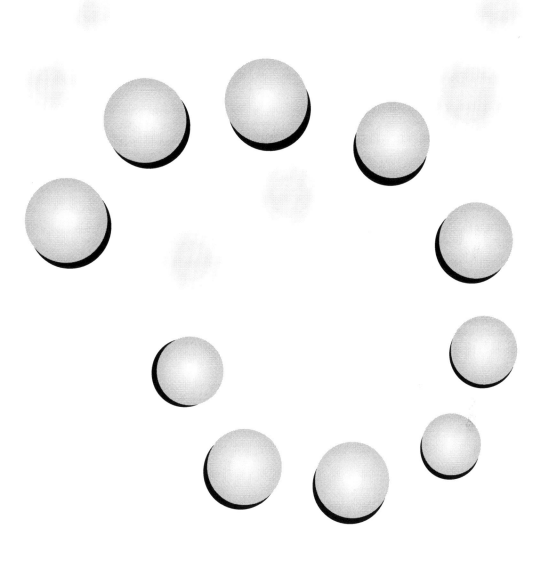

It was the end of another sorority year and a few sunny days shy of summer when I was admitted to the hospital. I was placed on suicide watch in a psychiatric hospital after I had been bullied for months in the workplace by a new supervisor who took exception to my complaints against him through the chain of command. I had exposed an extremely hostile and dysfunctional work environment led by an unethical and dishonest senior manager.

If I could put it into context with a twist of embellishment, for nearly a year it felt like I had been cumulatively hazed by every member of the Divine Nine from the past century. It was no wonder that survivors of hazing continue to carry the scars from their pledging days long after becoming members of their respective fraternities, sororities, and other outside and exclusive school club organizations.

I nearly paid the ultimate price for standing up for integrity, fairness, and a remarkable 23-year career as a public servant. The retaliation for calling out an inappropriately behaving manager was lightning fast swift, hard, heavy, intense and regrettably, allowed. I had long complained of a workload that had already robbed me of sleep, shrunken my appetite, and cheated me of overtime wages. After I had blown the whistle on management's unsavory work practices, my assignments began to triple while the deadlines for completing those assignments had been shortened to half of the amount of time.

I was told I was unqualified, inadequate, immature, incompetent, and a failure, and that I should look for a job someplace else. Its effects drained my spirit, sacked my faith, and spiraled me into a state of despair and hopelessness like I had never experienced before. I was a David against a Goliath and fighting for the cause of one that would potentially benefit a multitude to follow. The notion was unfathomable that I did not have the support of an agency I had devoted over half of my life to, and this hurt me to the core.

When I now look back, I am totally amazed I survived for as long as I did under the ill treatment and bad will. Adversity and hardship were no strangers to me, but this was new and unchartered terrain. I didn't know exactly what I was dealing with or what I was going through. The depression manifested slowly over the course of time. I thought it was just another one of life's trials where eventually I would see the light of day again. But then my thoughts started to take on some beliefs of their own, something I was not managing or overcoming very well.

From the outside looking in, all appeared as usual. I reported to work, went to church, attended chapter meetings, and maintained my household with a typical consistency where nothing appeared out of the ordinary. By nature I am unassuming, quiet, and low key, so there was nothing about my demeanor that would have alerted anyone that I was at the beginning of a significant medical crisis.

From within, my thoughts seemed completely logical to me. If I could not remove the source of my pain then I would remove myself from the bully inflicting the pain. I absolutely, positively, unequivocally hated reporting to work each day. I knew before the workday began that nothing good would come of the day accept the time to get off and head home at the end of the day. Getting off was the only thing I looked forward to each workday. Anything prior to clock out time was a blur. I was just grateful at the end of every day that I did not slam my car into a tree or drive it off a bridge. This became my new routine – working in a fog induced stupor, getting off, and keeping my car on the road until I made it home to begin another day of hell the next day.

I began to understand why victims of bullying checked out. They took the expressway on the road to suicide for the fastest and easiest route out of here. I also understood why the people closest to the victim of bullying never saw the suicide coming. These were the rose-colored glasses I looked through from a depressed state of mind, only I didn't know I was depressed at that time. I knew there were family and friends who loved me and would grieve my death, but a hurting spirit only saw pain that needed self-annihilation.

Surprisingly enough, living through the daily abuse from my job had not affected my perfect attendance at chapter meetings or impeded the good works I had been doing on behalf of the chapter. It was only after my hospitalization that I learned the devastating effects of an illness that had bound my joy and robbed me of my desire to live. I was depressed according to every textbook definition there was, but didn't grasp it or everything that came with it until I was out of crisis and in recovery.

I thought about people I knew who were functioning alcoholics. They would consume high amounts of alcohol while managing and balancing very successful careers, family, and self without considering themselves having a drinking problem. If there was an analog in the mental health realm, I think I would have been considered a person functioning with depression. I held it all together while managing life and all that came with it. I acknowledged to myself that I was dealing with extreme sorrow, but put on that resilient cap I had donned many times before and tried my best to carry on with life the way I knew how. That meant trying to present my normal and maintain my routines when I knew all was not well, and I was not myself.

As much as I despised going to work I did so and was never late and rarely absent. I continued my worship, ran my household, took care of my family, and poured myself into Zeta Phi Beta Sorority, Inc. I sat beside you in chapter meetings and provided my reports, spearheaded multiple community service projects, and supported the chapter with my time, talents, and treasures while going through or coming out of depression. To you, chapter Sorors, there was nothing different about me. To me, I did not want to hurt anymore, and had very wrong thoughts for what I considered to be the right reasons.

So when you emailed me asking me to attend the African American Health Program Executive Committee Meeting on behalf of the chapter, I would not have hesitated under normal circumstances. The African American Health Program (AAHP) was created to eliminate health disparities and improve the number and quality of years of life for African Americans and people of African descent in Montgomery County, MD. Zeta Phi Beta Sorority, Inc. – Eta Pi Zeta chapter was asked to be a partner in raising the community consciousness of health disparities disproportionately affecting African Americans in our county and to advocate for health education and awareness programs through outreach activities. This was a shining moment for Z-HOPE, Zetas Helping Other People Excel. Our chapter would inform, engage, and empower our community by reaching out to populations who would benefit most from the monumental and groundbreaking Affordable Care Act, signed into law by President Barack Obama in 2010.

Unfortunately, the timing of your email requesting I represent the chapter at this meeting could not have been worse. I had to officially acknowledge to myself that I had been more ill than previously thought, as I took residence in a psychiatric hospital. I had been there for two days when I opened your email from the common patient computer we had on our ward. All I told you was that I was in the hospital, and did not know when I would be discharged. I had not revealed to you why I was in the hospital; I suffered a psychotic episode and had been rated a high suicide risk. Two days earlier, I was moments away from taking my life, and had begun the long road to recovery.

Could you imagine seeing me at a chapter meeting or event on a Saturday and then receiving word on the following Tuesday that I had committed suicide? That almost became a reality had it not been for God's grace and intervention. I had been fighting to keep my then undiagnosed depression at bay. Staying active in the chapter and doing the work of Zeta in the midst of my ordeal meant I could use that time constructively to focus on doing good deeds and works for people in the community who depended on our services. Rightfully and selfishly, I believed when I had a part in making others feel good, I would in turn feel good.

That would be time well spent not thinking about the events or people responsible for my depressed state. I needed the love of my sisters to permeate my soul and fight this battle with me that no one but me knew I was fighting. I was upbeat when chapter meetings were in session, and we were happily and proudly serving our community. It gave me life for which I thrived in doing the work of Zeta while upholding our founding principles. But when the meetings were over and the services completed, I returned home very aware of my hurt, and went from high to low in a matter of minutes.

A few months prior to my medical emergency, you did catch me at a more opportune time. You asked me to represent the chapter regarding a disparity of a different kind among African Americans. The Chief Engagement and Partnership Officer of Montgomery County Public Schools invited Zeta Phi Beta Sorority, Inc. - Eta Pi Zeta chapter to a community dialogue on the academic success of the African American student. I was more than happy to accept this invitation on behalf of the chapter.

I am not an educator by trade, but I am a staunch supporter of higher learning. As a first generation college graduate and the only member of my family to graduate from college, I worked up to three jobs to provide an opportunity for my daughters to get a college education. How incredibly blessed were we when both of my daughters received enough scholarship support to complete their respective programs and graduate from college debt free! Because of these very doors opening up for this single parent, who not that long ago had to go to the food bank to feed her family, I had made it my personal mission to assist students with finding scholarship resources. Zeta Phi Beta Sorority, Inc. had long been about scholarship.

It is a personal labor of love for me to help hundreds of students in our community increase their chances of getting into college and remaining there until they graduate without financial hardships interrupting their pursuit. Hundreds of stake holders attended this forum, and

I got to represent the chapter as one of the many community partners involved who would continue and grow dialogue with The Office of Community Engagement and Partnerships (OCEP) for a brighter academic future for Black or African American students. The chapter was committed to the educational excellence of our students, and it began with preparing them for careers or college.

I participated in this forum while I was in the early to middle stages of manageable depression. I was at a place where I was being treated by my primary care physician for exhibiting symptoms of depression, yet I was still highly functioning in my personal, professional, civic, and social duties and responsibilities.

During this dialog we talked about solutions to address the specific issues related to Montgomery County's Black or African American academic achievement gap. Montgomery County was known for being one of the most affluent counties in the United States, and its schools were among the finest school districts in the nation. Home to Montgomery County were leading biotechnology companies and biomedical research institutions such as Johns Hopkins University's Montgomery County Campus, the Howard Hughes Medical Institute, the Food and Drug Administration, the National Institutes of Health, the Uniformed Services University of the Health Sciences, and the Walter Reed Army Institute of Research. Because of this, STEM (Science, Technology, Engineering and Math) related education curricula were heavily prevalent in our immediate surrounding area.

While Montgomery County Public School African American students fared better than their state or national counterparts in educational assessments, they still fared much lower than their White and Asian counterparts. They still lagged behind in graduation rates, in having competitive SAT and ACT scores, and in meeting entrance requirements for the University System of Maryland by double-digit percentages. Montgomery County Public School African American students exceled unfortunately, in having higher suspension rates.

While the event was meant to tap youth-serving organizations and share best practices in serving Black or African American and other students, our chapter was already proactive in addressing the academic achievement gap at its earliest level with the Adopt-A-School Initiative and by spending quality time with the students of Greencastle Elementary School. In addition, our chapter youth affiliates were engaged in social awareness, health and wellness, helping the less fortunate, academia counseling and mentoring, college and career preparation, and volunteerism. They pursued a higher quality of life, encouragement, and positive motivation for self and others with the guidance of our chapter.

I was halfway through a six-month medical leave of absence from work when the new Sorority Year began. I picked up right where I left off by taking the lead for the chapter for the Mt. Calvary Baptist Church HBCU College Fair in Lincoln Park, an enclave of rich African American heritage in the county expanding over a century. The College Fair had attracted hundreds of middle and high school students from across Maryland and the surrounding Washington, DC area. Zeta Phi Beta Sorority, Inc. – Eta Pi Zeta chapter had been supporting this college fair since its inception as a sponsor and exhibitor and was the only historically Black Greek Lettered Organization (BLGO) of the county's National Pan-Hellenic Council to have supported the college fair every single year. Honoring the founding principle of scholarship, Sorors manned a table and distributed Eta Pi Zeta chapter scholarship applications to the high school seniors in attendance. The chapter also marketed information on the three Zeta Phi Beta Youth Affiliates for girls and young ladies ages 4-18.

From there, I led Sorors to serve dinner at the Wells Robertson House for men and women who were transitioning from homelessness; coordinated the Zeta Prematurity Awareness Program, which included writing and designing marketing materials and a hosting a table at a local church; and was the liaison between the chapter and the state's Women's Legislative Briefing, the longest standing premier women's legislative event in the state of Maryland. The briefing featured nationally recognized speakers, prominent legislators, policy makers, and activists from the most preeminent national women's organizations in the country.

I listed these tasks and accomplishments not in the spirit of boasting or cataloging every single deed, but quite to the contrary. I referenced them in the spirit of gratitude and humility to testify to His goodness for using an ordinary person who had an infirmity to do extraordinary things. It was hard to believe that only a few short months earlier, I had been lying on a hospital gurney contemplating suicide, but for the glory of God, I was now back in full swing doing the work of Zeta Phi Beta Sorority, Inc. and serving our community with love. And yet, chapter, you still had no idea what I had been through that erupted my life with an exploding mental health crisis.

Serving while battling an illness that was foreign to me gave me a sense of purpose, in spite of it all. Depression and suicidal thoughts had me believing my life did not matter. Whether I was a believer in the body of Christ, a Soror of Zeta Phi Beta Sorority, Inc., or an individual after God's own heart, my purpose in serving was to improve the lives of people who did matter. As much as I enjoyed doing the work of Zeta, I could not wait to celebrate our chapter's 40th anniversary, and I jumped at the chance to participate on our gala's planning committee. Only a few years young into the Sorority, this would have been my first time celebrating a landmark occasion as part of this chapter. Gowns, pearls, and elegance!

The evening was historic, exciting, glamorous, and unforgettable. Eta Pi Zeta Chapter turned 40, and many of our charter members came back for a night of celebrating. But before we had turned 40, the first and oldest graduate chapter to charter in the history of Zeta Phi Beta Sorority, Inc. was turning 90, and I was fortunate enough to be there when International Grand Basileus Mary Breaux Wright delivered an awe-inspiring message for our neighbor chapter Alpha Zeta of the Baltimore Metropolitan area in Maryland.

Heading into a new and revised membership intake process, I was paired with an aspirant and became her mentor and coach as she began her journey into our illustrious organization. I could not think of a more special honor than helping a young Soror along the way. Yet, unbeknownst to my chapter or the aspirant, my health was still in recovery, plus I had no income. Not a likely combination for coaching a potential new Zeta. However, the fact that you considered me told me that you saw the best in me, regardless of the harsh and ugly reality from which I had escaped. I adored this young lady to pieces, and shudder to think about all this beauty I would had missed had I not gotten to the hospital and received treatment.

Time went on, and eventually the beginning of the Phi Beta Sigma 100-year Centennial Celebration, and the tail end of my recovery, came up. How befitting was it for our chapter to partner with the brothers from Sigma Sigma Sigma chapter of Phi Beta Sigma Fraternity, Inc. to present the play *A Sisterhood is Born* to a sold-out audience for our Founders' Day celebration. My life had made a full circle back to happiness. I found a new job that I thoroughly enjoyed, had completed my outpatient therapy and no longer needed medication, and I was in love.

My love was life itself. Over the summer I attended my first Boulé alongside the loves of my life, the very fine gentlemen of Phi Beta Sigma Fraternity, Inc., as they celebrated their centennial.   I was a voting delegate representing the chapter in Washington, D.C. If you were not there for the Reaffirmation Ceremony between Phi Beta Sigma Fraternity, Inc. and Zeta Phi Beta Sorority, Inc., you missed a beautiful and moving moment that halted time and simply continues to bring tears to my eyes whenever I replay that ceremony in my heart.

I survived workplace bullying, overcame my depression, and was reaping the best of life. I thought about what might have been a year ago had I not sought help. Instead of being your chapter delegate, I would have been a Triumphant Soror whose name, Lisa G. Eley, would have been deleted from the roll. Sadly, those remnant thoughts from having developed Post-Traumatic Stress Disorder (PTSD), having survived the trauma, and dealing with the memories of the bullying will never completely go away. I will always be reminded of all I would have missed and the hurting people I would have left behind if I had taken my own life in the previous year.

Hello Sorors, I am here! Standing, breathing, living, and by some accounts, a miracle! I survived what an enemy expected to do me in. What was meant for evil shall be turned around for God's glory and used to improve the lives of others. I could not live with myself in good conscious if I did not to try to prevent an ordeal like mine from ever happening again to someone else. We all matter! And it started with me sharing my story for this anthology. It did not have to be this way, had an agency taken a stand to intervene and immediately denounce bullying tactics. I am prayerful that this will change now that I am talking about it. As much as I believe my enemy should be punished for doing what he did to me and who knows how many others, my motivation is about saving a life more than taking him down. I wouldn't be any better than he if I wanted revenge. That is being a believer in Jesus Christ. That is being Finer, Sorors!

I took you along the journey of my depression from being bullied in the workplace. I had no history of mental illness and in all honesty, was not aware of the gravity of my situation until I ended up in the hospital and was removed from the source of my stress, an abusive supervisor. Only my family and closest friends knew what was taking place in my life. It was not easy to talk about then, and was much harder to talk about after my crisis had boiled over. The community at large depended on us chapter. And I know you would have carried on in my absence had I disclosed I was ill and needed to step away from the chapter momentarily. But you have to understand I needed Zeta Phi Beta Sorority, Inc., more than you could know.

When I served in these transitional residences and cancer houses, the people were so genuinely happy to have us. Men and women were living on the streets until the Wells Robertson House provided them with a home and a structured regimen for becoming self-sustaining and model citizens. But because our chapter prepared formal meals to the delight and gratification of the residents, we were often a favorite among the community partners who also served dinner at the home. The residents showed us their appreciation with cheers and applause and wondered how soon it would be before we returned for an encore. They had never had a sorority serve them dinner before.

When I first went with the chapter to The Children's Inn at NIH, I wasn't sure I could serve and not break down at the plight of children being treated for illnesses for which conventional treatments had previously failed. To a pediatric cancer patient and their family, The Children's Inn would be like home, and was a happy place that met these families right where they were. It had the aura of euphoria from its décor alone and was instinctively warm and inviting. Their mantra at The Inn was to care for the family and child as one because they recognized that the emotional comfort and support provided by the family made the difference in the lives of their ill children.

Just as with the Wells Robertson House before, the chapter received a round of applause and cheers from the families staying at The Inn because of the dinner we provided from scratch and served with love. It was a wow moment for me personally because I entered The Inn expecting to see solemn faces and hopelessness. Nothing could have been further from the truth. The families were chatty, happy, and seemingly oblivious to why they were residences of The Inn to begin with. I envisioned the children I'd seen on television from the St. Jude Children's Research Hospital commercials looking just like the children we were about to serve. I expected to cry and excuse myself from the serving line. Tears did fall, but not for the reasons I expected. I cried because the families were smiling and complimenting the dinner we had just provided. Their babies were sick, yet they appreciated the small act of kindness from a sorority.

That wow moment spun into an "ah ha" moment that fueled me to give of myself and serve no matter what I was dealing with. Making someone else happy would reciprocate and make me happy. I believed in my depressed state that if I pushed and served, and gave then eventually my depression would go into remission.

In a roundabout way, serving for the love of Zeta did just that. I truly believe that I lasted as long as I did before collapsing because of all of the good work the chapter was doing in helping other people excel. And that is why you probably did not see any signs of my distress, and even as of this writing, would find it hard to believe all that I had been through.

To God be the glory, Sorors! I turned my pain inside out, around, and upside down to be a friend to man. And while I did momentarily fall to my illness, I did not succumb to it. Hallelujah!

I do not know what it is you may be going through right now, Soror, but may what I have gone through inspire you to know that weeping may endure for a night, but if you would just hold on, joy will sure enough come in the morning. Let my example be the reason why you will not give in or give up. I spent eight days in a psychiatric hospital, was without income while recuperating for half a year, and lost a lucrative job and the only career I had ever known. Look at your situation and ask yourself, "Is there anything too hard for God?"

Children won't listen, spouse underappreciates you, job is occasionally cuckoo, chapter in discord, health could be better, or you cannot catch a break with your finances. Whatever your issue, Soror, look at what I have been through and believe it will be okay. You are awake, you are alive, and you are blessed! I absolutely hate what I went through but I love what I have become as a result. I already had a servant's heart, but now I have gained a far better appreciation for life and a purpose greater than anything I could have dreamt or imagined. I didn't choose this mission; it chose me. I will advocate until I can advocate no more to bring about changes to the workplace to deal with bullies and stop them in their tracks.

The eyes of my daughters were upon me, as they were not used to seeing me crumble. I was their buffer of protection and safety, absorbing and taking most of life's bumps and bruises so they would not have to. I lived my life as an example for them to more than emulate. There were many battles and conversations where I worried if they actually got it. My experiences came from the school of hard knocks. This was life, and it didn't always play fair.

Though there were setbacks we always seemed to manage. There was a time when we were the beneficiaries of strangers' kind donations, so I had instilled in my daughters since they were tots to always reach back and help someone else along the way. They remembered firemen coming to our apartment and delivering boxes of food, and the firemen letting them sit inside their fire truck.

I worked and sacrificed my comfort for them to have the basics and for others who were struggling far worse than we were. As a family we delivered Christmas toys to one family and a dinner to another family because the father of the family was dying from brain cancer. We did not know either family. These were examples of values that I wanted to instill in my daughters. Zeta Phi Beta Sorority, Inc. was a huge launching pad for me extending my service throughout the community. I taught my daughters to help other people and because of that I think they developed a greater appreciation for the charity work I do within and outside of the sorority. I also think I have their admiration and respect for the example I set.

I had worth and value when I became a member of our "Keeping it Finer" Zeta Phi Beta Sorority, Inc., and no one had the right to take that away from me. For me, it was a supervisor. In the name of sisterhood I pray it would never be a sister of Zeta on another sister. Valleys come and valleys go, and there will always be tests of faith and endurance. Having survived workplace bullying, I must do all I can so this does not happen to anyone else. By the time this story is in print, my prayer is there is legislation in the works to address bullying in the workplace and have it cease and desist.

I am healed, I am well, and I am grateful to be alive! In my darkest hours, I tried to ensure that my Zeta light shined. Did I act justly, love mercifully, and walk humbly while in the belly of adversity? Was I a tried and true living sanctuary even when no one was looking? Was my moral compass strong and sufficient? Did I use whatever gifts I had to serve others and lighten their burdens? Did I lead by example in upholding the founding principles of Zeta Phi Beta Sorority, Inc.? Were others blessed through me? I believe in my heart that I can answer each question in the affirmative while I was deep in the wilderness. I pray my God would be pleased with how I had managed it all and that I responded in a way that was pleasing to Him. Finer is as Finer does, women of Z Phi B!

Merriam-Webster can only define Finer Womanhood by dissecting its words into individual objects. I'll be the first to admit when I interviewed for Zeta Phi Beta Sorority, Inc. and was asked what Finer Womanhood was, I nervously fumbled and I'm pretty sure, amused the interview panel when I left. Simple and elegant, Finer Womanhood is a brand and quality unique to Zeta Phi Beta Sorority, Inc. and embodies the consummate gentlewoman. Never needing to be reformed in any way to the different times, it is now as it was then in 1920 synonymous with the eloquent and virtuous women of Zeta Phi Beta Sorority, Inc.

There is a saying that goes you never know how strong you are, until being strong is your only choice. The same could be said about being Finer, and could not have been truer for me personally when I was challenged to be poised, elegant, and respectful in the midst of anything but. Naked, unmasked, and stripped to the core, I did not know what was in me until "me" was all I had left. Out from a fiery pit and elegantly sculpted, I became more determined, much stronger, and forever Finer in living the best life I could.

While you may have initially expressed an interest in a sorority premised by scholarship, service, sisterhood, and Finer Womanhood, it was Zeta Phi Beta Sorority, Inc. that ultimately chose you, Soror, for having "the distinguishing characteristics of a woman, one superior in kind, quality, or appearance; marked by or affecting elegance or refinement."[1] This virtue does not end simply because you have checked it off your list of prerequisites for receiving membership consideration; it is a manner and quality for life.

If Zeta Phi Beta Sorority, Inc. ran a recruiting campaign for Finer Women today, would you be recruited to mold the sisterhood into the preeminent and finest sorority of our time just as our foremothers had? If your Finer went on sabbatical, then it is time to bring it back. When someone hears the word Zeta, they should instinctively know who those Finer Women are.

Take heart Sorors. There is indeed something to be said for branding and a name. In all that we do, we are beautiful, we are strong, and we are Finer!

"The best way to find yourself is to lose yourself in the service of others." — Mahatma Gandhi

FOOTNOTES

1. Zeta Phi Beta Sorority, Inc., *Finer Womanhood defined,* http://www.zphib1920.org/website-guidelines/, Accessed 14 February 2015

Let This Bond Be Unbroken

Jae Henderson

Dedicated to our mothers, Lillie Bell Marshall and Bobbie Collins Sanders

In June of 2013, I sat in front of my computer and hit enter to post my latest thoughts on Facebook. It was a brief statement that read: *Sometimes I just need someone to tell me that it's going to be okay.* A few minutes later, I received a response from my friend, Soror, and former roommate, Gwendolyn Sanders Woods. *It's going to be okay, Jae,* she wrote.

From someone else it might not have meant as much, but from her it was like cool aloe vera gel on a painful sunburn. I stared at those words and meditated on their meaning with a spirit of gratitude. They served as a virtual hug from my sister. Then, I went to check on my mother. She laid in her bed trying to grab a few hours of rest before she was awakened. She didn't sleep well during those days. I think it was stress and worry of what was to come. My mother was fighting full kidney failure and congestive heart failure, and there was only so much I could do to make it better. Dialysis, medication, doctor's visits and brief hospital stays had become a way of life us. A routine (minus the dialysis) my Soror knew all too well. Gwen and I not only shared the bond of sisterhood, but we also shared the unfortunate experience of watching our mothers deteriorate before our very eyes. I don't wish such a fate on my worst enemy.

My mother was my first example of Finer Womanhood: intelligent, articulate, quiet, poised, quick to praise, slow to insult, and always willing to lend a helping hand to others in need. When I was younger I thought she was boring because she was so even tempered, kept a small circle of friends, and was very much the homebody. She was also very good at minding her own business. I was told by family that even when my mother was young, she was an old soul. As I grew older and saw how similar to her I am, I realized that she gave me a life absent of drama, but filled with reflection, knowledge, and God's love.

As I took care of my mother years later, Gwen and her family were waging a war on that demon known as dementia, as it slowly robbed her mother of her mental function and mobility. Our spirits were tied as we tried our best to remain hopeful. We each petitioned God constantly for the miracle of healing. We also prayed for strength to see us through some of the darkest days of our lives. Our task was daunting. Yet, there was light. We reveled in little victories we referred to as "good days" – those days when our mothers seemed to be feeling well and more like their old selves. We cherished the time we were allowed to have them because having them in a weakened state was better than not having them at all.

I met Gwen while in college at The University of Memphis. We both worked at the YMCA near the campus. We hit it off right away. We later became sorority sisters after I joined the Rho Gamma Chapter of Zeta Phi Beta Sorority, Inc. in Spring of 1997, a semester after she did. We had some good times in college, and a few years later, we shared an apartment for a few months and the good times continued. As I grew to know Gwen better, I realized that she had a zeal for life and amazing faith which she attributes to her mother, who had even stronger faith. Gwen has an infectious sense of humor and her loud boisterous laugh can fill a room and spread joy to anyone within earshot. She was and is a blessing to me. Throughout her time as a caregiver, she maintained her sense of humor and encouraged me to do the same.

Somehow, knowing that I was not alone and that one of my dearest friends had the ability to empathize with me gave me some comfort. We spoke often, sharing our experiences and sharing information about Medicare and Medicaid, medication, and health care providers. Anything we thought could help the women who gave us life and lessen the financial strain ongoing medical treatments can bring.

As the months went by, we both saw our mothers' health continue to decline. I went to the hospital the day I received the text that her mother didn't have much time left. In January of 2014, Mrs. Bobbie Collins Sanders left this earth quietly, surrounded by her loved ones. Weeks later, when my mother entered the hospital for what would be the last time, Gwen sat in ICU with me for hours as my mother lay connected to heart monitors and other apparatuses designed to alert the staff to the condition of her vitals.

We talked while my mother slept. When she awoke, I introduced them. My mother was in good spirits that day and looked happy to meet her. I knew she didn't feel well, though. She had a tear in her intestines that prevented her from getting proper nourishment, and she looked almost skeletal. Surgery was scheduled to repair the tear. My mother was still fighting. I was still fighting and praying she would win. Little did I know, that would be the last day she would be able to speak to anyone. The next morning, my mother asphyxiated on something and had a ventilator placed down her throat to help her breathe.

Gwen never came back after that day. She later told me how hard that visit was for her because it reminded her of the passing of her own mother. Even while dealing with her own tragic loss, my friend was able to extend some support to me. I am grateful for her selflessness. My mother stayed in the hospital another two weeks and Gwen continued to call or text to check on us. Words of comfort and encouragement were ever present on her lips. I tried to give the same to her and her family.

The surgery to repair the tear in my mother's stomach was successful, but her bowels didn't return to normal function and she had to receive her nourishment via IV. She could no longer breathe on her own. She still received her dialysis treatments every other day, but her body was retaining so much fluid that it needed to be removed daily. Her prognosis was grim. No one should be forced to live that way. My family and I made the tough decision to let her go. Being merciful to her took priority over our desire to keep her with us. My mother died March 12, 2014.

Gwen and I both shed tears that flowed from the same type of heart wrenching pain. We both questioned why that had to happen and if there was anything we could have done differently. We'll probably never understand, but we've learned to focus on the positive. We still share stories of the last year of our mothers' lives. Some funny. Some not. Gwen took lots of videos and pictures of her mother. Ms. Bobbie looked vibrant and happy in them. In many of the videos, she cracked jokes and laughed. I saw where Gwen got her joyous spirit.

After our mothers' deaths, we spoke on the phone and met for lunch a time or two. On Mother's Day and Christmas, Gwen and I checked on one another to make sure we were okay. Those were the firsts of many holidays that we would be forced to face without the women who helped to make us who we are. I know Ms. Bobbie is smiling down on Gwendolyn Sanders Woods, who is one of the most thoughtful, caring, loving individuals I know. So, it came as no surprise to me that she had been extending her kindness to another Soror, Jameka Diggs, whose mother passed a few weeks before ours. I am grateful that God saw fit to place Gwen in my life. This experience has bonded us to one another in ways I will never be able express. Seared into my heart is a gratefulness that time will never diminish and a love that will never die.

I never thought I would lose my mother at the age of 37 and the pain of doing so is still there but Gwen was right, it's okay. I'm okay. We're okay. Life is not perfect and never will be because of the void. Yet, we are the daughters of two strong black women who taught us that when life gets hard, cling to your faith and pray. I pray that in times of calamity the people reading this will have a friend and Soror such as Gwen to help you get through. Finer Women take care of the people they love despite the odds, and in times of adversity we stand together and help keep one another intact. Our circle remains unbroken because our bond is strong.

Made in Seoul Sister

Jaynene Smith

*"Me and you, us never part. Makidada. Me and you, us have one heart. Makidada.
Ain't no ocean, ain't no sea. Makidada. Keep my sister away from me."*
– The Color Purple

Sisterhood is the tie that binds like-minded, but uniquely different, women for life. No matter the circumstance, even after the proverbial smoke clears, Sisterhood is the glue that without fail, holds it all together. It is a bond that constantly ebbs and flows throughout my experiences from the beginning of my ascent to Zeta in Seoul, Republic of Korea in Spring 2005. Although geographically separated from my extended family, and many of the Sorors whom I met while residing in Korea having relocated, I've had the pleasure to meet many inspirational women that to this day I call Soror, Sister, and Friend.

I've had constant role models throughout my life who exemplified our sorority principles of Scholarship, Service, Sisterhood, and Finer Womanhood. Becoming a member of a sorority does not prepare you to live these principles; it is, in fact, the other way around. Membership in our Sorority is an opportunity to give back, uplift, and to raise our collective voices to make a positive difference in our communities.

From my earliest memories, my mother, grandmother, and biological sister were constant reminders of what Finer Women should be. They educated me by providing a sound moral compass, mannerism, and daily examples. A Finer Woman is forged out of perseverance, compassion, strength, humility, and respect for herself and others. These three women were all of these.

I was raised in Southeast Washington, D.C. in what was then a respectable working class neighborhood. The women, an unofficial sisterhood, stood sentry over all neighborhood children. It was not uncommon to be disciplined by several of them before facing my mother Harriett, a 5'2" giant. My father worked to pay the bills, but my mother worked to provide my sister, brother, and me with beautiful clothing, an immaculate apartment, and a feeling that we were rich morally and spiritually. Providing for our existence was, for her, a constant source of worry. She was a strict disciplinarian; it was necessary to protect us from the 'streets.' It was my mother who the neighborhood children would exclaim, 'uh oh, you're gonna get it', when she walked outside and stood scanning the sector to find me, my sister or brother when the streetlights came on and we weren't in the house.

Chores were non-negotiable. They were completed on Saturday before anything else occurred that day. I, as the oldest, bore the responsibility for my siblings and all that they did, whether right or wrong. This 'ride or die' mentality was instilled in me at an early age. I rode, loyal to the end, for family and those whom I considered friends. So I learned how to fight, albeit physically (at that time) or verbally to protect those I loved.

My mother worked two jobs for as long as I can remember; her work ethic is unmatched and her compassion to help others continues to this day. I learned to 'make a way out of no way' from her; failing to provide for her children was never an option. She embodies all things: a black woman with an infectious smile, soft spoken words (but don't doubt that she meant every one), confidence, and grace, even under pressure. She is a Finer Woman.

Through my mother's positive reinforcement, she instilled love for myself and for others. She taught tolerance and appreciation for our material and spiritual blessings. My mother was the first 'sister' that I knew without a doubt would always be there, no matter what, to guide, correct, and encourage my dreams. Her dedication to provide the best for her children, discipline, and unconditional love, through the good and bad, provided me a firm foundation to grow. For that's what sisters do…

Granny, my mother's mother, also known as Ms. Wilhelmina Pearl Conyers, was a strong, stern woman who was well respected in her community. She was a single parent and raised my mother, the baby of the family, with strict rules that she abided by and passed on to her girls. If someone in the community was ill, Granny was there – she stayed until 'the fever broke'. She prepared meals (her gift) to celebrate, mourn, or to provide comfort. It was Granny who could be counted on to 'give you a good talking to' if you dared to show your behind, whether you were an adult or child.

Granny was also the resident fashionista in the neighborhood and church. Her hat and shoe collection was legendary. At age 96, she wanted me to 'chastise' my mother for taking her many heels because she could no longer walk in them. They were hers, and she felt that my mother was overstepping her 'authority.'

It was not until Granny's death in 2012 that I learned that she was a member of the United Order of the Tents for more than 60 years. The organization, which has chapters throughout the East Coast, was formed in 1867 as an Underground Railroad for slaves fleeing the South. The group took its name from the tents the fugitives used as shelter during their escapes. The mission has changed little since the group's earliest days. It continues to care for the sick and elderly, helps the poor and needy, instructs the young and makes sure the dead (no matter their financial circumstance) receive a proper burial. They've attended countless funerals, hosted annual Thanksgiving services, and raised untold amounts of money for orphanages, cancer research, homes for the elderly, and other causes.

The burial ritual to honor my grandmother by her Sisters and outpouring of love from the community moved my family to tears of appreciation for this woman who gave so much to so many. Ms. Wilhelmina Pearl Conyers was a testament to what a black woman should be, displaying true sisterhood and service. She was a force in the local black community, a self-less servant who gave to others without question, fanfare, or reimbursement. Granny was, without a doubt, Finer.

My sister was my total opposite while growing up. She toed the party line while I was deemed the rebellious one. Stacie was the voice of reason while I moved with my crowd, exploring the city, becoming obsessed with music, movies, and fashion. While she studied and took the traditional road to a college education, I partied. Although she was younger, she unknowingly served as my role model to educate myself and overcome any and everything that stood in the way of my education.

She was the scholar of the family. I was in awe of how she could focus on her education while dealing with the tragedy of losing some of her close friends to the streets. Education was her escape; I wanted to escape too. My sister made success look easy, she knew early on that she would attend college and made it happen. She taught me, through her example, that education opens all doors, so I worked so hard to catch up to her, to make my mother proud, and serve as a positive role model for my children. Sisterhood, as I learned from my sibling, is about motivation, setting goals, and achieving them all while pulling others with you. I wonder if she knows how she inspired me.

I joined the Army initially on a dare. My associates at the time didn't believe I would do it. Looking to leave D.C. and provide a better life for my son, I walked into the Army Recruiter's office initially to join the reserve component, but left prepared to enlist in the Active Duty Army. The fact that the Reserve recruiter was out of the office that day would change my life.

One of the most difficult things I would ever have to do would be leaving my son in the care of my mother and his father to join the Army. My mind said it was for the best, but my heart was slow to embrace this drastic move toward success. The Army literally saved my life. It provided opportunities to educate myself, global travel and a deep seated desire to give back – to help others like my sisters and brothers in arms helped me along the way. I met my husband, Jesse, while in the Primary Leadership Development Course in 1990. We vowed to make the Army a career, through thick and thin, for better or worse.

I also vowed to prove the naysayers wrong and become a college graduate like my sister. I chose, by my actions, to take the road less traveled to complete my education while working full time, raising my children, and serving in a dual military family with my spouse. I studied in and around the many military commitments, youth sporting events, PTA meetings, homework sessions (for me and my children), and rare moments when my spouse and I were in the same place at the same time between deployments. While at times it was extremely difficult, I wouldn't change a thing. My road to scholarship was non-traditional and didn't leave much room for error. My ability to multitask was the result of necessity, and it continues to serve me well.

My education, as well as the lessons I learned from my mother, grandmother and biological sister prepared me for my ascent to Zeta Phi Beta Sorority, Inc., on a sunny May afternoon in 2005 with my three other equally amazing Sorors. They prepared me for unconditional sisterhood, 'to be there' for my thousands of sorority sisters, those close and those who are loved from afar. Our relationships are complex – some are easier than others – but each encounter with our sisters should serve to teach and make us better personally and professionally.

Throughout my time in the Sisterhood, thousands of miles have separated us, but when Zeta called, we've answered. My sisters have been there for me, and I them, to provide counsel, celebrate and mourn relationships, births, and sometimes death. Where one of our sisters is weak, we are strong. We fight, cry, but throughout it all, we love – hard. When wrong, we apologize. When wronged, we forgive. We share our unique experiences, knowledge, and talents with our communities in our most noble cause – to uplift.

Our youth auxiliaries and undergraduate Sorors are the future of Zeta. My legacy, my daughter, follows in my footsteps. Asia was a former Archonette and joined our beloved Sisterhood in March 2013 at Tennessee State University. I surprised her and traveled approximately 14,000 miles (Seoul to Nashville and back) to be present for her and her 17 sisters' community introduction. I arrived on a Friday evening and departed early Sunday morning to travel back to Seoul.

My Soror continues to amaze me with her strength, resiliency, and zeal for knowledge. Asia is a quiet warrior, demonstrating a sincere spirit of compassion for others. She routinely greets others with the word Namaste, which, loosely translated, means a divine blessing that honors sacredness and equality in everyone. Seeing the good in everyone and every situation, she sometimes 'chastises' me when I refuse to change my way of thinking. Please charge it to my military mindset. Asia's taken the road less traveled, blazing her own path. I realized that as she matured, she was a Finer Woman in her own right. I'm so proud of the young woman she is and will evolve to become in the future.

I've also been inspired by many Sorors (they know who they are) who've provided sound counsel, experience, tough love when necessary, encouragement, and honest feedback. Sometimes adversity serves to humble and improve you; they would tell me when I was wrong and needed to 'have a seat.' So matter how long we've gone without talking, when we do, we just fall back in as though no time had passed. Our Code Blue meant that you stopped and answered the call, literally.

During my tenures as chapter Basileus and Asian-Pacific State Director, these ladies were extremely instrumental in my personal and professional growth. I was taught, by their example, to gracefully stand for what I believe is right, even when in the minority. I was shown that what you don't say can be just as powerful as what you do say. Even when I thought I'd reached by breaking point, my Sorors said, Stand! And Stand I did, with my sisters in front of, beside, and behind me. These relationships, many forged across the miles, are precious and lifelong. I will never forget or take for granted how these beautiful ladies have changed my life. There is no love like Sister Love.

Trying to be the best person you can be every day affirms your reason to be on this earth. Adversity, like pressure applied to coal, can serve to refine you. Believing that things will work out and putting forth the work to make it so is an exhibition of faith. Being thankful for what you've been given and paying it forward assures more abundant blessings in your life. Experiencing tragedy and encountering those less fortunate than you teaches humility. I strive to learn from my mistakes and to leave each thing I touch better than it was when I found it. I smile often, because I know that I have much to be thankful for. All of these experiences, both good and bad, improve you, creating a Finer individual in its aftermath.

The ties that bind us in our beloved Sisterhood are our call to service, quest for scholarship, and above all, our example of Finer Womanhood. Our beloved Founder, Viola Tyler Goings said, 'There's a Zeta in a girl...' Zeta chose this rebellious girl raised in Southeast Washington, D.C. I strive each day to answer to call to service and live up to our rich legacy. The ties that bind us from my vantage point in Seoul, Republic of Korea where my journey in Zeta began cannot be broken because every beat of my heart and those of my sisters are tried, true, and Royal Blue. Although I've recently relocated back to the States, I know from experience that Sorors the world over cry Z Phi B and when called, we answer one and all!

Thank You: Excerpts from "My Mom is a Teenager"

Pamelia Readus

Imagine in one week you will celebrate your 16th birthday, and in less than two months you will give birth to your first child. It was not an imagination for my mom.

My mother was a 16-year-old "colored" girl living in the colored housing project in the fifties. Did I mention in the south? There is very little self-confidence or hope for a teenage single mom with very little education. Well one thing my mom possessed was the faith in knowing that when you fall in life situations, keep looking up. She was determined that she would do whatever it took to give her child the best of life opportunities. Her goal in life was to make sure her child got a college education. In her eyes she knew that an education would be the one thing to keep her out of the homes of white folks. She wanted to make sure that it would be her home she cleaned and her children she raised.

The first thing my mom did to change her life situation was to seek mentorship from Christian women in the community who were of strong family value. These were Christian women who did not see her as another colored girl with a baby and going nowhere in life. These women gave encouraging words that ignited her self-esteem and gave her a sense of hope. I would say these were finer women. It is good to have friends, but it's always a better plan to have a good mentor. A good mentor will critique your actions. A mentor will tell you when you are wrong and embrace you with love.

The next thing you must have is a vision. Create a "vision board." If you can see it, you can do it. Set goals in life and work to achieve them. Make sure you speak kind words to yourself. I like to call these the "I" words. "I can do it; I am good enough; I am ready."

I say to teenage and single moms of today to seek mentors and guidance from folks who demonstrate leadership qualities. Surround yourself with folk of like minds and similar visions. Be prepared to put in the work. Know that you are human and you will make mistakes. The key to success is to learn from the mistake. Remember, the opposite of success is failure. Never trying is failure. Quitting is failure.

My mother's death was more than a loss of a love one. I lost my best friend and biggest supporter. I was taught the spirit of serving and giving as a child and for so many years my mother was my service partner. We believed that two or more should gather for service projects.

I felt like something was missing in my daily walk until one day, while reading the local paper, I came across an invitation for service. I met with a group of ladies and from that day forward, my life was changed. That lovely invitation threw me into the fold of the mighty sorority of Zeta Phi Beta. The principles of Scholarship, Service, Sisterly Love and Finer Womanhood were not only what I was looking for, it was just what I needed. Something happens in my life every day that make me say, "It's a good day to be a Zeta." It led me to thoughts of how to say "Thank You."

Thank You

Looking for the perfect gift to show my appreciation

Wondering what would be more meaningful than a token of love.

What do you give Five Pearls that is suitable for recognition?

It has to be of elegant taste for ladies of the Dove.

How do you pay homage to trailblazers who provided service to those in need?

While longing to embrace scholarship and true sisterhood

Blazing paths as they plant the seed

Of ladies who exemplify Finer Womanhood.

I want to say I'm grateful for your foresight

I'll forever show kindness and gratitude

Stand for the right, rather than the might

I'll demonstrate grace and love as the attitude

Of Finer Womanhood.

Thank you, Arizona Cleaver Stemons,

Thank you, Pearl Anna Neal,

Thank you, Myrtle Tyler Faithful,

Thank you, Viola Tyler Goings and

Thank you, Fannie Pettie Watts.

Love of the Dove – Pamelia Readus

Reflections

Mendy Mack

Zeta is a business...Zeta is a brand - I am the brand

As a young woman born of Haitian descent (I am a first generation American), I was unaware of "Greek life" until my cousin went to college and became a member of Phi Beta Sigma Fraternity, Inc. It was the first time I was exposed to the idea of like-mindedness for the good of the African American community.

As I came to understand the history of Black Greek organizations and the tumultuous time during which they were formed, I later realized that an altruistic view of community aware-ness and uplift motivated the founders of these organizations to look beyond themselves, to take notice of the communities surrounding Howard University and later, the global community.

I remember seeing my cousin on campus wearing his blue and white Phi Beta Sigma shirt and crossing jacket, walking on campus with his blue and white cane. I remember crowds of people circling him to congratulate him and I wondered why—what did he do? What was this group that he joined, and what did his membership mean? He wouldn't answer my questions directly. It seemed one question followed another, and finally the best advice he gave me was to pick up a copy of "The Divine Nine" and read it. So I did, and being the avid reader that I am, I finished the book in a matter of days.

I was blown away by the history of these organizations—the Founders were so BOLD. I was enlightened, I was intrigued, I was enthralled, and by the time I finished the book, I was interested in meeting a Zeta. I was interested in joining a sisterhood of women who not only understood the importance of being a part of their communities in order to appreciate their needs, but who were not afraid to challenge themselves to live their creed—to be Finer in all aspects of their womanship.' I sought Zeta with vigor.

When I decided to pursue the Zeta light, there was a degree of nervousness and fear that overtook me the moment I stepped into the informational. I saw the women in royal blue and white with letters across their chests, on pins, on scarves, on purses and I thought, "Could this be me? What did they sacrifice to become members?"

I wondered if I, too, had the willpower necessary not only to become a member while in College but for the rest of my life. I became a member of Zeta Phi Beta Sorority, Inc., in April of 2003, right before graduating from College. I graduated in May 2003, had my first child in August 2003, and started medical school in 2004.

Unfortunately, Zeta became a beautiful symbol of greatness that lived in the crossing gifts on my shelf. Until I attended my very first Boulé (which happened to coincide with Phi Beta Sigma's Centennial celebration), I didn't understand the "big picture." Zeta Phi Beta Sorority, Inc. is a business, and when there is a need in the community requiring attention, Zeta becomes a verb. Our passion becomes service, becomes advocacy for civil rights, and equal access to community resources. I took part in business sessions at Boulé and voted on issues vital to the integrity of the Sorority. I held hands and sang the National hymn with women spanning decades of servitude in a sea of Royal Blue and White.

In this moment I cried. Overwhelmed by emotion, I envisioned our beloved Five Pearls smiling and thinking, "Yes, they understood our vision." I heard our International Grand Basileus, Mary Breaux Wright, speak to Zetas from all over the world, encouraging them to prepare for 2020! I immediately began seeing Zeta as an international organization that demanded professionalism and creativity from its members. I understood Zeta as a brand where every decision made while displaying Zeta Phi Beta on one's person reflects on the 100,000+ women who also call Zeta their home. In this light, I, too, am the brand. I began to see each member as a vital piece of our picture, every personal achievement contributing to our sisterhood's legacy.

I returned home with a deeper understanding of the Sorority and a renewed interest in growing as a Zeta. Though I was previously financially active the last few years prior to Boulé 2014, I was a non-productive branch on our tree, admittedly not very fruitful. After Boulé, I leaped from 2003 to 2014 and became the Basileus of my graduate chapter. Yes, Zeta Phi Beta became tangible, something I could touch, something I could feel when speaking to my sisters.

The Sorority is so much bigger than me, than my chapter's "issues." Every Zeta who wears her letters is a walking advertisement for every other Zeta. What are we doing in our daily lives that sheds a positive light on our Sorority? Every Zeta who serves her community with Zeta at the forefront, communicates Zeta's brand contributes to Zeta's legacy.

This, in my opinion, is what makes us Finer. We live our principles in our daily lives. We don't "put on" our letters; they are in our hearts, and we carry them everywhere we go.

Do I make sure I am treating Zeta as a business and my chapter Sorors as members of a team with the common goal of advancing the Sorority's ideals? Yes!

Do I make sure I look camera ready when my letters are on? Yes!

Our Founders founded Zeta with the precept that it would survive them. Today, I stand amongst more than 100,000 women who answered the call of Zeta, and accept the responsibility of educating, elevating and uplifting communities all around them—communities that extend as far as the Middle East, Belgium, London, Africa and Korea. Clearly, in keeping with the ideals set forth by our Founders, Zetas worldwide have a zest for trailblazing! Indeed we are sisters of the Dove, Finer Women of all races.

Their Vision, my Inheritance, our Legacy

In the darkest of nights
When fear tried to abide in the deepest of thoughts
Crippling victims across generations
Leaders were formed
Injustice brought forth a new idea

5 women braved these times
The pressure of societal norms
Turned sand into pearls
Our Founders answered the cries of our sisters, brothers and unborn children
Forming a legacy of triumphant firsts
Dedicating lives to Service and Scholarship, Sisterhood and Finer Womanhood

Did they know 100 years later still women would follow -
Speaking for those muted by fear
Wounded by society's nepotism
Did they know Royal Blue would spread beyond Howard University into Belgium and the Middle East?
Did they know that Pure White would shine bright in the darkest hours of our history?
Did they know that the Dove would bring hope to communities plagued
by poverty, unequal access to healthcare or education?

Yes! Zeta Phi Beta boldly resounds in the hearts of Finer Women across the globe!
Yes! The vision of our steadfast and purpose driven founders inspires new ideas and continues to create new leaders.

Archonettes on Finer Womanhood

Voices of Zeta Archonettes

In 1963, Lambda Zeta Chapter in Houston organized a teenage group from all the high schools in the city. The name Archonettes was added to the Zeta structure in 1968 for the national senior-high youth auxiliary. The Archonettes engage in a variety of social, educational and service activities such as charm clinics and sub-debutante cotillions. They also assist in operating the Stork's Nests and serve wherever teenagers are needed to facilitate Zeta's programs. Archonettes are a Youth Auxiliary Group for young ladies 14-18 years of age.

Finer Womanhood is knowing who you are and what you represent at all times.

– **Kayla Walker,** Archonette, Rho Iota Zeta, Mendenhall, Mississippi

Finer Womanhood is encouraging women to be better and not step out of character, not tearing another woman down.

– **Kashea Woman,** Archonette, Rho Iota Zeta, Mendenhall, Mississippi

Finer Womanhood is not succumbing to today's stereotypes and keeping your cool during the toughest of situations.

– **Alycia Triplett,** Archonette, Alpha Eta Zeta, Memphis, Tennessee

Finer Womanhood is the expression of a lady who embodies elegance in her demeanor, is educated to improve herself and others, elevates to help raise humanity, and endures to conquer the race of life with zeal.

– **Kaleeauh Steele,** Archonette, Alpha Theta Zeta, Savannah, Georgia

Finer Womanhood is being the best you can be and carrying yourself like a woman. Finer Womanhood is being different from the rest and being courageous.

– **Leia Kay,** Archonette, Gamma Nu Zeta, Camden, New Jersey

Finer Womanhood to me means a young lady who works to the best of her ability. It means seeing the bright side of things no matter how tough it is. A Finer Woman is always a leader and never a follower.

– **Julia Nobles,** Archonette, Gamma Nu Zeta, Camden, New Jersey

Finer Womanhood is to carry yourself like a good woman and fall on your own shoulders even if you do something wrong. It is working to the best of your ability.

– **Sasha Rayne,** Archonette, Gamma Nu Zeta, Camden, New Jersey

Finer Womanhood is to be a woman that can lead by example. She is a woman people extol. A woman that knows how to carry herself in a classy and respectful way.

– **Camrah Carter,** Archonette, Gamma Nu Zeta, Camden, New Jersey

Finer Womanhood is being an example of how a woman should conduct herself in society. Finer women care about the people and their community. They care about education and they take a stand in their community by participating in social change. Finer women lead by example and know how to carry herself in a classy way.

– **Kiearra Flowers,** Archonette, Eta Sigma Zeta, North Little Rock, Arkansas

Finer Womanhood means a woman is destined for greatness. She can do anything that God allows her to do. She can achieve any goal that she puts her mind to; there is no stopping her.

– Zoe Blackburn, Archonette, Tau Psi Zeta, Alsip, Illinois

Finer Womanhood is the paragon of every woman striving to be a leader, motivator and a better person than they were the day before.

– Bre'Anna Grant, Archonette, Gamma Nu Zeta, Camden, New Jersey

Finer Womanhood is something that all women should strive to achieve in their everyday life. A finer woman is a woman admitting her wrongs and learning from them.

– Kameron Johnson, Archonette, Gamma Nu Zeta, Camden, New Jersey

Finer Womanhood is being a finer woman, even in the hood.

– Tameah Young, Archonette, Gamma Nu Zeta, Camden, New Jersey

Finer Womanhood is leadership.

– Tamia Peguero, Archonette, Omicron Epsilon Zeta, Albany, New York

Finer Womanhood is being accomplished and successful in everything a woman does while carrying herself in a professional and/or social manner.

– **Jimara Thomas,** Archonette, Xi Mu Zeta, Markham, Illinois

Finer Womanhood is being respectful to yourself and others.

– **Lena Ramsey,** Archonette, Xi Mu Zeta, Markham, Illinois

Finer Womanhood is knowing that you're not perfect.

– **Jordan Gallon,** Archonette, Xi Mu Zeta, Markham, Illinois

Finer Womanhood is being a self-assured young lady.

– **Jada Lincoln,** Archonette, Xi Mu Zeta, Markham, Illinois

Finer Womanhood is respect for self, manners, knowing right from wrong, and showing leadership skills at all times.

– **Raiyana Montgomery,** Archonette, Xi Mu Zeta, Markham, Illinois

Finer Womanhood is a woman who thinks for herself and holds herself to high standards.

– Kyla Booth, Archonette, Omega Mu Zeta, North Brunswick, New Jersey

Finer Womanhood is significant because it emphasizes, morals, selflessness, obedience, respect, higher standards, and goals that people should strive for in life; it is unique and challenges a woman to become a more responsible and respectable person.

– Deja Marsh, Archonette, Tau Delta Zeta Chapter, Laurel, Maryland

Finer Womanhood is the way in which women come together to support their community, their family, and themselves.

– Jasmine Graves, Archonette, Tau Delta Zeta, Laurel, Maryland

Finer Womanhood is exhibiting all of the principals of Zeta and carrying yourself to a standard that is higher than normal."

– BreNae ToChana Scott, Archonette, Tau Psi Zeta, Alsip, Illinois

Finer Womanhood is having values and morals which will contribute to my transition from a young lady to a young woman. As I further my education, it will open doors for me to stand in good company of strong, vibrant and intelligent women of Zeta Phi Beta Sorority, Inc.

– Jayda Horn, Archonette, Kappa Rho Zeta, Highland Park, Michigan

Finer Womanhood is having dreams and believing you can do anything you put your mind to. Finer Womanhood is having a positive outlook on life and being a positive role model. Finer Womanhood is being elegant and having manners. Finer Womanhood is being brave and taking risks. Finer Womanhood is caring for others and being compassionate. Finer Womanhood is having power to stand up for what's right and not afraid to speak your mind. Finer Womanhood is being inspirational to others.

– **Jasmine Dixon,** Archonette, Phi Alpha Zeta, Waldorf, Maryland

Finer Womanhood is a finer woman who is not only a God fearing woman but a woman that when you look at her you know she stands for something.

– **Raven Hodges,** former Pearlette, Amicette, presently a graduating Archonette; Alpha Epsilon Zeta, Kansas City, Kansas

Finer Womanhood is the demonstration of the most exceptional characteristics of a woman. These characteristics typically include, but are not limited to respect, honesty, compassion, knowledge, accountability, service and feminism.

– **Daisha Tucker,** Archonette, Kappa Epsilon Zeta, Bronx, New York

Finer Womanhood is being the best woman you are able to be and showing it through actions.

– **Janae Lowe,** Archonette, Kappa Epsilon Zeta, Bronx, New York

Finer Womanhood to me means working to my utmost ability to excel in school, extracurricular programs, and community service. By being caring, compassionate, and respectful towards others, I show some of the numerous characteristics that exemplifies what Finer Womanhood means to me.

– **Tyra Henry,** Archonette, Kappa Epsilon Zeta, Bronx, New York

Finer Womanhood is giving a helping hand to others.

– **Abigail Asamoah,** Archonette, Kappa Epsilon Zeta, Bronx, New York

Finer Womanhood is life. You are being a better woman and carrying yourself in a respectful manner.

– **Akia Morrison,** Archonette, Delta Zeta, Charlotte, North Carolina

Finer Womanhood is when beautiful ladies join together as one. They learn how to be respectful young ladies. They learn good manners and how to be polite.

– **Taylor Wilson,** Archonette, Zeta Zeta Zeta, Denver, Colorado

Finer Womanhood is showing respect and having respect. Showing that you have manners and know how to dress appropriately, actually dress like you care about the way you look. When greeting someone you say hello with a smile and shake their hand.

– **Julyah Wilson,** Archonette, Zeta Zeta Zeta, Denver, Colorado

Finer Womanhood is a woman that is not shaped by the opinions of others, but knows her self- worth.

– **Gabriel Grant,** Archonette, Upsilon Psi Zeta, Oak Park, Michigan

Finer Womanhood is a being a lady at all times and a pillar in her community.

– **Rachel Grant,** Archonette, Upsilon Psi Zeta, Oak Park, Michigan

Finer Womanhood is a woman who respects and values herself. She knows her worth and has self-love.

– **Kyla Price,** Archonette, Upsilon Psi Zeta, Oak Park, Michigan

Finer Womanhood to me is standing your ground. Standing your ground is saying no to what you feel isn't right and sticking to what you say. Finer Womanhood means not giving in to pressure or losing your patience, even though it may be hard sometimes.

– **Beautiful Lawson,** Daughter of Anthology Editor, Belgium

ANTHOLOGY

Affirmations of
Finer Womanhood

Finer Affirmations

Karen Arrington

Be Finer…!

Put on red lipstick, stilettos and start a revolution!

Be the difference in the world that you want to see!

Be okay with who you are and where you are. Other women are not your competition. Finer women know who they are and comfortable in their own skin.

Rise up to your calling. Finer women pray and believe in a higher power!

Nothing of great significance is accomplished without the help of other people. Call it a clan, tribe, family or circle of sisters. Finer Women uplift other women!

Diverse in mind, body and spirit… Finer Women come from different backgrounds and walks of life. They always look, think and act Finer.

Stop waiting on permission to show up in the world. Finer Women stand up, speak up and raise the roof. Tell the world what you want and it will respond!

Leave the world better than you found it. Finer women are lights in their community.

Over the past 20 years, I've managed to rack up more than 100,000 hours of service,

and I'm just getting started.

Being Finer is a super power. Not everyone has the privilege of being extraordinary.

To the Finer Women of Zeta Phi Beta…I see you. I get you. I feel your power!

A Tribute to My Sister,
Maxine CarrieJones Bryant

Alpha Chapter - April 1970
(Alpha Zeta Chapter – Diamond Life Member)

Arlene MJ Taylor

God made her a sister first when our brother Richard was born, and again when I was added to the family. She loved and cared for us as only an older sister could.

Zeta later made her a sister to many, as she shared her love and knowledge with the Blue and White family. I watched, as a little sister would, the things she did with the Blue and White. Helping others and making a difference in the lives of those around them was their main goal, aside from keeping their grades up and graduating.

I watched as she and her new sisters carried themselves on Howard's campus in the early seventies, even seeing a photo of the Zetas at their 50th Boulé. Eventually, I, myself, was inspired to become a member of the Blue and White family. The guiding principles—Service,

Scholarship, Sisterly Love and Finer Womanhood—sounded like something that I wanted to be part of. I couldn't wait to go to college and become part of the Blue and White family and, most of all, a sister to my sister.

In 1974, my sister by blood became my sister again. We have always shared the love of our parents Mack and Gladys Jones, the love of our brother Richard, and the love of many family members and friends, but nothing beats that sisterly bond, first by blood and then by love, within the Blue and White family.

We have been fortunate to share many Boulés and Zeta events together, even sharing the 75th Anniversary Celebration in 1995. As Zeta looks forward to the Centennial, we look forward to sharing another major milestone together.

I am glad she set the example that made me want to be a part of the Blue and White family. Thank you, Maxine, for always being there for me. I Thank God for my sister, and I thank Zeta for making us Sister / Sisters.

Journey to Finer Womanhood

Cherline Pierre
Zeta Kappa Chapter

Finer Womanhood is more than eleganance, one's dress size and outer appearance, beauttiful hats and gloves, an event, or attritube. Finer Womanhood equates to becoming a superior person of character. Although the word "Finer" can be defined in several ways, my preferred definition is "to achieve or produce something better than." Achieving and producing something of quality requires some sort of journey. Being or becoming "Finer" is a journey through womanhood that simply becomes a way of life.

As ladies, we aspire to be better cooks, parents, sisters, sorors, friends, colleagues, mentors, business/civic leaders, employees, employers, students, wives, and the like. Exhibiting the disposition of being Finer requires one to remain passionate about exhibiting the fruit of the spirit in tone, words, reactions, inflection, thoughts, and gestures. Presenting one's self as a lady of Finer Womanhood is never about self, but rather it is about being of service to others.

Aspiring to become Finer impacts, inspires, and influences others and the communities one is a part of. Upholding the Finer characteristics of womanhood, requires that one remain meek enough to allow herself to be loved, forgiven, humbled, and hurt. Finer Womanhood ultimately becomes a reflection of one's inner being and outer spirit.

Finer Womanhood is a lifelong process that requires one to proactivly journey through life, passport in hand, in effort to ultimately achieve whatever goals one sets forth. The journey to Finer Womanhood is a participatory activity, and is certainly not for spectators. This journey is not confined to a boxed in approach; but rather the ability to creatively, progressively, and confidently, balance the various roles you play in life.

The passport you take along the journey is what identifies you as a woman who is not defined by the standards of others and society, but is defined by her own morals, values, and beliefs. In the end, the fruit bearing results of your journey are what grant you ulitmate access into your inner self and identifies you as a Finer Woman; a blue-tiful woman of Zeta Phi Beta Sorority, Inc.

Sharing My Thoughts on Finer Womanhood

Willa J. Godley

It gives me great pleasure to extend greetings to members of Zeta Phi Beta Sorority, Inc.!

Having pledged in 1962 at Saint Augustine's College (now University), I have watched the Sorority grow. Finer women are definitely blazing new paths, as evident in all the things Zetas have done. Looking at all the phenomenal paths our Sorors have traveled just makes me sit back and smile. They have blazed the path in their communities to advance the power of Scholarship, Service, Sisterhood and being Finer Women. Zetas have carved the path in many countries.

As you read this, you will gain an appreciation for the work that is happening in our local chapters, states, and regions. This work has truly been a shining example of the founding principles of Zeta. I would now like to share with you excerpts of an interview I conducted, reflecting on my experiences with Finer Womanhood.

1. *Where you were born and raised?*

   Rowland, N.C. (Robeson County)

2. *Where you currently reside?*

   Winterville, N.C. (Pitt County)

3. *What is the best part about being a Zeta?*

   Getting adopted by my younger Sorors

4. *What was it about Zeta that made you decide to become a member?*

   The unity that I saw within the chapter at Saint Augustine'e University and their bond with Phi Beta Sigma Fraternity, Inc. I also loved the fact they were very involved with providing service on campus and in the community.

5. *What was your first leadership role in Zeta?*

   Basileus at Saint Augustine's University- Phi Beta chapter

6. *Who was Grand Basileus when you became a member?*

   The Rev. Dr. Deborah C. Wolfe

7. *When did you meet your husband?*

   In 1988 at Pitt County Schools

8. *What is your advice to someone who aspires to be a Zeta?*

   Learn all you can about Zeta. Strive to be of service to others, get all the training you can, and remember: it is all about Zeta, not you!

Affirmation

Michele H. Pondexter

Nothing takes the place of authentic. Being a "reasonable facsimile" won't do. You must upgrade your thoughts, words, and actions to make room for your truly authentic self. It is said that an authentic woman who walks tall with her head held high has purpose, and usually knows where she's going. #yourauthenticpurpose

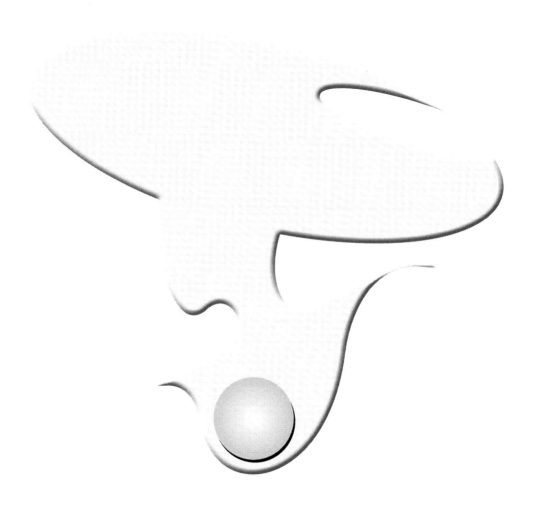

A Finer Woman Emerges

Kim D. Sawyer

We come into this world kicking and screaming to announce our arrival. Through the different stages of our life, the many experiences, the help and guidance along the way, the handling and navigation of the hand dealt by the Almighty, and the choices we make, a woman, a Finer Woman, emerges.

A **Finer Woman** who is sure of herself, confident but not arrogant;

A **Finer Woman** who carries herself with grace and sophistication and exudes pride and dignity;

A **Finer Woman** who is astutely aware that goodness is about character, integrity, honesty, kindness and generosity;

A **Finer Woman** who is courageous enough to do the right thing because it is right;

A **Finer Woman** who knows that no one who achieves success does so without the help of others;

A **Finer Woman** who respects herself and is respectful to others;

A **Finer Woman** who is faithful and loyal to what matters to her;

A **Finer Woman** who strives to help others in need.

And when the life journey is over, a **Finer Woman** will leave this earth knowing that she was a rainbow in someone's cloud.

ANTHOLOGY

Amicae

ZETA PHI BETA SORORITY, INC.

Zeta Amicae – The Finer Side of Friendship

Donnie Faye Hull and Renee Byrd

ZETA PHI BETA SORORITY, INC.

Just for a moment think about three words: **REASON, SEASON**, and **LIFETIME**. Every friendship exists for a **REASON**, **SEASON**, or a **LIFETIME**. Some friends come into your life for a **REASON**, you need them to be in your life for a **SEASON**. Some friends come into your life for **LIFTIEME**, this is the Finer Side of Friendship. Zeta Phi Beta Sorority, Incorporated and Zeta Amicae - are **TREASURED FRIENDS** for a **LIFETIME**. This friendship is truly a blessing and the relationship shared is a true gift. The **REASON** and **SEASON** will fade away but the **FRIENDSHIP** between Zetas and Amicae will last a **LIFETIME**. We have united our hearts, hands, and minds together to create a strong friendship as we serve God and mankind. Finer friends are friends forever. Let us hold our friends with both hands. **Zetas and Amicae – A FRIENDSHIP MADE IN HEAVEN.**

1948, the year where it all started at the Boulé in Philadelphia, Pennsylvania under the administration of Soror Lullelia Walker Harrison, 12th International Grand Basileus. Soror Lullelia Walker Harrison – one of God's beautiful masterpieces. A Woman of Faith…A Woman of Vision…and A woman with a compassion and love for the Amicae.

Charter Members

The First charter was granted to Zeta Amicae of Houston, Texas. These ladies set the standard for the Finer Side of Friendship that is still in effect today. In 2013 Zeta Amicae of Houston, Texas celebrated 65 years of continuous service. Amica Adelaide Forde served as the first Amicae president. One of the charter members, Amica Mary Hinton is still actively serving this auxiliary.

Adelaide Forde
of Houston, Texas –
First Amicae President

Amica Mary Frances Hinton
Only living charter member
of the Houston Amicae

Grand Basileus Mary Breaux Wright with Amicae at the Inaugural National Zeta Amicae Leadership and Empowerment Retreat held in Indianapolis, Indiana, July 2013

The Regional Zeta Amicae Presidents demonstrating the Finer Side of Friendship by presenting a sizable donation to Grand Basileus Mary Breaux Wright for the Capital Campaign at the 2014 Boulé in Washington, D.C.

This is a special moment in time as we salute our treasured friends for 67 years of friendship, love, and service. Congratulations for all of the accomplishments you have achieved in 67 years. All across Zetadom, you have truly been an example for others to follow. You have reached this milestone through your hard work, dedication, and love. We are proud to know you and be your friend.

ZETA AMICAE

Thank you for your spirit of love,

Thank you for your spirit of friendship,

Thank you for your spirit of service.

Your invaluable contributions to Zeta Phi Beta Sorority, Incorporated will always be remembered.

We challenge you to continue to preserve the legacy of love, friendship, and service by embracing and implementing programs, projects, and activities of Zeta Phi Beta Sorority, Incorporated. You are strong women getting engaged in all eight regions. Like women in the Bible on a Quest for Excellence, You display the Finer side of Friendship.

For the Love of Zeta, Be like Miriam – Be Women of Service.

For the Love of Zeta, Be like Rahab – Be Women of Deliverance.

For the Love of Zeta, Be like Ruth – Be Women of Loyalty.

For the Love of Zeta, Be like Hannah – Be Women of Prayer.

For the Love of Zeta, Be like Dorcas – Be Women of Good Works.

For the Love of Zeta, Be like Eunice – Be Women of Faith.

The BEST IS YET TO COME as you continue to "**BE A FRIEND** and to **BE OF SERVICE**" to Zeta Phi Beta Sorority, Incorporated. We salute our Finer Friends, the Amicae!

From the History Books

The Blue Book and Archons

Compiled by
Marjay D. Anderson, PhD

THE BLUE BOOK

THE ARTS AND FINER WOMANHOOD

Mme. Lillian Evanti

*'Women are the books, the arts, the academies
that show, contain and nourish the soul.'*
Shakespeare

Every woman is born with some germ of artistic appreciation, the development of which depends upon the individual, and environment will condition its degree.

Appreciation of and participation in the Arts is the greatest wealth a woman can enjoy. Finer womanhood when it reaches toward perfection must embrace a constant and consistent absorption of the fine arts. A richer consciousness for introspection is its gift to womanhood. It gives her that glimpse of ecstatic vision for which the soul hungers in its search for the infinite.

Rhythm, order and balance are the three organic principles of life. A woman should feel this trinity in all life, especially when contemplating or listening to a work of art. Reflect for a moment and consider this ever present trinity in Music (be it vocal or instrumental) in the dance, in poetry, weigh its inherent values in architecture, painting, and sculpture. What great literature or drama can live without them? To appreciate Art one must seek it often and absorb its intrinsic beauty. A real work of art will either fill you with a quiet harmony or inspire a feeling of exaltation. Have you ever beheld a Rembrandt while listening to Beethoven Music? It is a glorious experience that tunes the spirit to the unity of all greatness.

The cinquecento period gave us a rather static art which was also characteristic of the people of that epoch. Modern art is in tune with the twentieth century and has that freedom and spontaneity which characterizes its pulse. There is no longer an attempt to make a photographic copy of nature, but to express beauty through form and color. Even the space which surrounds a picture takes on its own vibrations and the rhythm is so compelling that it seems to continue outside of the frame. The new color and form that Debussy gave to his musical palette was inspired after having read the poems of Jean Moreas, the English pre-Raphaelites, and Shelly. (Here again we find that spirit of unity in the arts). It was the wax sculpture of Schelomo. (Which is the Jewish name for Solomon) by Catherin Barjanska that inspired Earnest Blochoto to write his masterpiece "A Hebrew Rhapsody for Cello and Orchestra."

The inspiration that Berlioz, the great French Composer, derived from the works of Benvenuto Cellini, the Italian Sculptor of the 16th Century, gave birth to an opera with Cellini as the protagonist. Florence Price, our noted woman composer, was inspired by nature

1936

THE BLUE BOOK

in writing her latest Symphony "Mississippi." She starts with its source in Minnesota, and caries this main artery through its narrow winding journey to its exodus in the Gulf of Mexico.

What relationship does art appreciation bear to our every day life? You will find yourself giving more taste and originality to your interior decoration. Your personal wardrobe will have more charm and individuality, its influence will be stamped indelibly on your professional contacts, be it in school, office or business. No one of us will question the cultural development of the fine arts. It gives you that ease and grace of personality and poise that makes you feel at home in any group. What finer theme for conversation can one have than to discuss a recent art exhibit, a symphony concert, a fine drama, your preferred poet? Woman's philosophy of life embraces her attempt to interpret experiences and adjust herself to ever changing conditions.

To be in tune with the arts, she will through their rhythmic symmetry and harmony better understand the relationship of life. They are an antidote for unhappy thoughts that open wide the gates to let beauty in. Hidden deep in the breast of every woman, is her own Symphony. Tell me what woman has not heard within, the vibrations of an Allegro, or an Adagio-ossai? Or a Scherzo or Largo? There will be dissonance and unresolved chords until she uses her power to resolve them. Be it sorrow, ecstasy or fortitude, she must meet the challenge.

What can the arts mean to women of Zeta Phi Beta? A closer harmony one to the other

with an ever widening circle of influence to all other women. An added consciousness of the three organic principles of Rhythm, Order and Balance. A fuller understanding of that Unity inherent in all God's Creation.

FINER WOMANHOOD

Observed by every Chapter of the Zeta Phi Beta Sorority annually, the last full week of February.

To Soror Eugenia Chiles of Atlanta who has gone on to join the innumerable caravan, but whose memory will forever be green in the annals of the Zeta Phi Beta Sorority, goes the honor of our annual observance of Finer Womanhood. It was suggested by her to Epsilon Zeta in 1928 and became a National Obligatory Observance.

In every community where there is an active Chapter of our sorority, there is a consciousness that Zeta stands for something more than social activity and whiling away of precious hours, in the week that begins the month of February. Services are held in churches. Sorors present the work of the organization in High and Normal schools and universities, every Zeta at sometime during the week renews her pledge of loyalty and fealty to her sorority. Lecture Teas, formal dances, closed dinners and luncheons, visits to charity institutions, Hobby shows, theatre parties, awarding of scholarships, Vesper services, Zeta Sigma council meetings, all these are but an outward sign of the inner consciousness of every Zeta woman that finer women live full lives, and are

1936

THE BLUE BOOK

fine in every occasion and circumstances that goes to make up that full life.

From all over the jurisdiction came most satisfying reports to the National office in 1936. Especially noteworthy were the efforts of every Chapter to secure the service of outstanding guest speakers and those of our sorors who are gifted with eloquence, were much in demand.

Especially noteworthy were the observances and we have reports from Alpha, Beta, Gamma, Epsilon, Theta, Iota, Nu, Sigma Tau, Zeta Zeta, Eta Zeta, Theta Zeta, Iota Zeta, Kappa Zeta, Nu Zeta, Xi Zeta, Omicron Zeta, Pi Zeta, Beta Alpha, and Epsilon Alpha. It is with pride and confidence that we look forward to the 1937 observance and the reports that will come from every Chapter.

————

Finding balance between the right wing of tradition and the left of adventure.
Idling for naught save when hands will not grace the soul.
Never becoming slave to good dreams of no bottom.
Earning our bread with sixty minutes worth of distance run.
Rising toward a mountain of transfiguration, but remaining not.

Walking with queens; nor spurning the cry of the herds.
Opening our minds to the dictates of the stored-up wisdom of the ages.
Moving toward the star of ideals; when salvaging the sum of humanity.

Approving the handicraft of the weave by checking his pattern.
Naming ourselves as preceptresses of our fate.
Holding naught as queen, save honor and love.
Obeying only our convictions.
Offering nothing to the world when we would keep the best.
Delving deeply or delving not, into the tasks we give our lives to.

Stella Louise Parker

————

HOW FINER WOMEN ACHIEVE

Harriett La Forrest

The women of Zeta Phi Beta Sorority reach the needs of those in their environment through service. These women have illuminated an otherwise dark picture. The flaming torch whirling through the chaotic conditions of civilization reveals women both brilliant and luminous, the center of intrigue, plot, and conspiracy, dynamic forces behind gigantic movements, the instigator, the foil, the despoiler, the pawn, the reward, the cause, the Alpha and Omega. Her multitudinous achievements have been by their cosmic, and deep powers of gravitation. She is the moulder of destiny, the creator of history.

The women of achievement or the "Finer Women" have a very forceful individuality ever using its strange drawing powers. This radiant

————

1936

THE BLUE BOOK

individuality is never lost in a crowd, because they have the courage of their convictions.

Can women leave an immortal record? They do because they are dominated by a mighty purpose, per-faculty to take life from their other faculties, "Resolve and thou art free," said Longfellow. Tis foolhardiness to dally with ones purpose. To hang forever in the balance, is to lose one's grip on life. The inability to make decisions indicates the lack of control which slackens achievement. Finer women do not wait for favorable conditions, events must submit themselves to her not vice versus. Great opportunities not only seldom come to the most fortunate, but are also sometimes as quickly gone.

In retrospection of the achievements of women we find that they have a vision of clairvoyance that enables them very quickly to bring themselves to a decision so eliminating the dissipation of energy which executes nothing. We find that no woman owns her body and soul. She gives as regally as sovereigns. She is invariable; not only accepting the rosy tasks, but pursuing them steadily when thorns appear.

BETA ZETA — WASHINGTON, D. C.

Beatrice S. Catlett, Basileus
Harriet L. Collier, Anti-Basileus
Louise Madella, Jerveler
Mary M. Jones, Epistoleon
Esther Peyton, Tamiouches
Mary T. Sumner, Grammateus

Helen C. Williams

Beta Zeta boasts of the largest membership in the sorority and is composed of "Wise Women of the East" for in their midst is a Dean of Women at a university, professors of English, several principals of schools, Doctors of Philosophy, those who have encircled the globe not once but several times, and several who have visited Europe numbers of times, singers, artists. Washington, the university city for our group, boasts of two Chapters and a third about to be organized at Miner Teachers College, where a very fine pledge club is learning the Zeta way.

1936

THE BLUE BOOK

Evelyn Frazier

The Finer Womanhood programme was a most educational one, a panel discussion on "The relation of College Sororities and Fraternities to the community" and the panel was conducted by Sorors Edith A. Lyons, Mayme H. Plummer, Mary Mason Jones, Mary R. Reid, Beatrice Catlett, Sarah Mc Gowan and Soror Lucy Baker of Alpha Chapter, in conjunction with Brothers Jesse W. Lewis, National President of the Phi Beta Sigmas, Dr. John A. Turner, Dr. B. H. Early, Mr. Langston Taylor and Mr. Frederick Mennis. The guest Speaker was Mrs. Virginia H. Mc Guire, President, Washington Branch the N. A. A. C. P. and her theme was "Woman's place in Our Changing Civilization."

An active participation in the Zeta-Sigma Council, very definite activity in the educational work of every kind at the Nation's Capitol, is credit to Beta Alpha.

Recently at the Washington Educational Week the Recreational Project of Zeta Phi Beta Sorority held no mean place both as to exhibit and discussion of its success. From Washington came the director of the Project, Soror G. L. Hamm, the assistant and instructor in Handcraft, Soror E. Peyton, and the guest speakers as well most of the volunteers for service.

In the social life of Washington, Zeta Phi Beta always plays a very definite part. All in all Zeta lives up to the traditions of the ideals of Zeta, Zeal, Scholarship, Sisterly Love and Finer Womanhood.

Two national officers come from its ranks, Soror Grace Collins, Chairman of the Executive Board, and Soror Beatrice Carlett, Chairman of Scholarship, as does Soror Anita Turpeau Anderson, the composer of our National Song, and original chairman of the Project.

Beta Zeta and Alpha were hosts to the National Conclave last year and proved themselves worthy and charming hostesses as well as educational leaders.

Much credit is due Soror Beatrice Carlett who as Basileus for the past two terms, has kept Beta Zeta well in the foreground in every worth while activity.

During the year Betz Zeta presented three scholarships to students at high schools, who were chosen by the principals for highest rating.

1936

THE BLUE BOOK

Xi Zeta: St. Louis, Mo.— Organized December 5, 1935

Charter Members
Lucille Ogden
Juanita Ocrey
Carolyn Williams
Ella Walker
Lue Swarz
Josephine Turner
Beatrice Tate

Hattie Gilliam
Vivian Hayes
Jeanette Irving
Mary Newman
Edith Johnson Procope
Inez Pegues
Elsie Gearin

Present Officers
Lue Swarz, Basileus
Hattie Gilliam, Anti-Basileus
Bernice Bolar, Grammateus
Juanita Ocrey, Anti-Grammateus
Lucille Ogden, Tamiouchos
Beatrice Cooper, Jerveler
Audrey Anthony, Parliamentarian

1936

THE BLUE BOOK

Justine Townes

Soror Josephine Muse received her M. A. at Oberlin; Sorors Mary Reid and Grace Collins received their Masters degrees at Columbia University. Soror Mary M. Jones has been made president of the Washington Local Teachers Union.

Beta Zeta was active in a movement condemning discrimination in stores owned by Jews in Washington and succeeded in having practices inimical to the group discontinued.

One of the outstanding achievements of the year was the giving of a $200 scholarship to a student at Lincoln University, Wilie C. Davis who promises a brilliant future.

Xi Zeta Chapter, St. Louis, Missouri, was organized December 5, 1935 by the national organizer Sadye L. Dunham, at Poro building. This Chapter is exceedingly fortunate in having as it members women who are very efficient in their vocations. We have teachers in the public and vocational schools, dramatic artists, musicians, writers, etc. On February 5, 1936 eleven girls were pledged. During Finer Womanhood Week Zi Zeta gained much publicity with its programs and especially the Dramatic Recital. The artist for this memorable occasion was none other than our national organizer—Sadye L. Dunham. This program was counted as most unusual and the best program of its kind given this year. Following the recital a "Supper with Greek Friends" was given. Representatives from all the sororities in the city were present. Soror Dunham as always acquitted herself most creditably and was graciously acclaimed by the St. Louis guests of Zeta.

Xi Zeta Chapter was formally presented to St. Louis at a dance given by the Phi Beta Sigma Fraternity.

Xi Zeta is working hard trying to increase its membership to fifty, and also to make St. Louis Zeta-conscious. Under the capable leadership of its Basileus, the Chapter has tried earnestly to carry out all the requirements in both national and local call. Xi Zeta has as

1936

THE BLUE BOOK

its Basileus an artist and personality in Lue Swarz whose dramatic interpretations are outstanding.

Xi Zeta was hostess to the West Central Regional in June and it was hard to convince the delegates that they were not attending a Boulé. Two days of intensive work interspersed with dances, teas, cocktail hours, and pression of Xi Zeta's hospitality that will not soon fade even though the hand-carved wooden brooches bearing the words "St. Louis Regional" will have gone the way of all brooches.

1936

THE ARCHON

ZETA'S FINER WOMANHOOD

By Iris Holden

The Zeta Phi Beta Sorority in its many chapters throughout the country are at this time observing Finer Womanhood. The term Finer Womanhood is such a comprehensive one and bears elaborate possibilities for its achievement.

A man builds a house but he calls upon a woman to turn the house into home. It is she who softens the harsh surroundings and brings sunshine into the darkest corners.

Present day woman has been granted many privileges that were denied the generations of women that preceded her. Today she can enter the portals of the greatest institutions of higher learning, there to compete on equal footing with her brother. The beginning of the 20th century found woman unable to take part in the legislation of our great country, but today, only 20 years after, she has been granted her franchise, she has become a most powerful factor in state life. This position now held by the fair sex was achieved through years of persistent fight when naught but failure could be gleaned on the horizon.

Over twenty-three hundred years ago Euripides declared, "A woman should be good for everything at home but for nothing away from it." Men, as a whole, have been reluctant to abandon this point of view. The average man thought that if women were granted a voice in the conduct of the nation they would decide the fitness of political candidates in Shakespearean fashion.

"I have no other but a woman's reason; I think him so because I think him so."

Among the many women who have distinguished themselves are Mrs. Ferguson, ex-governor of Texas; Mrs. Frances Perkins, Secretary of Labor in President Roosevelt's Cabinet; Alice Roosevelt Longworth, congresswoman; Anna Moskowitz Kross, Justice Supreme Court, and in New York City a young woman of color, Eunice Hutton Carter, assistant district attorney.

There are not many men who would willingly agree with Shakespeare, for in the short period that woman has enjoyed her civil rights she has proven herself a most rational individual. In public office she has set a new record for fearless, clean government in executive, judicial and legislative bodies.

Members of our race have a particularly difficult road. Economic conditions set up almost unconquerable obstacles. Racial prejudice and intolerance often raise their ugly heads to make an already heavy load greater. But to the woman of fine calibre these are accepted as mere hurdles in a race which she must win. She is ever mindful of the responsibility that rests upon her shoulder. She must take advantage of

1939

THE ARCHON

every opportunity that presents itself, because success for her also means advancement for her people. It is to these women that the Zeta Phi Beta Sorority is devoted.

Women have long been educators. Did you not learn your first lessons at your mother's knee? It was she who impre3ssed upon your plastic mind your responsibilities to community, church and state.

Bettie V. Magill
Grammateus Pi Chapter, Tulsa, Oklahoma

The Dame Schools of the Colonial period organized by women represented an early step toward public education in America. They were often the only institutions of learning that the children of the colony could hope to attend. Still these women were not free to teach the pupils. They mastered two jobs at once. While tending their many household duties they found time to teach the three R's, probably from the only book available, the Bible. These are the contributions that have been made to American democracy by women who have stood the test of Fine Womanhood.

In New York City we are proud of Mrs. Eloise McDougall Ayer, who has distinguished herself as a great educator. At the present time she enjoys the honor of being the only Negro principal in our public school system. Those of you who have journeyed to the capital of our great country were probably curious enough to visit that great institution of learning and culture, Howard University. An able woman spent most of her best years at this institution, guiding and directing the thousands of young women with whom she came in contact. She fought always for the maintenance of a high standard of education. She was known throughout the country as Dean Slowe. Her outstanding ability as an educator caused her to be called to the rostrums of many of our great colleges and universities, among them Columbia University and Smith College. She has gone on, but her memory lingers on as light to brighten the pathway of those who would follow in her footsteps.

Our sorority boasts of many women who have carried the torch in the field of education, among them, Mrs. Mary H. Plummer, principal of a junior high school in Washington,

1939

THE ARCHON

D. C.; Johanna Huston, for many years assistant dean of women at Howard University; Dorothy Teasdale Payne, supervisor of music in the public schools of New York City, and many others that time will not permit to mention. These women were fired with the desire to achieve and so they worked untiringly to attain their goods.

Mrs. Mary McCleod Bethune, another educator, has distinguished herself nationally by lifting her voice to demand an equal right for the young American Negro student. Today, as a member of President Roosevelt's National Youth Administration, she has aided indirectly thousands of students in the completion of their education. It takes a fearless woman of vision to do the job that she is mastering.

One does not have to turn the page of history to discover these women. We read about them daily. You observe such a figure in Mme. Chang Kai Chek of China and Mrs. Sarah Delano Roosevelt, mother of our President.

Woman Must Adapt Herself

If you have ever delved into the biographies of the great men who have served their fellow men and sacrificed their lives to the betterment of mankind, you have often found somewhere in the background a devoted mother or probably a wife who encouraged and inspired them to greater heights. It is this virtue of woman so understanding, so full of sacrifice, that makes her a priceless jewel.

A group of Washington Zetas

Left to Right, front row:
Sorors Jean Dent and Faustina Brown.
Back row: Sorors Geraldine Elliott,
Rosalie Reid and Antiionette Bowler.

1939

THE ARCHON

During these trying days of economic stress and turmoil, women have been called upon to bridge the gap, and they have rallied to the cause with a zest that has amazed their fellowmen. Effective agitation on the part of women has led to legislation reducing the working hours, controlling child labor, and making the factory or mill a sanitary place in which to work. These improvements spell more employment for able bodied men.

Women have become famous for their organizations which crusade against crime. Such a body as the Woman's Christian Temperance Union, the world's largest organization formed exclusively of women, has done much for social reform. Largely through the agency of this society, many states established laws which placed in the curriculum of the public schools the study of the effects of the use of narcotics and stimulants. It has secured police matrons, industrial homes and houses of refuge for girls and women. The passage of many laws for the protection of these women can be traced to the work of this organization.

Throughout the United States women have organized for the sole purpose of aiding widows and orphans, building libraries and better school houses. For women realize that the children of today are the citizens of tomorrow.

While Negroes were bound by the shackles of slavery, our women were crying out for freedom, with a voice that quickened the hearts of their oppressors. It was Sojourner Truth, slave girl, who saw the vision of the Negro freed of his bonds, and petitioned to God for his deliverance. Dauntless, self asserting, having the courage of her convictions, she sought freedom for her fellowmen.

The Jews were sore and oppressed by the Israelites and God sent Moses to lead his people into the Promised Land, but Harriet Tubman led the Negro slaves to freedom. Through her so-called underground railroad, she gave new hope to beaten, persecuted slaves who were condemned to a life of bondage.

Soror Marjorie Hunt Sills, loved for her charm and personality, serves as assistant secretary to the president of Shaw University. Among her many activities, she writes poetry as a hobby, much of which has been published in the leading newspapers, white as well as colored. One of her poems, "Your Friend," was read over the "Moon River" program.

1939

THE ARCHON

Someday she hopes to publish these poems. Soror Sills is active in other civic and social organizations among the younger group of Raleigh, besides Zeta, where she serves as Omicron Zeta's Epistoleus.

The Negro woman has not permitted her Caucasian sister to crowd her from the horizon. She, too, has ventured into the fields hitherto held sacred to men. Throughout the country women are entering the various professions. In New York City we have outstanding Negro physicians, among them Doctors Mae Chinn, Vera Joseph, Muriel Pettioni, Hyacinth Davis and Myra Logan. Dentistry, too, has claimed many brilliant women, namely Doctors Bessye Delaney and Stephanie Davis.

The fine arts have not been neglected; our women are making a place for themselves in the various fields of art, music and drama. Such names as Augusta Savage, sculptress; Marian Anderson, Katterina Jarbora, Mme. Lillian Evanti and Mercedes Gilbert have made history for our race.

Last but not least of the finer women is the mother. Words can not color her deeds for her sacrifices have already covered her in glory. The rapid progress made by the Negro since his emancipation can be heaped in a great part at the door of his mother. She has been the impetus for this onward march. Our ministers, doctors, lawyers, educators, engineers and college presidents, have achieved because they were inspired by their mothers. These women were often unlettered and ignorant, but they knew no end to sacrifice.

The life and letters of Paul Lawrence Dunbar tell of the encouraging words that his mother would write to him. During his long period of illness her words of cheer urged him on to pen the words that today stand as a monument to his name and race.

Women are constantly contributing to this vast drama called life. Their deeds are many; their achievements a thousand fold.

Soror E. M. Van Dyke, the head of the Business Department of the College, is the sponsor of Nu Alpha Chapter. She is also a charter member of the chapter, and is to a very great extent responsible for their success thus far.

1939

THE ARCHON

SATISFACTION

I've had joys looked for in life
Between the days of war and strife;
I've lived well, laughed often, too,
Learned much and loved you;
I've respected intelligent men
And kind to little children been,
Accomplished many a fruitful task,
Given to the world as well as asked.

Cherished through song and poems sweet
Despondent souls I've chanced to meet,
Seen the beauty displayed on earth,
Praises in prayer and song—gave birth;
I've looked for the good in every man,
Gladly extending a welcome hand.
My wish—my life be an inspiration new;
Respect for what I say and do.

—Marjorie Hunt Sills

ZETA'S FINER WOMANHOOD

Zipporah Taylor, Nu Chapter, Richmond, Va. Formerly principal of Second Union School; recently elected to Richmond Public Schools.

Soror Rosa Lee Stewart, Grammateus of Nu Alpha Chapter. She is a Junior and formerly attended Prairie View College, where she was an honor student.

Soror Margaret T. Shelton, Pi Chapter. Assistant principal of Wheatley High School, Boynton, Oklahoma. (Soror Margaret T. Shelton Anderson, mother of soror Marjay D. Anderson.)

1939

THE ARCHON

RE-PLEDGE CEREMONY TEA
FINER WOMANHOOD WEEK, FEBRUARY 1939

Sorors of Epsilon Zeta Chapter of Zeta Phi Beta—it would seem that this re-pledge service, coming at the time of the observance of Finer Womanhood Week, should be of especial significance to us; that it should serve to enlarge our vision and make us keenly aware of our stewardship. I think it is fitting that we should at this time ask ourselves just what we are doing to foster and develop finer womanhood and what is its true significance.

It is heartening to see that we have paused and taken stock of ourselves and the oneness of our purpose and realize that we of large opportunities and advantages—by these very reasons—are charged with a definite and distinct obligation to our community, our fellows, our sorority and ourselves to join hands with the forces of advancement for the best development of all, to the end, that as a chapter and as an individual we see to it that we do the very best that we can do—forgetting all strife and putting away all pettiness—fully realizing that we are a part of the whole and that Zeta has a right to expect—through this fine fellowship and spirit that we are doing—the best that we can do.

The story of a King and his Garden brings home to me the finest illustration of this great truth:

It is said that in the olden times there was a king, who in a nearby village to his kingdom, had the most beautiful flower garden throughout the land which was the pride of his heart an in which every specie of flower was grown.

It was his custom to pay an annual visit to this village in order to view and browse around in this garden, which was the delight of his heart. Upon one of these annual visit, it was nightfall when he reached the village, since the mode of travel then was by horseback., so he retired early so as to be fresh and certain to arise early the next morn; he scarcely slept at all that night because of his joyous anticipation, and at the very first peak of dawn he arose hurriedly, performed his toilet, and rushed out to view his garden. As he swung wide the gates, stepped inside and beheld what was in his view, his heart sank within him and tears streamed down his face—for everything in it had died—even the grass underfoot had withered.

As he sorrowfully wandered over the garden, he walked over to what had once been a beautiful rosebush and said, "O beautiful roses that once were, how does it happen that you died?" The rose said, "My leaves were not waxen like those of the lily, my fragrance was not like that of the peonies, and I didn't think it made any difference, so I just died." Then he

1939

THE ARCHON

wandered over to what had once been beautiful peonies and said, "O beautiful peonies that once were, how does it happen that you died?" And the peonies answered, "My colors were not like those of the roses, my fragrance was not like that of the roses, my petals were not shaped like those of the roses, and I didn't think it made any difference, so I just died." He then walked over to what had once been beautiful lilies and said, "O beautiful lilies that once were, how does it happen that you died?" And the lilies said, "My fragrance was not like that of the roses, my leaves were not like those of the peonies and I didn't think it made any difference and so I just died." He then walked up to what had once been a graceful pine tree and said, "O pine tree, how does it happen that you died?" And the pine tree said, "I was not strong and sturdy like the oak tree and I didn't think it made any difference, so I just died." Then, utter despair, he slowly and sorrowfully walked over to what had been a sturdy oak tree and said, "O oak tree, how does it happen that you died?" And the oak tree said, "I was not tall and slender and graceful like the pine tree and I didn't think it made any difference, so I just died."

Slowly the king wandered over the garden, tears blinding his eyes, going over to each flower, and each gave the excuse that because it was not just like the other nor had the same color, nor gave off the same fragrance that it didn't think it made any difference as to whether or not it lived—when, suddenly, in a far-off corner, he found a little patch of violets blooming for all they were worth! He fell down upon his knees before them, this time tears of joy raining down his face, and cried out aloud, "O beautiful violets, how does it happen that when everything around you died—you lived!!" The violets said, "I knew that my leaves were not white and waxen like those of the lily; I knew that my fragrance was not like that of the peonies, I knew that my color was not like that of the roses, I knew that I was not strong and sturdy like the oak tree, I knew I was not tall and graceful like the pine tree— but I did know—that you wanted me to be the very best that I could be—and so I just lived!!"

And so, Sorors, I think it would be well that we keep in mind that we shall have to give an accounting of our stewardship and strive to do the "very best" and be the "very best that we can be."

Frances Lamor Blackshear,
Anti-Basileus,
Phi Zeta Chapter, New York City.

1939

THE ARCHON

THE CORRELATION OF OUR GOAL AND OUR LEADERS TO OUR FINER WOMEN

By Soror Velma C. Bunch

For nearly a quarter of a century there has been much development and growth of Zetahood into a potent organization of the finest there is of Greekdom. Onward and onward our sorors have been motivated by our goal and led by the far-sightedness of our leaders to do bigger and better things—to build finer Negro women.

It is the goal, "Finer Womanhood," that we are rushing ahead to reach. In every field there are our Zetas—playing the game—and, "it's not for the sake of the ribboned coat or the selfish hope of a season's fame"—but, it is because our leaders hands on our shoulders smote, and we hear them say, "Play us, play us, and play the game!" Through willingness to cooperate, consideration for others and desire to win—through these three laws of attaining the summit of one's hope—we achieve our mark admirably.

As Goethe thought,
"A good man does his honest share
In exercisi8ng with the strictest care
The art bequeathed to his possession,
Dost though thy father honor, as a youth?
Then may his teachings cheerfully impell thee.

Dost thou, as man, increase the stores of truth?
Then may thine own son afterwards excel thee."

Mrs. Bunch

1939

THE ARCHON

—so may it be with Zetas. Already over one hundred of our initiates have won enviable places in their fields and have gained recognition for ranking among the better women of this generation. There are those who have actually tackled with almost unsurmountable obstacles; yet, being alert, determined and committed to some cardinal principle, they represent the creditable number of our sorors included in today's "Who's Who."

Mingling with these inspiring leaders of the present, and being heir to a rich heritage of culture as left by such departed ones as Violette N. Anderson, Eliza A. Coppage, Edith D. Green, Zetas are bound to grow into finer women. We are following in their footsteps, absorbing the finer stuff that our pioneer women were made of an contributing to mankind those ideals that our predecessors would have us give—truth, beauty, service—or, in short—finer Womanhood.

Making This A Better Place In Which To Live

By Soror Sarah G. F. Holmes

Living is the essence of all life. Living together is a natural and necessary constituent of life. Living together in peace and harmony should be the supreme desire of all mankind.

When we hear talks of war all around us; when we see the hurt that human beings inflict upon each other, we can but marvel that the Infinite continues to bear with and strengthen us.

There must be some reason for this. It is the belief of the writer that each of us has a particular job to perform. It is true also that some of us do not perform our tasks, either because we are too lazy, or we have not found ourselves.

Whatever our job, it is the duty of each of us to do that thing well.

This is the age of opportunity. The world is ever eager to receive the individual who can do a thing superbly well.

Opportunity, however, is not something that we find standing with outstretched hands beckoning us. Yet opportunities are ever present. Every life is full of them, every lesson in school or college, every business transaction—an opportunity to be police, an opportunity to be manly, an opportunity to make friends, an opportunity to be honest. Make the most of each of these and help make your world a better place in which to live.

Pay attention to trifles, for trifles make perfection and perfection is no trifle.

Every day is a little life and all your life but a day repeated. Those that dare lose a day are dangerously prodigal; those that dare misspend it, desperate.

What is the happiness of your life made up of? Little courtesies, little kindnesses, pleasant words, genial smiles, a friendly letter, good wishes and good deeds. All trifles, but ho, how important in this world of ours.

1939

THE ARCHON

Do not struggle to do something great and wonderful, for you will miss the little happinesses, the sum of which would make your lives sublime.

Find yourself before it is too late. Live with and for others.

Ah, what a sad world this would be
If no one were here but you or me!
No one to see, no one to hear,
No one to talk to, no one to fear.
But what a happy world we hope to see,
Filled with people like you and me,
Working with a purpose, a love and a will,
Climbing the heights, however steep the hill.
This is the Zeta spirit kind and true,
Giving and loving as we work our way through,
Always remembering, no matter how heavy the load,
To build a Zeta house by the side of every road!

1939

THE ARCHON

THE CHALLENGE TO FINER WOMANHOOD

By Soror Ann G. Sasser
A. and I. State College, Nashville, Tenn.

The challenge facing Finer Womanhood today is to help Americans reconstruct their economic, their political and their personal lives on the basis of Christian principles.

The first requisite in reconstructing anything would be understanding of the construction and second an accurately or intelligently designed plan for the reconstruction. Let us consider for a few minutes some elements in the construction or structure of our economic life.

1. Labor is a basic element. It is up to Negro Women to broadcast information that if the millions of blacks who live in the South are supplied with purchasing power in the form of wages the South will become one of the most prosperous sections of the nation.

We should feel and execute our obligation to encourage workers to join unions. Two-thirds of Negroes in this mechanical age, where there are said to be 10,000 employable tasks, are segregated in two fields of endeavor, agriculture and domestic service. These two fields offer no protection to workers measured in terms of wage and hour security. Therefore, the Need of Extension of coverage of social security to agricultural and domestic workers is a challenge facing Negro Women.

Our first consideration in the whole matter of reconstruction was labor. That choice was made with purpose. Finer Womanhood—Negro Leadership indeed—so called prosperous people generally—tend to separate themselves—their plight from the masses. We must identify ourselves with the masses. Our plight is inextricably bound with theirs. We must start Economic Reconstruction at the bottom. We must listen to C. C. Spaulding when he says that the only two efforts that may be successfully started from the top are ditches and graves.

Dr. Griswold told a group of V. University Graduates, "One of the important things we may have learned during this war is that our fine doctrines of political freedom will be nearer realization when we understand that they have real meaning only to those who are in an economic position to act with the liberty such doctrines provide. It is the money in the consumer's hands that keeps the economic machinery going," Dr. Griswold asserted, "not the money at the top." This last comment brings up the important matter of Taxation. Are our numerous complaints about taxation sound? To what extent are present forms of Taxation methods of decentralizing and redistributing Wealth? I do not propose to be able to answer this question. I do know however, that the Question of Taxation should challenge Negro Women.

1939

THE ARCHON

Zeta Brides—Alpha Eta Zeta Chapter, Memphis, Tennessee

Seated at Piano, Bernice Roberts McClelland. Standing left to right, Sarah Reid Dixon, Mattie Brown Tyus, Bernice Eskridge Callaway, Beatrice Boyd Helm, Virginia Dortch Edwards, Helen Williams Waterford, Bertha Polk Ray. Not pictured, Maggie Donelson Jordon.

I can think of no challenge facing Negro Women greater than that of creating among Negroes an awareness of their collective economic strength. Negroes must learn to control and effectively wield their spending power to greater advantage. Out of two billions dollars spent annually by Negroes for food, clothing and shelter, government figures show Negro merchants have a turn over of not exceeding one hundred ten million. To mention collective economic strength naturally brings to attention cooperatives. The Cooperative Movement has not meant to Negroes what it should have. The Cooperative Movement constitutes a challenge to Negro Women and, if Negro women seriously set themselves to the task of undertaking any type of Cooperative Movement—they would succeed. For, as someone has observed, "I have yet to see a movement for the good of the community which women got behind that

1939

THE ARCHON

did not result in success." Great is the power of womanhood. We should put that power to good use.

Herbert Agar: "Behind the Negro Problem" there looms the vast problem of the colored races throughout the world—a problem which contain within itself—the problem of the survival of our democratic faith. In the light of Agar's unquestionable truth—how do you feel when you hear the following accusation by Earnest E. Johnson, Chief of Washington Bureau of Associated Negro Press, "There is today no understanding between Ethiopia, Liberia, Haiti and American Negro Leadership." (Of course Agar was thinking of all dark people.)

Do you know that there are many more dark people in the world than there are white people? To teach Negroes to see their own political interest bound up with those of the dark peoples of the world is a challenge facing Negro Women.

Now we come to the Reconstruction of Personal Lives on a Basis of Christian Principles. "The crisis in which modern man finds himself is spiritual." It will be surmounted by reaffirmation of spiritual values. Civilization's sickness—referred to in introduction—is a spiritual sickness. We must be reminded that Christianity is socially relevant. We must get away from the type of Religion which promises a piece of pie up in the sky when you die by and by. Appeasement—smoothing over is not the teaching of Christianity. Christianity teaches Reconciliation.

The point is—if we are to reconstruct our personal lives on Christian principles, we cannot simply look on wrong and say, Oh that's too bad and let it go at that. A socially relevant religion demands that we join whatever group is fighting social and economic inequality, injustice in any form whether it is a church group, a union, a local chapter of NAACP or the Urban League or a political party. To any of these fighting groups, you or I should bring the effectiveness of one more voice, one more letter to state legislatures or congress or business groups, one more dollar bill and above all each individual must be convinced of the importance of his action.

Good Way of Life—Planned for—Not Drifted Into!

Some people seem to think that just being passively good will make the whole world better. They expect America to drift into some better state. Whatever our city, state or nation may be, or our international scene becomes—it will become that because of coordinated measures—because of some actively good or actively bad people's coordinated efforts.

To convince people that the Great Christian Religion is a basic necessity in our everyday living is a challenge facing Finer Womanhood.

1939

THE ARCHON

RELIGION:

Get Religion like a Methodist
Experience it like a Baptist
Be sure of it like a Lutheran
Conciliate it like a Congregationalist
Be proud of it like an Episcopalian
Simplify it like a Quaker
Glorify it like a Jew
Pay for it like a Presbyterian
Practice it like a Christian Scientist
Work at it like the Salvation Army
Propagate it like a Roman Catholic
Enjoy it like a Negro.

I don't know what the writer intends these lines to mean. One thing is certain—we have a larger number of different opinions on Religion than any other group. This story which I'm going to tell will indicate this fact: A little colored boy in the South was carrying a rabbit in a bag to a clergyman whose address he had in his pocket. Somehow the rabbit worked a hole in the bag, jumped out and ran. For a moment, the little lad stood confused, puzzled and then light seemed to dawn on his mind as he cried out in derision, "Run, you little rascal, but you ain't got the address!" Well, we dare not say or even think which of those many faiths have the right address; but we are sure that the one that can boast of the most socially relevant practices must be the one with the right address.

It is imperative that we reaffirm some definite belief in the principles of Christianity. We must regard respect for others and practice respect for others as a basic principle of Christianity. "Be noble," wrote Lowell, "and the nobleness that lies in other men, sleeping but never dead, will rise in majesty to meet thine own." Everyone is sure that many white people do not respect others (especially Negroes) and every person very likely would hate to admit that some Negroes have not learned to respect others.

If we would reconstruct our personal lives on Christian principles we must preach and practice the strategy of Good Manners.

In the January issue of the Negro Digest, Oswald Garrison Villard discussed the importance of the strategy of Good Manners for Negroes. (I eagerly commend the article for your reading.)

Speaking about the many instances of bad manners of Negroes on buses and trains etc., he says—"It may be alleged that these are trifling incidents. On the contrary they are of vital importance for the incidents are told and retold fifty times and perhaps steadily exaggerated. The unfortunate but stubborn fact is that when a Negro is ill-mannered, his enemies spread the untruth that all Negroes are ill-mannered. We resent this, of course. Our resentment does not change the ugly untruth. Hence this challenge to Finer Women: To incessantly preach to young and old alike that reprisals don't pay, that personal aggressiveness and bad manners are certain to do more harm to Negroes than anything else except outright crime. William Hard mentioned Science, master of matter, that will not only forever devise new methods of hurling matter against the enemy, but also new methods of repelling

1939

THE ARCHON

those hurlings. To bring these hurlings and counter hurlings to an end is not the function of scientific man who seeks only to release the power of the physical world; it is the function of moral man, who to his own uneasiness, hears himself eternally bidden by something above himself—to strive to release the power of the world of the spirit—the power of truth and justice.

All of that can be summed up in these words: The Defensive Weapon against the Atomic Bomb is the reconstruction of our personal lives on the basis of Christian principles.

It is a row of empty houses that gets its windows broken. Empty heads, empty hearts and idle hands are sure to come to grief. Zetas be wise!

ALWAYS A WAY TO ZETA

There is always a way to rise, my pledge,
Always a way to advance,
But the road that leaders to FINER WOMANHOOD
Does not pass by the way of chance;
It goes through the stations of Work and Strife,
Through the valley of Persevere,
And the one who succeeds while others fail,
Must be willing to pay most dear.
But there is always a way to fail, my pledge,
Always a way to slide,
And the ones you find at the foot of the hill
All sought an easy ride.
So on and up, though the world be rough,
And the storms come thick and fast;
There is room at the top for the pledge who tries,
And victory comes at last.

By: Mildred Bowers, Archonian
Gamma Beta Chapter of Zeta Phi Beta

1939

THE ARCHON

SERVICE THROUGH FINER WOMANHOOD

Delivered by Soror Augusta White, Alpha Alpha Zeta Chapter, Z O B, Salisbury, N. C.

In considering the celebration of Finer Womanhood week, many thoughts arise as to the position and achievement of woman. Although at one time she was considered the inferior sex, she has definitely proved herself worthy and capable of performing the tasks which have become hers. While less restricted in her religions than in her social contracts, her position has changed from that of a menial worker in the fields and in the home to one of responsibility in civic, religious, educational and industrial life. Even in the present age of progress and knowledge, the battle for equal rights, especially for women of our race, is not yet won.

With the dawn of a new age, the Negro woman has seized happily the opportunities of education and work. Since the late nineteenth century, schools of nursing, education, and the like, have opened their doors and through them have passed hundreds of young negro women who have become the leaders of their communities. With the courageous example of women like Sojourner Truth and Harriet Tubman, pioneer leaders of an enslaved people who exemplified great service through finer womanhood, the women of our race have overcome innumerable obstacles and marched bravely on their road to freedom.

The Twentieth Century era—the period of the worst world conflict in history—offers no less aspiring an array of leaders in both races. Such women as Judge Mary Bolin, Labor Secretary Frances Perkins, Editor Minnie Singleton of the Macon Telegraph, Lucy Laney, prominent educator in Georgia, Mary McCleod Bethune, Charlotte Hawkins Brown and others serve as examples of women leaders.

In keeping with the ideals of rendering service through finer womanhood, true Zetas will never be sorry:

For living a pure life;
For doing their level best,
For being kind to the poor,
For looking before speaking;
For harboring clean thoughts;
For being generous to an enemy;
For stopping their ear to gossip;
For asking pardon when in error;
For giving an unfortunate person a lift;
For promptness in keeping their promises;
For rendering true service and leading some soul to Christ.

Service through Finer Womanhood implies direct application of virtuous traits—service through Finer Womanhood exemplies true traits of character. Too numerous to mention are the women who have succeeded in life because of respect for self and others, because of perseverance, tolerance, humility, courage,

JULY 1946

THE ARCHON

truthfulness, kindness, courtesy, honesty, good-will and love. Who can deny the words of the immortal Sage—Solomon? Who can deny that a "good name is rather to be chosen than great riches?" He wisely declares that the price of a virtuous woman is far above rubies.

If you can hear the whispering about and never yield to deal in whis-
    pers too!
If you can bravely smile when loved ones doubt you, and never doubt
    in turn what loved ones do.
If you can keep a sweet and gentle spirit in spite of fame or fortune,
    rank or place,
And though you win your goal, or only near it
You can win with poise or lose with equal grace.
If you can meet with unbelief, believing and hallow in your heart a
    simple creed,
If you can meet deception, undeceiving, and learn to look to God for
    all your need;
If you could be what girls should be to mothers, chums in rags and
    comrades in distress,
And be unto others as you'd have them be unto you—no more and
    yet no less.
If you can keep within your heart the power to say that firm uncon-
    querable "No"
If you can have a present shadowed hour, rather than yield to build a
    future—
If you can love yet loving master and keep yourself within your own
    self's clasp;
And not let dreaming lead you to disaster nor pity's fascination loose
    your grasp.
If you can lock your heart or confidences,
Nor ever needlessly in turn confide,
If you can put behind you all pretenses of mock humility or foolish
    pride;
If you can keep the simple, homely virtue of walking right with God,
Then have no fear that anything in all the world can hurt you,
And—what is more you'll be a woman, dear.

JULY 1946

THE ARCHON

FINER WOMANHOOD AND SERVICE

By Helena Armistead Scott

The Zeta Phi Beta Sorority fosters two of the highest types of ideals — Finer womanhood and Service.

We owe all of the appreciation and gratitude that our hearts can summon to the founders of this organization; those five young women, who on the campus of Howard University, in 1920, conceived these lofty ideals. They saw the many changes going on in their mode of life and religion; and foresaw the place the nobler woman would have to hold to balance the uncertainty and ever changing conditions of the world. They knew that no nation could rise above the status of its womanhood. They, like Crawley, knew that, the hand that rocks the cradle rules the world For it is the woman who trains the new generation and molds its destiny.

We look about ourselves, the many changes we see puzzle us. What seems to be a new age keeps us wondering what to do to keep in line with the progress of our time. The world is changing so rapidly that we can hardly keep grasp on it. What constitutes the right development of the Negro woman in this age of the world? What part has she to play in the world in the future?

The answer comes by adhering to the principles of Finer Womanhood. Times and seasons may change; but the axiom of growth and development are the same in all ages. A man may plant corn with a machine instead of by hand but the law of its development from the kernel to the stalk is the same. A woman's sphere may seem different from the sphere in which her grandmother lied, but it is essentially the same. So no matter how the women of our race may expand their activities, in education, in business, in professions, in politics, all of these activities should rest o f the basis of maternal instinct. Indeed, it is not necessary that a woman should have children of her own, to be an intelligent mother of her race.

The two greatest factors necessary to give the Negro woman her rightful place are: First, the development of her intellectual powers through education. Second, the development of her spiritual nature by holding before her the high aim of her existence; that of sponsoring a better race.

The members of this sorority, throughout this land, at this very time are banded together, concerting every effort to establish what we proclaim to be the essence of our civilization, Finer Negro Womanhood. Now, we are only at our best when we are engaged in a task immortal and divine. Such a task is nothing more than some bit of service we may render some fellow being. But few of us have yet grasped the deep significance of the blessed

JULY 1946

THE ARCHON

utterance of the Prince of Peace, who said, "He that would be great among you, let him be servant." Then, too, the finest things are begun in humility, and expressed in service. Service is the most natural expression of the unselfish soul. It is the sweat that drops from the brow of one who strives to serve his fellowman. It is the act of causing your heart to beat and your life to live again in the breasts of others.

The woman who is ever thinking and striving to do what she feels best for those around her, will influence those, and they, in turn, will inevitably influence others. She realizes that she journeys this way but once, and tries to crowd into her life as much good as possible. Her soul echoes the thought the poet immortalizes with his words:

I want to give good measure running o'er,
And into angry hearts I want to pour
The answer soft that turneth wrath away,
I'm sure I shall not pass again this way.

Let us aim to achieve these things through the right moulding of each new generation as it appears. So, my dear sorors, let us pray, that the things we leave undone, which will be carried on by our sisters yet to come.

For to her who lives, prays, and is so imbued with the qualities that make the nobler woman; so that those around her desire to emulate her, we say, she has wrought magnificently well!

JULY 1946

THE ARCHON

THEME FOR 1946

SERVICE THROUGH FINER WOMANHOOD

Serving
  Energizing
    Reviving
      Vitalizing
        Inspiring
          Constructing
            Emphasizing

ZETA

Tactful
  Honest
    Reliable
      Obedient
        United
          Gracious
            Hopeful

WOMEN

Firmly
  Industriously
    Nobly
      Enthusiastically
        Religiously

SERVE

Wounded
  Oppressed
    Misguided
      Anxious
        Needy
          Humiliated
            Obstructed
              Outraged
                Doubting

HUMANITY

JULY 1946

THE ARCHON

ALPHA PI ZETA HONORS 'WOMAN OF YEAR', 'ZETA'

San Antonio, Texas—Alpha Pi Zeta Chapter, culminated Finer Womanhood Week observance in a proverbial-blaze of glory! . . . when two outstanding women were honored at a tea given in the East Wing of the Municipal Auditorium on Sunday, March 10, from 4 to 76 P.M.

More than a thousand guests turned out to honor Mrs. C. Austin Whittier, 1956 "Woman of the Year"; and Soror Velma S. Butler, 1956 "Zeta of the Year". The two deserving women were selected for honors by Alpha Pi Zeta chapter because of outstanding contributions made by them to the civic and social growth and development of the community.

Mrs. Whittier organized the Alamo Cancer Aid Society in 1953, an auxiliary to the Alamo-Bexar Cancer Aid Society. She has steered its operation since that time and at present is serving as its president. The needs of many cancer patients are met through this organization.

Mrs. Whittier is identified with religious, social, and local and state civic organizations. She worked with the Women's Progressive club in operating the Ella Austin Children's Home; promoted the idea of giving Yuletide cheer to needed children while serving as chairman of the health education committee of the Pine Street Branch YWCA; served as president of the Alamo Medical Society and as secretary of the Lone Star State Medical Society. She is the wife of a local physician and surgeon, Dr. C. A. Whittier.

Soror Velma S. Butler was signaled for honor for her outstanding contribution to Alpha Pi Zeta chapter and to Zeta Phi Beta Sorority. It was under her leadership, immediate past basileus of the chapter, that San Antonio was given its first undergraduate chapter of Greek organizations among us, Delta chapter of Zeta Phi Beta Sorority. She is now serving as direct sponsor of the new chapter.

Soror Butler is identified with religious activities and many social, civic and professional organizations. At present she is National Associate Director and Regional Director of Amicae Affairs. She is vice president of Alamo-Bexar County Teachers' Credit Union. She is a teacher of exceptional children in the Japhet Opportunity School of the local school system. She is the wife of a local businessman, Mr. Payton Butler.

Guests were received by members of the sorority and registered by Sorors Mayme Cabiness and Myrtle Williams. In the formal receiving line were: Soror Velma L. Blair, basileus of Alpha Pi Zeta chapter; Mrs. Whittier, an honoree; Mesdames Mildred Stevens and

APRIL 1957

THE ARCHON

Mattie Landry, 1955 women of the Year; Soror Velma S. Butler, one of the honorees; and Soror Mable Booker, anti-basileus of Alpha Pi Zeta chapter.

Mistress of ceremonies for the delightful occasion was Soror Mavis Whitson, grammateus of the chapter. Incidental music was afforded throughout by Sorors Anna Jo Walker, Jewel Haynes, of Corpus Christi, Texas; Violet Cook, Miss Mary Rutledge, Miss Bertha Wilson, Mr. Bryant Walker and the Royal Knights Male Chorus.

Highlights of the afternoon were the presentation of the Woman of the Year, Mrs. Whittier, which was made by Basileus Blair, while Mrs. Stevens placed on her the pin of award; and the presentation of the Zeta of the Year, Soror Butler, which was made by Anti-Basileus Booker, while Mrs. Landry placed on her the pin of award. Adding a touch of congeniality and charm to the occasion was the recognition of former honorees as Women of the Year since 1947. The immediate past Women of the Year who placed the pins of award on the honorees made congratulatory remarks to this year's recipients. Both honorees made gracious responses.

Throughout the afternoon and evening cake, coffee and tea were served the guests by members of the sorority presiding over the beautifully arranged table which carried out the sorority colors of blue and white. Punch was served from another table with similar décor.

Zeta sorors serving in the many capacities extending every guest hospitality throughout the reception were: Sorors Lela Watson, Vera Thomas, Catherine Huff, Lucille Boyd, Hazel Hayes, Ouida Merchant, Helen Bradley, Myrtle Fields, L. B. Stevens, Ursiline Allen, Dorothy Miller, Narva L. Jefferson, Violet Cook, Vera Parker, Bettye Hurd, Margaret Johnson, C. M. Rutledge and Lenora McGee.

Friends of Zeta assisting in serving the guests were: Mesdames L. Calhoun, L. Smith, E. Murray and G. Robinson.

The honorees received many, many telegrams, flowers and orchid corsages from friends and relatives, far and near, which made the place a picturesque setting. Soror Butler was presented an orchid corsage by Soror Booker from her husband, Mr. Payton Butler; and a basket of Bird of Paradise flowers from her relatives in California. Mrs. Whittier was presented a basket of rich-red roses by Mrs. Scott Foley from her sister, Mrs. H. B. Pemberton, Jr., Dallas, Texas; Dr. and Mrs. Clay Jones, Chicago, Illinois.

Highlights of the affair were televised on KENS-TV, Channel 5, the same night at 10:30. The program was recorded by the KCOR Radio broadcasting station and was rebroadcast the following Monday night, March 11th, at 10:30.

During Finer Womanhood Week Zeta sorors and friends worshiped in a group on Sunday, February 24th, at Bethel A. M. E. Church, Rev. J. F. Baker, pastor.

An impressive pledge renewal service was held in the beautiful and spacious home of Soror L. B. McIntyre, 515 Hays Street, with

APRIL 1957

THE ARCHON

Sorors Lucille Lamkin, L. B. Stevens and McIntyre hostesses. The table for the pledge service was laid with white Bibles and individual candles embedded with a white rosebud by Soror Lamkin. A delicious repast was served.

Chairman of Finer Womanhood Week activities was Soror Mavis Whitson with Soror Vera Parker, co-chairman. Others serving on the committee were: Sorors L. B. McIntyre, Dorothy Collins and L. B. Stevens.

The sorority expresses its appreciation to those who came from out of the city and joined in to make this year's tea a tremendous success.

Alpha Pi Zeta chapter, San Antonio, Texas, honored Mrs. C. Austin Whittier, left, as 1956 "Woman of the Year," and Soror Velma S. Butler, as 1956 "Zeta of the Year".

2 HONORED BY WASHINGTON ZETAS IN ANNUAL OBSERVANCE

Washington D. C.—The 36th annual observance of Finer Womanhood Week began with the Sorority members attending the religious service at the Rankin Memorial Chapel, February 24, 15 11 A. M., and was followed on March 2, by the Ninth Annual Youth Conference at the Engineering Building, Howard University, the theme of which was: "Good Citizenship—Our Responsibility to America." The conference included a panel discussion of the topic: "Gateways to Opportunity", led by Mr. Charles Carter, principal of Ambush-Bowen School, and was followed by group conferences during the morning session. The afternoon speaker was Mr. Carl L. Perian, research director, Senate Sub-Committee on Juvenile Delinquency.

On Saturday, March 2, at 8 P. M., the undergraduate chapters of Zeta had a "Round-up" at the Y.W.C.A. Annex in order to bring into active membership all delinquent Zetas.

The observance of Finer Womanhood culminated in a public meeting held in Baldwin Hall, Howard University, on Friday, March 8, at 8 P. M. At this meeting two honorees were named. Mrs. Agnes E. Meyer (wife of the chairman of the Washington Post, a leading D. C. newspaper) was named "Woman of the Year" for her contributions to civic, national,

APRIL 1957

THE ARCHON

and international affairs. Mrs. Josephine C. Smith was named "Zeta Woman of the Year" for outstanding service to Zeta. The theme for this year's observance was: Revealing the ideals of Finer Womanhood through the fine arts—music, dancing, and art.

Music was represented by piano solos by Miss Joan Carter of the Washington conservatory of Music and by Miss Margaret Williams of the Sorority; vocal solos by two prominent soloists, Mrs. Mildred Austin Smith and Miss Roberta Long, both Zetas; and chorus work by the Youth Choir of Mt. Carmel Baptist Church, Mr. Malcolm Taylor, director.

Three members of the Howard University Dance Group, Shirley Proctor, Norma Spriggs, and Barbara Insley, danced a number entitled "Impending".

Mrs. Lois Pierre-Noel of the Art Department of Howard University sent a representative from the department to discuss briefly "Art Today" along with one of her own pictures.

Epsilon Lambda Zeta Hears Dr. Maggie Browne Daniels

Prairie View, Texas—Epsilon Lambda Zeta chapter sponsored the morning worship for Prairie View A. & M. College on February 17 during Finer Womanhood Week. This service was observed in the auditorium gymnasium on Sunday at 11:00 A. M. with Dr. Maggie Browne Daniels, National First Anti-Basileus, guest speaker.

Dr. Daniels

Soror Daniels greatly inspired the audience as she delivered the impressive message, "A Call For Leadership," emphasizing each Greek's obligation, as well as responsibility, to fellow citizens in the community. She held the faculty and over 2,700 students' attention during the entire hour.

Mrs. C. L. Wilson was assisted in conducting this service by Mr. Don White, organist, and the college choir, singing the anthem, "O Praise Ye" (Tschaikowsky) with Dr. R. von Charlton, head of the school of music, director.

Immediately following the worship service the sorors retired to the Phillip home for rededication service to greater Zetadom. Soror Daniels presided over this pledge service.

A very delicious buffet luncheon was served to sorors and their special guests, Dr. Daniels and her husband; Dr. Anne Campbell, head of the English department at Prairie View. Soror Kirkwood presented a gift from the chapter to Soror Daniels.

While Dr. Daniels was guest of Epsilon Lambda Zeta chapter, a reception was given in the C. L. Wilson home honoring her as the Finer Woman of the week.

The faculty and employees of Prairie View and friends of nearby communities came by

THE ARCHON

to meet and greet Soror Daniels. Mrs. L. C. Phillip introduced a few persons, but placed much surprise on the presentation of Soror Daniels as she is very well known all over the United States. Mr. and Mrs. C. L. Wilson received the guests with Dr. Daniels. Brother Wilson is one of the oldest members of Phi Beta Sigma fraternity. Sorors Jewel Smith and Eunell Sadberry Martin presided over the coffee service and punch bowl respectively. Soror Jessie Kirkwood registered the guests.

Several messages of congratulations and best wishes were sent here for Soror Daniels, also a gift from Soror Kathryn Suell Gibson who is now on leave in graduate school at Columbia University, New York City. The Phi Beta Sigma fraternity brothers of the campus, sponsored Soror Daniels' motor trip from the Houston Airport to Prairie View.

GAMMA NU ZETA CHAPTER CELEBRATES FINER WOMANHOOD

Camden, N. J.—Soror Ida B. King was heard by a thrilled audience on Sunday, February 17, 1957, at the Kaighns Avenue Baptist Church in Camden, New Jersey.

Miss King's address, The Pursuit of Happiness, was most enlightening and will be long remembered by all who were fortunate enough to hear her.

Upon arriving at Philadelphia's International Airport, Soror King was met by a group of sorors, among whom were Sorors Sadie H. Fernanders, Basileus of Gamma Nu Zeta Chapter; Soror Alberta Meekins, public relations chairman, and Thomas Allison, who is president of the Sigma Rays, a group of high school youths, affiliated with the Zeta Lites.

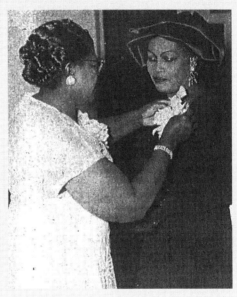

Soror Sadie H. Fernanders pins a corsage on Soror Ida B. King at Gamma Nu Zeta's Finer Womanhood Tea, at which she was guest speaker. Soror Fernanders is basileus of Gamma Nu Zeta chapter.

In the evening, Soror Fernanders held "Open House" at her home in honor of Soror King.

Among organizations attending the "Open House" were Delta Sigma Theta Sorority, The National Sorority of Phi Delta Kappa, Business and Professional Women's Club of Camden

APRIL 1957

THE ARCHON

and Vicinity, New Jersey Organization of Teachers, N.A.A.C.P. and O.E.S.

The Woman of the Year was presented during this Finer Womanhood program.

Mrs. Mary Smith of Lawnside, (a suburb of Camden City), was honored at a Finer Womanhood Tea on Sunday, February 17, 1957.

Presentation of an orchid and a Zeta Key were made to Mrs. Smith in recognition of her outstanding work in her community.

Among her many accomplishments are the founding and maintenance of a hospital and convalescent home, in which she cares for patients sent directly through the State Agency. She also cares for some patients absolutely free of compensation.

She established the Lawnside Parent Teacher Association.

Soror Helen L. Shockly was the chairman of this very outstanding event and she is also the Grammateus of the chapter.

Activities of the Zeta Lites and Sigma Rays

Among the many activities carried on by our teenage clubs was a visit to Radio City Music Hall, New York City. Sorors who chaperoned the trip were Soror Estella Hall, Soror Alberta Meekins and Soror Olive Brown, sponsor of the Zetalites.

Zeta Lites and Sigma Rays attended the Mitch Thomas Television Show in Wilmington, Delaware. The highlight of the program was the personal appearance of Steve Gibson and the Red Caps with Damita Jo.

The Basileus of the Philadelphia Sigmas, Brother Bryant Williams, was the guest speaker for Sigma Rays who honored their parents at a banquet. Among their platform guests were Soror Alberta Meekins, Soror Olive Brown, sponsor of the Zetalites, and Soror Sadie H. Fernanders, Basileus, Gamma Nu Zeta Chapter.

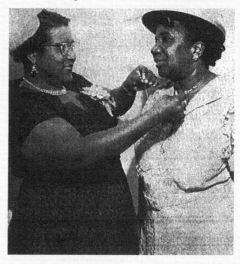

Soror Mary E. McPherson is shown here presenting the Zeta Key to Mrs. Mary Smith, Gamma Nu Zeta's "Woman of the Year."

APRIL 1957

THE ARCHON

PETERSBURG, VA. ZETAS PRESENT "WOMAN OF YEAR"

Petersburg, Va.—Alpha Omega Zeta Chapter in celebrating Finer Womanhood Week, worshipped at Zion Baptist Church in a group and presented Mrs. Leolia R. Valentine as "Woman of the Year." Mrs. Valentine is a retired school teacher, and is outstanding in religious and civic affairs n the City of Petersburg. She is also a member of Alpha Omega Zeta chapter of Zeta Phi Beta Sorority.

Members of the chapter are: Sorors Antoinette Boone Florence Branch, Jane Byrd, Deloris Churchill, Mae R. Delaney, Evelyn Duck, Mary P. Goode, Van Burean Hall, Mattie Izzard, Cornelia Jackson, Ethel B. Johnson, Grace C. Johnson, Gwendolyn B. Jones, Marie King, Geneva Myster, Mary W. Neugent, Marie Pegram, Pearl Perkins, Geraldine Spike, Emily Turner, Theophile Taylor, Leolia Valentine, and Marguerite M. Watson.

Soror Valentine, left, is shown receiving gift from Soror Marguerite M. Watson, basileus of Alpha Omega Zeta chapter.

APRIL 1957

THE ARCHON

*ALPHA *** KAPPA ALPHA *** BETA ZETA*
HOWARD ZETAS OBSERVE 40TH YEAR

FOUNDERS DAY

The history of Zeta Phi Beta Sorority was related in song and story at the 40th Founders' Day Celebration on Friday, January 22 at Baldwin Hall, Howard University.

Soror Josephine C. Smith, Eastern Regional Director and Supervisor in charge of Elementary D.C. Schools, presided.

After the welcome by Soror Gwendolyn Hall, Basileus of Kappa Alpha Chapter, there were greetings from the following: Phi Beta

Baldwin Hall at Howard University was the scene of the public meeting and reception which was sponsored as part of the Finer Womanhood observance by Beta Zeta, Alpha and Kappa Alpha Chapters. Sorors who took part in the program are shown at the speakers' table, left to right (seated): Soror Josephine C. Smith, Eastern Regional Director; Soror Mary R. Reid, Beta Zeta Chapter Basileus; Soror Anita Turpeau Anderson, who wrote the words to our National Hymn; and Soror Edith A. Lyons, Past Grand Basileus, Assistant Superintendent of Public Schools, District of Columbia.
   (Standing): Soror Susie E. Miles, National Tamias; Soror Audrey B. Robinson, composer of music of National Hymn; Soror Nona H. O'Neal, Alpha Chapter Basileus; Soror Georgie S. Johnson, Beta Zeta Chapter Founder; Soror Idella M. Costner, Beta Zeta Chapter Second Anti-Basileus; Soror JoAnna Toney, and Soror Patricia Simon.

MAY 1960

THE ARCHON

Sigma Fraternity by Mr. Clifton Felton, Alpha Chapter of Zeta Phi Beta by Soror Jeannette Burell, Zeta Amicae by Mrs. Streets, Sigma Shadows by Mrs. Felton and the Pan-Hellenic Council by Soror Fannie C. Offutt of Beta Zeta Chapter.

"Zeta Throughout the Years," written by Soror Jennie Gross was a narration of the history of the Sorority related in periods from 1920 to 1960. Throughout the narration there was skillfully interwoven a background of music which depicted the general character of the activities of the Sorority during that period. For instance, during the 20's, in which the Sorority was formed and began its growth, the theme which was used was sung to the tune of "O Solo Mio." After the period of the 30's, the depression days, when many o f the Zeta projects were initiated such Correction and Prevention of Juvenile Delinquency, Housing and so forth, came the song "We Were Sailing Along." At the end of the 40's, during which time many executive offices were created, the song was "Working Together" to the tune of "Oh, What a Beautiful Morning!" During the 50's, which was characterized by extensive growth, even to Africa, "Is It True What They Say About Zeta?" was sung.

Soror Jennie Gross was the narrator throughout and Miss Cozette Carter, in addition to accompanying each song also played beautiful and appropriate music between each period. Other music was furnished by Soror Margaret Williams, who played brilliantly "Barcarolle" by Liadov and by Soror Virginia Moore who sang very effectively "The Star."

Also included was the presentation of officers and guests by Soror Mary R. Reid, Basileus of Beta Zeta Chapter.

After the Sorority Song, The Rev. George A. Parker, who opened the program with the invocation closed it with the Benediction.

Soror Geneva C. Turner

FINER WOMANHOOD WEEK

Beta Zeta, Alpha, and Kappa Alpha Chapters held the Public Meeting and reception of their Finer Womanhood Week Program on Friday, February 26, in Baldwin Hall on the campus of Howard University. The theme for the program this year was "Preparedness: Key to the Doors of Opportunity." The guest speaker for the Public Meeting was Soror Anita Turpeau Anderson, educator, scholar and an eloquent speaker.

Music was furnished by the Roosevelt High School Choir, Soror Frances R. Hughes, Director. The program was under the chairmanship of Soror Idella M. Costner, Second anti-Basileus, Betz Zeta Chapter.

Prior to the Public Meeting all members attended the All Religious Service at Rankin Memorial Chapel, Howard University. This service was followed immediately by a Pledge Service.

The week ended with the Twelfth Annual Youth Conference which was held February 27 at Howard University under the chairmanship

MAY 1960

THE ARCHON

of Soror Hilda Alacorn, Principal, Garfield Elementary School. The theme for the conference was "Preparedness for the Soaring Sixties." The keynote address for the morning session was given by Dr. Halson V. Eagleson, Professor of Physics, Howard University. The leaders of the six group conferences which followed were: Mr. Floyd H. Agestinelli, Advisor, D.C. Commissioners' Youth Council; Mr. William F. Benedicy, Executive Director, Social Hygiene Society; The Rev. Joseph Haskins, Pastor, St. Marks Methodist Church; Mrs. Lorraine C. Knupp, Principal, Ruth K. Webb School; Mrs. Margaret Noble, Teacher of Science, D.C. Public Schools; and Mrs. Dovey J. Roundtree, Attorney at Law.

The luncheon speaker was the Rev. E. Franklin Jackson, Pastor, John Wesley A.M.E. Zion Church. All youth of the area were invited to attend.

Soror Geneva C. Turner

INKSTER, DETROIT ZETAS CELEBRATE 40TH YEAR

The beautiful Le Moyne Garden Community Center of Inkster, Michigan was full of warmth and the old Zeta Spirit when Zetas from Detroit met with the local Zetas to commemorate Founders' Day.

Soror Marie Clifton, Chairman of the Founders' Day Committee was capably assisted by the following Sorors: Glennie Cox, Mildred Mickles, Emma Sink and Maude Reid.

Soror Thelma Down, past National Trustee was in charge of the program which featured a history of the Sorority by Soror Mary Grey and a history of the local chapter by Soror Ione Gibson who was also performed in the role of a vocal soloist. Soror Gibson was accompanied by Soror Alberta Powell.

Soror Ethel Nelson, Basileus, made special presentations to past Basilei of the local chapter. Special honor was given to Soror Elizabeth Nelson who was recently listed in "Who's Who in American Education for 1959-60."

Soror Maude Reid received a lovely corsage for being the most recent Zeta to earn a Master of Arts Degree. A lovely corsage was presented, also, to soror Juanita Vaughn, the oldest Zeta present.

Greetings from the local Sigmas were extended by Elon Mickels.

White Carnations tied with blue satin accented the table where refreshments were served.

"Eyes on Africa," a symposium sponsored by Beta Iota Zeta, highlighted that chapter's Finer Womanhood observance. The meeting featured Dr. Babatunde A. Williams, Associate Professor of Political Science, Northern Illinois University; Miss Patricia Tucker, University of Chicago; and Miss Grace Alele, Professor of Mathematics, Queens College, Ede, Nigeria who is currently a Visiting Professor at the University of Vermont.

A public meeting, the symposium was held at the International House in Chicago, Illinois.

MAY 1960

THE ARCHON

ALPHA PI ZETA HONORS FIVE — FINER WOMANHOOD

Principals at five of the public schools in San Antonio, Texas, the honorees are: (left to right) Mrs. Bella H. Cameron, Mrs. Grace T. Luter, Mrs. Elizabeth T. Wrenn, Mrs. Balmer T. Oliver, and Mrs. Wilethel W. Brooks.

Alpha Pi Zeta Chapter, assisted by Delta Chapter, hosted their fortieth anniversary tea Sunday, March 20, in the student lounge of St. Phillip's College. The tea was a culmination of "Finer Womanhood Week" activities during which five women principals of San Antonio Public Schools were presented as "Women of the Year," coinciding with the five Pearls who organized the Sorority in 1920.

Honorees chosen for dynamic community leadership and service to children were

FIVE OUTSTANDING. Soror Velma S. Butler (right) and Mrs. C. Austin Whittier (left), honored at Alpha Pi Zeta Chapter during Finer Womanhood Week last year, were on hand to congratulate the San Antonio chapter's five "Women of the Year" who were named at the recent celebration of the annual event.

MAY 1960

THE ARCHON

Mesdames: Bella H. Cameron, Balmer T. Oliver, Grace T. Luter, Wilethel W. Brooks and Elizabeth T. Wrenn.

Guests were greeted and registered by the sorors and directed to the receiving line which included Alpha Phi Zeta's Basileus, Soror Lottie B. Stevens and past honorees Mrs. C. Austin Whittier, Woman of the Year, 1956 and Soror Velma S. Butler, Zeta of the Year, 1956 and this year's honorees.

Sorors dressed in the sorority colors, serving in various hostess capacities were: Sorors Viola Inman, Lucille Lamkin, Bennie Rutledge, Lizzie Randle, Katherine Huff, C. M. Bedford, Lina B. Carrington, Lelia Watson, Edna Hills, Mayme Cabiness, Patricia Rainey, Emma Broady, Goldie Hannah, Lena Katherine Jernigan, Tommie Mann, Dorothy Collins, Lenora Robinson, Gaynell Sapenter, Hazel Hays, Ouida Rainge, Erma Evans, Margaret Johnson, Louvonia Norwood, Myrtle Fields, Myrtle Nichols, and Dorothy Miller. Visiting sorors present were Sorors Allie F. Pitts and Alclair Pleasant of Corpus Christi.

Zeta color scheme was carried out in the table décor. Each table was covered with a beautiful embossed white linen cloth, with five blue streamers laid horizontally, and touching the floor, representing five founders. The five ribbons intersected a breathtaking "space" type arrangement of blue and white flowers in a tall crystal and silver bowl, carrying out the local theme of the special observance, "Women in Pace with Space." This arrangement was flanked by silver candelabra, holding white lighted tapers. One end of the table held the beautiful coffee and tea silver service and on the opposite end was a huge mounted, tiered white cake with "Zeta blue" spun sugar decorations.

THE ARCHON

Alpha Eta Zeta
Service, Fellowship Highlight
Finer Womanhood Week Activities

Alpha Eta Zeta Chapter observed Finer Womanhood Week with a variety of activities centered around the Boulé theme "Strengthening the Cultural, Civic, and Moral Values of Today's Youth" during the week of March 6 through 13. Soror Earline M. Somerville, General Chairman, and seven very capable sorors steered the week of worthwhile activities.

Sunday, March 6 at 6:00 P.M.—"News of the Week" over radio station WDIA—Soror Freida Marr, Chairman. All Chairmen were interviewed by Mr. N. D. Williams, well

AMICAE REMEMBRANCE — *Sorors surprised Amicae members during their meeting at the YWCA. Mrs. Annie Wiggins (center), president, and other officers seated. Also, Basileus Kateo, Amicae sponsor Somerville and Past Director of Amicae Affairs Callaway.*

MAY 1960

THE ARCHON

THEATRE PARTY—A group of forty top high school honor students and sorors pose in front of the new Daisy Theatre. They enjoyed "Porgy and Bess" and refreshments.

known disk jockey, and highlights of each day's activity were given. Special emphasis was placed on "The Holiday On Ice" presentation which benefits the charitable projects of the chapter.

Monday, March 7 at 4:00 P.M.—"Amicae and Remembrance to Friends." Cards were sent for all occasions. A group of sorors attended the Amicae Meeting where they were busy making plans for the South Central Regional Meeting, April 15-16. A social hour followed with refreshments served. Soror Earline Somerville, Amicae sponsor, was chairman.

Tuesday, March 8—"Toys for Africa"— Soror Larcenis Cain was chairman. Toys were collected from sorors to be sent to Africa. Alpha Eta Zeta was anxious to participate in this new project of service to youth.

Wednesday, March 9—"Theater Party" at New Daisy Theater—Soror Erma Clanton, chairman. Sorors and forty top Honor Society students of the eight high schools enjoyed "Porgy and Bess." Alpha Eta Zeta plans other activities to include youth groups of forty during this our Fortieth Anniversary Year.

Thursday, March 10—"Eyeglass Project Day"—Soror Hazel Pyles, chairman. Letters and financial reports of services rendered to children in the Memphis and Shelby County Schools were mailed to the schools. Nearly $1,000.00 expenses for eyeglasses and treatment has occurred for six months. The "Holiday On Ice" presentation benefits this project.

MAY 1960

THE ARCHON

FIRESIDE CHAT—Mr. Sam Rutherford, director of Children's Bureau, held the attention of the Colored Case Advisory Committee and Sorors at the residence of Soror Helen Waterford.

HOSPITAL VISIT—Sorors spread cheer during this hour of stories and games and delighted the children with gifts during their visit to the Crippled Children's Hospital.

Friday, March 11 at 8:00 P.M.—"Fireside Chat," Soror Bernice A. E. Calloway, chairman. Sorors and members of the Colored Case Advisory Committee of Children's Bureau, lead a discussion on needs of children in foster homes in the area. The Committee on the Prevention and Control of Juvenile Delinquency is interested in what the chapter can do. Much information was gained. A lovely tea table added to the fellowship.

Saturday, March 12 at 3:30 P.M.—"Las Cheerios" at Lamar Crippled Children's Hospital, Soror Manae Stanback, chairman. The little patients enjoyed story-telling, games and singing with Sorors Maggie Jordon, Leatha Haley, Hazel Pyles, Celia Chaplin, Sara Dixon, and Earline Somerville. A gift box of toys, crayons, and books delighted the little patients.

Sunday, March 13 at 8:P30 P.M.—"Holiday On Ice" at Ellis Auditorium — Sorors Carlotta Stewart Watson, chairman. The fourth annual presentations of his world-famous spectacle again brought a capacity audience of about 4,000. Memphis and the Tri-State area patrons of all ages have lauded the chapter for such a cultural and thrilling presentation, which benefits the Eyeglass Project and Scholarship Fund.

At the performance, a $500.00 check was accepted by Mr. Fred T. Gattas for St. Jude Hospital, a proposed interracial establishment for the treatment of children's diseases, especially leukemia. Danny Thomas, of CBS television, is spearheading this drive over the country.

MAY 1960

THE ARCHON

"HOLIDAY ON ICE" presentation — (left to right): Soror Carlotta Stewart Watson, General Chairman; Mr. Fred T. Gattas, who accepted the $500 check for St. Jude's Hospital; Soror Sara Lewis, "Princes of the Ice"; Soror Maggie D. Jordan, Pi Alpha sponsor; Soror Bernice Callaway, Publicity Chairman; and Soror Sara R. Dixon, Co-Chairman.

"PRINCESS OF THE ICE"—Soror Sara Lewis of Pi Alpha Chapter accepts flowers from "Holiday on Ice" stars Jinx Clark and Arnold Shoda.

Crippled children of Keel Avenue School were special guests of the chapter. Through cooperation with the Zuber-Bynum Council, tickets were purchased for all children in the Special Education classes of Memphis City Schools.

Lovely "Princess of Ice," Soror Sara Lewis, Anti-Basileus of Pi Alpha Chapter, was selected on the basis of an outstanding scholastic record at LeMoyne College. She has been chosen for mention in "Who's Who" among students in American Universities and Colleges, a Senior, and Vice-President of Alpha Kappa Mu Honor Society. She was presented flowers during intermission by the star of the show, Jinx Clark.

This busy week of activities commanded the attention of the public with emphasis on service to children and youth. Much recognition has come to the chapter because of its significant contributions to the community in this area. Under the competent leadership of Soror Loretta H. Kateo, Alpha Eta strives to further justify the recent commendation of being the outstanding chapter regionally and nationally.

MAY 1960

THE ARCHON

GENERAL COMMITTEE and ticket chairman pose in the lobby of Ellis Auditorium before the show. These are the hard working Zetas of Alpha Eta Zeta Chapter who find pleasure in successful community building endeavors.

MAY 1960

THE ARCHON

EASTERN REGION

BETA ZETA CHAPTER: WASHINGTON, D. C. 1981 FINER WOMANHOOD OBSERVANCE PUBLIC PROGRAM

The 1981 Finer Womanhood Public Program was held in March. Speaker for the occasion was the Hon. Dr. Charlene Drew Jarvis, Washington, D.C. City Council. Dr. Jarvis's address centered on the provision for handicapped persons made by the city of Washington, D.C. with respect to travel accommodations, use of public facilities, and proposed benefits.

The chapter's selection for the 1981 "Zeta of the Year" recipient was Soror Lucile W. Brown who was cited for outstanding public and private record of service to her profession, civic organizations, and Zeta Phi Beta Sorority, Inc. Soror Brown is the retired director of Food Services at Howard University. The Amicae of the Year was Friend Ruth P. Dial, president of the Washington, D.C. Zeta Amicae group. A special award was presented to Soror Dola A. Walker for her untiring efforts despite her physical handicap. The program centered on aspects drawn from the universal celebration of 1981 as the "International Year of Disabled Persons."

Other 1981 Finer Womanhood Observance activities included worship services at Rankin Chapel, Howard University and an inspirational rededication service during which Soror Thelma Fisher rendered thoughts on the meaning of service and sisterhood.

Soror Lynette F. Smith was chairman of the Finer Womanhood activities.

THE WASHINGTON D.C. STATE MEETING

On December 5, 1981, the components of the Washington, D.C. State were called together by the State Director, Soror Lynette F. Smith, for the second annual State Meeting. Delegates from the Zeta chapters— Beta Zeta graduate chapters; the Amicae, and the Archonettes met for a day of workshops, forums, and a luncheon at the Blackburn Center, Howard University.

SPRING 1982

THE ARCHON

The theme of the meeting was "Will our Communities Survive? Mobilization for Political and Economic Power." The workshop leader for Zetas was Soror Attorney Lucy T. Edwards and the workshop leader for the Amicae was Brother Gerald D. Smith, Executive Director of Phi Beta Sigma Fraternity, Inc. City Councilman John Ray was the luncheon speaker with greetings brought by Attorney Terrell, the aide for City Council Chairman Arrington Dixon, and from Brother Sam Wilkins, the local chapter president of Phi Beta Sigma Fraternity, Inc.

During the general session, greetings to the group were brought by Soror Ellis D. Jones, Director, the Eastern Region, and by Dr. Marjay D. Anderson, Basileus of Beta Zeta chapter. The Basilei of the college chapters, Sorors Jan Vincent and Danita Byrd, were also in attendance. More than 60 delegates were in attendance.

Soror Lynette Smith, the State Director, received a money corsage from the group in recognition of her splendid work in the planning and implementation of the D.C. state meeting. Members of the planning committee included Sorors Lois Brown, Josephine Saunders, Louise Howard, Naomi Pemberton, and Friend Joan Johnson an Ann Reed.

BETA ZETA CHAPTER INITIATES TEN (10!) PROBATES

On December 12, 1981, Beta Zeta chapter initiated ten probates into the Sorority. The ritual was a moving one attended by more than 70 members of Beta Zeta chapter. Members of Alpha and Kappa Alpha college chapters also attended. The Dean of Pledgees for the Fall, 1981 line was Soror Ellis D. Jones, assisted by Soror Virginia Brockington and members of the pledge committee. Basileus, Dr. Marjay D. Anderson, presided. Sorors were resplendent in the white attire mandated by the ritual for the initiation ceremony as were the pledgees.

For their service project while "on line," the pledgees collected more than 500 cans of food to be distributed to charitable agencies and institutions in the Washington, D.C. metropolitan area. They also prepared "blue and white goodies" for Sorors to partake of while attending information sessions.

The new Sorors entering the sisterhood are Iona Black, a chemistry teacher; Jean Childs, a bank employee, Freddie Dixon, PhD, a university biology professor; Frances Jackson, a community volunteer and retired teacher, Lila Lewis, a retired teacher, Claudia Privott, R.N., a university nursing instructor, Barbara Reeder, a metro transit employee; Marion Shields, a school teacher; Lois Sylver, a corporate recruiter, and Barbara Wright, a technical editor.

SPRING 1982

THE ARCHON

These ladies were treated to a scrumptious banquet at Hogates Restaurant after the ceremony. Welcome to Zeta Phi Beta!

BALTIMORE ZETAS OBSERVE FINER WOMANHOOD WEEK

Alpha Zeta Chapter culminated its observance of Finer Womanhood Week with a Public Meeting and Tea on Sunday, March 7, 1976, at the Sharon Baptist Church. Speaker for the meeting was Soror E. Fran Johnson, Director, Division of Consumer Education, U.S. Consumer Products Safety Commission. Awards and Citations were presented to several community women and youth. Ms. Maria Broom, local television personality, was named "Woman of the Year." Soror Althea S. Cornish was named "Zeta of the Year." Mrs. Ruth J. Norris, employee development specialist, Social Security Administration, received the "Community Service Award." Misses Michele Johnson and Margaret Harriday were named

as "Girls of the Year." Eta Epsilon, Alpha Zeta's undergraduate chapter at the University of Maryland College Park, received a Citation for high scholastic achievement as a group.

Basileus Mary E. Fields presents Plaque to Soror Althea S. Cornish, the "Zeta of the Year" at the Finer Womanhood Week Tea of Alpha Zeta Chapter.

THE ARCHON

Alpha Zeta Chapter participated in the Third Annual Women's Fair held at the Baltimore Civic Center. Displays in the booth highlighted Stork's Nest and the Zeta Educational Center. Shown here staffing the booth are (Standing L to R) Sorors Isoline Crowner, Ethel Hall, Alice Hall, LaReesa Smith, and Bernice S. White. Seated are (L to R) Elizabeth Demby, Beatrice Hall and Beatrice Mayo.

SPRING 1982

A Pictorial Journey of Finer Womanhood

Compiled by Amber Pratcher

PHOTO COLLAGE KEY — (Left to right, top to bottom)

PAGE 344
Fayetteville State University, 1974
Louisville Municipal College, 1951
North Carolina Central University
    (2 photos), 1962
North Carolina A&T University, 1958
Nettie Napier
Kentucky State College, 1954
Winston Salem State University, 1968
Autherine Lucy
Annie Turnbo Malone
Bethune Cookman College, 1956
Winston Salem State University, 1971
Dr. Elizabeth Duncan Koontz
Wiley College, Marshall, Texas
Shaw University, 1947

Fisk University, Circa 1950
Johnson C. Smith University, 1957

PAGE 345
Boulé Honorary Members Induction, 2014
    Congresswoman Donna Edwards
    Elizabeth Omilami
Mississippi State College, 1954
Tau Delta Zeta, Baltimore, MD 2010
Florida A&M University, 2010
Southern Region Undergrad Retreat, 2011
Greensboro Debutante Ball, 2013
50th Anniversary March on Washington, 2013
NC Central University, 2013
United Arab Emirates, 2014
Okinawa, Japan, 2013

The Vision:
Be Finer In 2020

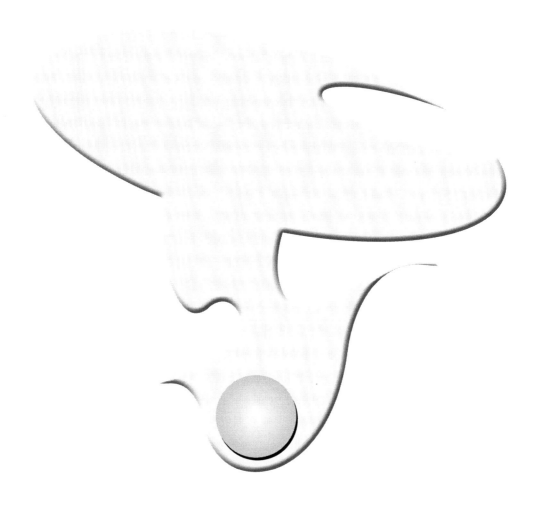

The Centennial Charge:
Excerpts

Jylla Moore Tearte, PhD

ZETA PHI BETA SORORITY, INCORPORATED

Delivered by

Jylla Moore Tearte, PhD

20th International Grand Basileus

2020 Centennial Commission Chair

January 17, 2015

Baltimore, Maryland

===

Mary Breaux Wright

International Grand Basileus

Nell Williams Ingram, EdD

National Executive Board Chair

Janet Y. Bivins, Esquire

Atlantic Regional Director

Danielle Green

Maryland State Director

Be Finer in 2020!

Our vision is to "Be Finer in 2020!" What does being finer in 2020 look like for you? What personal and professional goals will you record in your passport that you will strive to achieve between now and 2020? What have you always wanted to do but just never took the time to do it? What place have you wanted to visit, but you just haven't taken the time to plan the trip? Who have you wanted to collaborate with that you just haven't decided that the time is NOW? We must all commit to doing things differently so that in 2020 and beyond, we can ALL say, we are FINER for having made today the first day of our Journey to Centennial.

Let's start the journey by being grounded in our purpose.

On January 16, 1920, five co-eds on the campus of Howard University in Washington, District of Columbia, founded the Greek letter organization, Zeta Phi Beta Sorority, Incorporated. They dared to be different and established the principles for the Sorority of Service, Scholarship, Sisterhood and Finer Womanhood. Known to some as the praying band, they built a foundation based upon Proverbs 31… Who can find a virtuous woman?

As we launch our Journey to Centennial, we remember five virtuous women… our Pearls… our FOUNDERS.

> **Arizona Cleaver Stemons**
>
> **Myrtle Tyler Faithful**
>
> **Viola Tyler Goings**
>
> **Pearl Anna Neal**
>
> **Fannie Pettie Watts**

May their spirit be invoked today and each day for the next five years of our Journey to Centennial as we honor their legacy. Our vision is to "Be Finer in 2020". We commit to our mission of being the preeminent community-conscious, action-oriented organization that delivers world class service to help other people excel by blazing new paths.

Our Founders taught us through their courageous vision for Zeta to directly affect positive change; to chart a course of action for the 1920s and beyond; raise the consciousness of people; encourage the highest standards of scholastic achievement; and foster a greater sense of unity among its members. They were not like other women of their day.

They believed that sorority elitism and socializing overshadowed the real mission for progressive organizations and failed to address fully the societal mores, ills, prejudices, and poverty affecting humanity in general and the black community in particular. Since its inception,

Zeta has continued its steady climb into the national spotlight with programs designed to demonstrate concern for the human condition both nationally and internationally.

Soror Teraleen Campbell has penned our Centennial Prayer that will be a source of guidance when we lose our way. Soror Melissa Jones has energized our spirit with our Centennial Song so that we will keep moving when we have not a drop of energy left to make it to the next service project that will help somebody… because we know that if we can help some-body along the way, our living will not be in vain.

Yes, we know that to whom much has been given, much is expected. We are still the talented few. We are still the Sorority that dares to make a difference. We are the Sorority that shut down a television show whose reality was NOT the reality of Arizona, Myrtle, Viola, Pearl and Fannie. It was not who we are or who Zeta will ever be. Zeta will not let anyone, any show or any body define who we are on our Journey to Centennial.

Now is our time as we begin our Journey to Centennial to reflect upon the past, deepen our commitment to service while plotting our path for the future. As Barbara West Carpenter, our 21st International Grand Basileus shared when asked about the Centennial, she said:

> "In order for Zeta to be viable in the next 100 years, we must have a cadre of the best and the brightest women with vision and fortitude who are dedicated to carrying out the precepts that our Founders bravely set forth for us in this great Sorority to follow. Failure to consider such exceptional women for membership will certainly set us up for demise. Our mere existence for the future depends solely on what we do as a Sorority today."

It's time that we tap Zeta talent. It's time that talented Zetas step forward and serve, not for self-aggrandizement, but FOR THE TRUE LOVE OF ZETA! Our precepts are long standing. Our instructions are clear. Yet, we must translate how the past aligns with the present in order to be positioned for our tremendous future. So, please allow me to share a quote from Founder Stemons.

In the 1955, 35th Anniversary Edition of our magazine, the ARCHON, Founder, First President and Grand Basileus Emeritus, Arizona Cleaver Stemons said:

> "When Zeta Phi Beta Sorority had its' beginning at Howard University, Washington, D. C., in January 1920, the first World War had not been long ended. Woman was still kept on a pedestal; the chaperone was in vogue; the cigarette belonged only in the male realm; the tap-room was unheard of, and no 'lady' entered the 'Women's Entrance' of the old-fashioned saloon. Curse words did not pass her lips, and even a bit too much make-up made her character questionable. The greater aspirations of college women were the ascertainment of knowledge and the exhibition of the fine qualities of womanhood."

Let today be the first day of the rest of your life. Plan to BE FINER in 2020. Are we doing the work that we are meant to be doing on earth? Have we impacted the lives of someone through giving of our time, talent and treasure? Are we living in the right place, at this time, doing work that truly matters?

Do good things so that people can say good things about you when your voice is silenced. What would someone say if asked to share a few words about how you lived and the impact you had on their life or the lives of others?

People don't care how much you know, until they know how much you care. I would venture to say, people don't care what you dress like if you haven't addressed your genuine heart. I would venture to say that people don't care what you say until the words of your mouth and the meditations of your heart are acceptable in the sight of the Lord. I would venture to say that what you do in the dark behind closed doors always comes to light. Yet, I know that, no matter how dark the night… JOY COMES IN THE MORNING.

Amicae are Friends to Zeta. Established in 1948 in Houston, Texas, we work together to insure that our communities know that they have friends in Zeta and Sigma. Amicae travel with us when we venture to Capitol Hill to be the voice of the voiceless. Amicae support our efforts to insure that students have the resources to get a college degree. Yes. Amicae. Our Friends.

Zeta is a commitment for a lifetime. Starting with our Pearlettes at 4 years of age… to a member who most recently turned 106 years young in the Southern Region, we work with, we work for, we think about the continuum that is Zeta.

I would ask that you join me today in making five commitments for the Founders… yes, five for the five Founders.

1. Get fully engaged with the Sisterhood of Zeta

2. Find a cause and serve with PASSION

3. Document five personal goals that you will achieve by 2020

4. Become a 2020 Visionary

5. Contribute to the historical journey of Zeta

Zeta Phi Beta Sorority, Incorporated is embarking upon our Journey to our Centennial. I charge each of you to join us for the ride. It will be the ride of a lifetime. It will be a trip to remember. Zeta and Zetas will "Be FINER in 2020!"

The Finer Woman: An Acrostic

Evelyn L. Foster
1935 X-Ray (Now Archon)

The finer woman is

> **F**aithful to duty;
> **I**deal of womanhood;
> **N**oble in character;
> **E**ngaging in manner;
> **R**esponsible to a trust;
>
> **W**omanly in conduct;
> **O**bedient to a higher self;
> **M**agnanimous in spirit;
> **A**ffable in receiving others;
> **N**oteworthy in deeds;
> **H**ospitable to strangers and guests;
> **O**bliging to neighbors;
> **O**pen-hearted to poor and needy;
> **D**eserving of praise.

Finer...Defined in 2015 for the 2020 Journey and Beyond

Tamara Manning Gordon
Co-Founder of Z-BLUEtique with Dola Edwards

F...Finer, Fly, Fierce, Fabulous, Focused, Friendly, Fervent

I...Impelled, Intelligent, Independent, Inspiring, Innovative

N...Noble, Nurturing, Nice, Needed, Never Tiring

E...Expressive, Energetic, Engaging, Empathetic, Elegant

R...Radiant, Refined, Respectful, Remarkable

Z-PHI-B Be Finer

Danielle R. Green

I am a Woman of Z-PHI-B who holds the ideal of *Scholarship* so dear to me.
Education, ability, intelligence and more,
A woman of knowledge, unlocking Zeta's door.
I Am A Woman! I Am A Scholar! Z-PHI-B…Be Finer!

I am a Woman of Z-PHI-B who holds the ideal of *Service* so dear to me,
To support, assist, care and provide.
A woman of substance with resources and more,
Yet a helping hand and friend to the core.
I Am A Woman! I Am A Servant! Z-PHI-B…Be Finer!

I am a Woman of Z-PHI-B who holds the ideal of *Sisterhood* so dear to me.
Friendship, unity, faithfulness and love,
A woman bound to the pledge of Zeta's call,
Answering one and answering all.
I Am A Woman! I Am A Soror! Z-PHI-B…Be Finer!

I am a Woman of Z-PHI-B who holds the ideal of *Finer Womanhood* so dear to me.
Elegant and gracious, with class and style,
A woman of excellence is what I seek,
Proverbs 31 filled, wholesome and complete.
I Am A Woman! I Am Fabulous! Z-PHI-B…Be Finer!

I am a Woman of Z-PHI-B who holds *Scholarship, Service,*
Sisterhood and *Finer Womanhood,* so dear to me.
Community-conscious, action-oriented, principle driven and destiny-bound,
To uphold and live the dream our Five Pearls found.
I Am A Woman! I Am a Zeta! Z-PHI-B…Be Finer!

Acknowledgments

This Anthology was conceived by Rhonda Lawson as a 2020 Visionary Project with the assistance of the following resources:

Doris McAdams Stokes, Copy Editor
Jylla Moore Tearte, PhD, Project Editor
Malica Fleming, Cover Design

Proceeds from the sale of this book will be donated to the 2020 Centennial fund raising campaign of Zeta Phi Beta Sorority, Incorporated. Chapters, states and regions of the Sorority who order 25 or more copies from the Centennial Exchange will be credited with a 2020 Visionary Contribution. For more information, visit the Centennial website at:

www.zphib2020.com/CentennialExchange

Many thanks to the Anthology contributors and we trust that this publication will be a lasting reminder of all that "Finer Womanhood" means to the Sisterhood of Zeta Phi Beta Sorority, Incorporated.

Jylla Moore Tearte, PhD
20th International President and
2020 Centennial Commission Chair
Zeta Phi Beta Sorority, Incorporated

CEO, Crystal Stairs, Inc.
Project Director

The Final Word

A Tribute to Amber Renee Curtis Pratcher

One Pin, Five Pearls

Amber Renee Curtis Pratcher was born on June 14, 1979 and departed this life on July 20, 2015. She joined Zeta Phi Beta Sorority, Incorporated, Mu Tau Zeta Chapter, Speedway, Indiana in 2001. An uninterrupted active and financial member throughout her years of service, she was the Founder of RealZetas, a network of progressive thinking Zetas who formed strong sisterly bonds through their engagement as sisters. A trailblazing social media professional, the #IAMZETA campaign was widely acclaimed as the most innovative and successful publicity campaign for the Sorority.

She served in many positions of leadership at the local, state, regional and national levels including chapter Basileus and charter member of Upsilon Kappa Chapter, Bloomington, Indiana. At the national level, she was the National Director of Instructional Design and a member of the National Publications team. A voice for social activism, she served as the webmistress and social media coordinator for the Great Lakes Region and editor of the Zeta Zest, the region's official publication.

A member of the Centennial Commission, Amber was the keeper of historical and contemporary records and photos that chronicled the history of Zeta. She completed the compilation of the photos presented in "A Pictorial Journey of Finer Womanhood" in this Anthology the week prior to her passing. She also compiled the photos in the Centennial Passport. Amber completed her 2020 Visionary Charter Donor pledge and was visionary #205.

Amber, wife of Jonya Pratcher; mother of Jaden Benjamin Pratcher; daughter of Benjamin Franklin Curtis and Cora Tucker Curtis; sister, friend, colleague, advocate, activist, and so many other connections to her life, she was a "Phenomenal Finer Woman".

Forever Finer… The Final Word of the *"Keeping It Finer Anthology"* is dedicated to Amber!

Soror Amber Pratcher
Mu Tau Zeta Chapter
Speedway, IN

I am Creator and CEO of RezlZetas and I executed this campaign tirelessly through long days and sometimes even longer nights, creating the designs and images. I have a B.A., 2 M.S. degrees and am a devoted wife, mother, daughter and sister, all while working as a Senior Administrator at a top-ranked University, integrating emerging technologies and managing millions of dollars in scholarship monies. I am a visionary and I make things happen, particularly when it comes to my beloved sorority. I have held almost every position on the local level, including chapter president, and have chartered a chapter. I currently serve on every level of my sorority in elected and appointed positions. RealZetas has stood in gaps for many years and I intend to continue to shine a light on the best my sorority has to offer. I am professional, I am game-changing, I don't blaze trails, I INCINERATE them. I AM ZETA.

Love always, Amber

ANTHOLOGY

Personal Reflections on Finer Womanhood

Made in the USA
Columbia, SC
13 November 2024

46407352R00204